Stillness on Shaking Ground

A Woman's Himalayan Journey Through Love, Loss, and Letting Go

Stillness on Shaking Ground

A Woman's Himalayan Journey Through Love, Loss, and Letting Go

Carol A. Wilson

BOOKS

Winchester, UK
Washington, USA

First published by O-Books, 2017
O-Books is an imprint of John Hunt Publishing Ltd., Laurel House, Station Approach,
Alresford, Hants, SO24 9JH, UK
office1@jhpbooks.net
www.johnhuntpublishing.com

For distributor details and how to order please visit the 'Ordering' section on our website.

ISBN: 978 1 78535 533 2
978 1 78535 534 9 (ebook)
Library of Congress Control Number: 2016941420

A CIP catalogue record for this book is available from the British Library.

Design: Stuart Davies

Printed and bound by CPI Group (UK) Ltd, Croydon, CR0 4YY, UK

CONTENTS

Acknowledgements viii
Dedication xi
Note from the Author xii
Preface 1

Part I

Meltdown 9
By the River 31
Escape 33

Part II

Training for Tibet 49
Tibet from Nepal 61
Nepal: Last Resort—Manika Graveyard—Nuwakot 125
Retreat 131
Caste and Culture 147

Part III

Gorkha 7.8 Earthquake 175
On Ground Earthquake Relief 193
Dolakha 7.3 Earthquake—Hijacked 211
Magical Pokhara 233

Part IV

Dark Clouds 249
Letting Go 273
Motherland India 279
References 283
About the Author 286

Illustrations

Figure 1, Parasol

Figure 2, Golden Fishes

Figure 3, Vase

Figure 4, Lotus

Figure 5, Conch Shell

Figure 6, The Endless Knot

Figure 7, Victory Banner

Figure 8, Dharma Wheel

GisaTom, TibetanArtDesign

Photographs

Nepal Flag, Carol A. Wilson

MUCH love, Carol A. Wilson

Acknowledgements

I pay homage to my spiritual teachers: His Holiness the 17th Gyalwa Karmapa, Trinley Thaye Dorje, spiritual head of the Karma Kagyu Buddhist tradition; the late 14th Shamarpa, Mipham Chokyi Lodro; Lama Ole Nydahl and the late Hannah Nydahl, who were the first Western students of His Holiness the 16th Gyalwa Karmapa, Rangjung Rigpe Dorje. Appreciation is extended to Maggie Kossowski, translator and personal assistant to the late Lopon Tsechu Rinpoche, who organized and led two of my pilgrimages to Nepal, India, and Bhutan, and gave me many transmissions from Lopon Tsechu Rinpoche. I am grateful to the honorable Professor Sempa Dorje, a teacher and private tutor to Gyalwa Karmapa and a living pandita of Buddhism and Hinduism, for his profound teachings. I am also grateful to Khenpo Chodrak Tenphel Rinpoche, Shangpa Rinpoche, Duping Rinpoche, and Khenpo Tsering Samdrup for their teachings. A thank you is extended to Khenpo Mriti, Secretary at the Karmapa International Buddhist Institute (KIBI), for his role in inviting me to teach Academic English Writing at KIBI. I am thankful for the friendship of Ani Karma Zangmo, Ani Tenzin Sangmo and my students who continue to inspire and motivate me.

My gratitude and deep appreciation is forever extended to the Tibetan and Nepalese people who taught me about loving-kindness, courage, and perseverance in the wake of human suffering. I thank the many big-hearted, compassionate family members, friends, and donors who supported me in providing relief aid to the Nepalese people following the 7.8 Gorkha and 7.3 Dolakha earthquakes. To the creative Janet M. Bass, *Lightning Tree Films, Ltd.*—who produced films that documented and promoted my on-ground relief aid efforts—endless hugs for your friendship. I thank my long term Nepali friends: Neel Shahi, *President, Team Nepal's Children's Home* for always watching my back, and Rajendra Lama, *Friends Adventure Team,* for his undying friendship and the incredible photograph of the Himalayan range utilized in designing the cover of this book. Finally, much love is extended to my enormously talented daughter, Lindsey Myer (LEL studio+design) for the design of this book cover and for her consistent support over the years. To Trevor Greenfield, Dominic C. James, Elizabeth Radley, and the staff at John Hunt Publishing, thank you. To *all* of you—you are forever in my heart.

Dedication

For the People of Nepal

May all of my merits gained be dedicated to the benefit of all beings, limitless in number.

May they accumulate the causes for happiness.

May they be held by the Victorious Ones in protective embrace.

Note from the Author

At the outset, please note that this book is appropriately written in none other than the third person position of careful observer. However, because the book is based on a true story, the names of the main characters have been changed—although all of those characters probably would have agreed to full disclosure of their identity. This decision was based out of respect; after all, who would get involved with Olivia knowing that they would become a character in a book—and in some cases, dissected down to pulp. Yet, the story unfolds as a meandering—and often relentless—river takes its course. Let's only hope that between the box of Kleenex and bouts of laughter, it opens out into a magical reservoir that embraces and enlightens your life in some extraordinary way.

Preface

It's easy to sit complacently within the walls of the world as we know it; however, this complacency can change, as if a gust of wind activates a seed within us and drives us to become nomadic, exploring beyond the safety-security fence we have erected around our existence—not only a physical exploration but an exploration that is psychosocial-spiritual. Yes, after six high-adventure trips to Nepal with detours to Tibet, Bhutan, and India, Olivia recognized that she was a nomad. Being raised in the military didn't groom her for this wayfarer life, but rather, having an appreciation for the world beyond what she knew. Her deepest karmic connections, including teachers and Gurus, seemed to lie in the East—not in America. However, traveling to the East meant traveling to a different world, especially when it included the Communist country of Tibet (China) and the third world country of Nepal, a severely underdeveloped, poverty-stricken, landlocked, and disaster prone country, divided into three distinct topographic areas that each exhibit their own hazardous profiles: steep mountains in the north, hills, and terrain, all subject to volatile weather. It often meant surrendering to a huge learning curve that required functioning without expectation, accepting the unexpected, and settling into spontaneous suspense and adrenalin-producing, cliff-hanging adventure—even when it meant danger.

There was a 30-day Maoist-guerilla cease-fire when Olivia first explored Nepal during a time of protracted civil war. She trekked through the top of the world in Tibet while under the scrutiny and surveillance of Communist China, hung prayer flags at Mt. Everest Base Camp in high-speed winds as a storm approached, survived Mt. Everest's freezing temperatures in a wrongly pitched summer tent, disembarked from a plane moments before it crashed near Lamidanda Airport, killing all passengers on board; traveled on narrow, precarious mountain roads in blinding smog during the blackness of night, and sat on a bungee jump platform in Nepal with a 525 foot plunge. She survived the 7.8 magnitude Gorkha earthquake on April 25 and for 40 days afterwards, which included the 7.3 magnitude Dolakha earthquake on May 12 and over 300 aftershocks, scurried past and dodged in and out of damaged buildings on the verge of collapse; participated in recovery missions for the dead lying beneath rubble, traveled to rural, mountainous villages on a tractor to deliver relief aid to earthquake victims on treacherous roads, replete with grave-producing active landslides, and lived to tell how she survived a thriller action-packed hijacking—not en route from New York to Houston—but with 20 Nepali men, drunk on raksi, in a remote village in the middle of the night.

Olivia experienced Nepal through rose-colored glasses: The Land of Exquisite Beauty, The Land of the Majestic Himalayas, The Land of Ancient Art and History, The Land of Grateful Children, The Land of Gorgeous Wives, The Land of Men's Pointed Hats, The Land of Doting Mothers, The Land of Precious Little Girls, The Land of Nepali Smiles, The Land of Poverty and Bamboo Work Baskets, The Land of Colorful Umbrellas, The Land of Ineffective Government, The Land of Spiritual Strength, and The Land of Betrayal and Kindness. And through all of this, by virtue of her birth into a world of sickness, old age, and inevitable mortality, Olivia was confronted with her own sense of meaning. As she experienced and perceived the dynamics of our world, she went toe-to-toe with the suffering, challenges, and decisions that all beings face, which included the capacity to love deeply and then let go.

We have heard the adage that it's not what happens to us in life—it's how we deal with it that matters; yet, as "shit happens," we are ill equipped to understand the complexity of the suffering that we see and feel. We may sink into numbness and denial, believing that suffering will only happen to others. "Perhaps I'll get lucky and the stray bullet won't hit me, but him. I won't get cancer, I won't get old. I'll live happily ever after, surrounded by people who love me." Unfortunately, it is a misconception at the least, and delusion at the most, to believe that stray bullets dodge oneself and hit only others. It is only when *freed* from denial that we become acutely aware of pain and suffering, and we wish to be free from it. No one will deny that even insects will run from suffering. We all wish for happiness. None of us wish to suffer. Ironically, if we are confused or do not understand the root cause of our suffering, we are clueless about how to alleviate it. We grasp at solutions outside of ourselves that can actually create or exacerbate suffering. As the great 8th century Buddhist Master Shantideva (1979, p. 5) said:

> Although wishing to be free of misery,
> They run towards misery itself.
> Although wishing to have happiness,
> Like an enemy they ignorantly destroy it.

At the minimum, some of us are motivated to develop healthy coping skills, which are helpful, but not a cure for suffering. Others choose to self-medicate with prescription drugs, alcohol, nicotine, and recreational drugs that often become addictive. The outcome—we operate on autopilot with an unrelenting loss of freedom. Others reach for Starbucks, chocolate, and "comfort food." Many choose to blame other people for their pain and suffering, not taking self-responsibility by turning the pointed finger at oneself. Still others simply accept and succumb to occasional joy and suffering as if on a roller coaster, never knowing when the next up or the next down will hit or when the next land mine will detonate.

For others, like Olivia, suffering can motivate one to become a wayfarer and search for greater meaning in life. A positive trajectory, and for many, the beginning of a new life experience, begins with a wish for something more—something not seen with the eye—something so deep that a compass seems to point the way in a new direction. There is a tug, a nudge, a knowingness that another perspective will help us make sense of the undertows and currents that have pulled us under on one too many occasions. This is what the greatest of all psychologists—the Buddha himself—sought. He searched for meaning beyond cyclical birth, old age, sickness, and dying. He was determined to identify the cause of suffering and defined it as rooted in the kleshas of ignorance, attachment, and aversion (the three poisons), which lead to other kleshas that also create karma. Western psychology would best define these three poisons as narcissism, desire, and anger but without an understanding of the role of karma. Logically, if one does not understand the cause of suffering, how can one possibly uproot it?

Like many of us, Olivia experienced a perpetual cycle of emotions—joy, the frustration of being squeezed and shaken when buttons were pushed, and the subsequent pain experienced after falling in love with someone and then having to let him go. This kind of suffering was delineated by the Buddha: *Suffering has a cause, and the cause is desire (attachment).* We tend to cling onto things as if they are permanent, when in reality, those things are temporary, impermanent, and do not last. We develop attachment that can give rise to craving, a feeling of possessiveness and obsessiveness, which causes suffering and clinging that makes letting go very difficult. Letting go is especially difficult before or after the pain of alteration occurs—suffering caused by change, a violated expectation and failure of happy moments to last. All temporary happinesses are subject to change and lead to suffering when we are attached to them.

For Olivia, an "a-ha" light bulb moment occurred when she realized that suffering was created in her own mind. When that truth is recognized and accepted, we then realize the prudence of working with mind, identifying the cause of our feelings and emotions in order to uproot their effect—suffering. It was not any one man who had caused Olivia's suffering, but rather, the attachment and feelings that she had developed about him. But why? Why are we innately wired in such a complicated way that our mind is the source of misperception of self (ignorance) and, thus, suffering?

People often wonder why Buddhists want to understand suffering, but not in a cryin' and dyin' Patsy Cline kind of way. Logically speaking, one must know that there is suffering, the cause of the suffering, and a diagnosis must be made in order to treat it with a prescription; however, this diagnosis and treatment is contrary to Western approaches. Most of us do not need to delineate our suffering as listed in the DSM-IV (Diagnostic and Statistical Manual of Mental Disorders). We do not need a 301 diagnostic code in which to bill an insurance company for medical reimbursement for the treatment of suffering. More importantly, if we take a close look at the complexity of the karma we create for ourselves, it is logically quite impossible for another person or professional to evaluate, assess, purify, or change that karma, especially when it has accumulated throughout many reincarnations. Conclusion: we must put on our own boots and pull them up by their bootstraps. No one else can do it for us.

Olivia reflected upon her own common sense over and over again—only to validate what she already knew—"The buck truly does stop with me." However, the procrastination of someday syndrome is insidious. Someday I'll do something about these afflictive emotions. Perhaps tomorrow, which becomes the next day—and then the next. Olivia learned that she had to go back to Go over and over again in order to understand the cause of suffering and the cure for it—applying knowledge, reflection, and meditation, the only manner in which we can train the mind. She developed a motivation to achieve stillness on the shaking ground in which we dwell in a manner that actually worked; however, it involved discipline and perseverance—beyond instant gratification, the turning of a page, and the clicking of a mouse. This is her story.

Carol A. Wilson, PhD
New Moon Day, the 30th day of the 12th month in the year of the Wood Sheep (Tib.)
February 8, 2016
Kathmandu, Nepal

Part I

Meltdown

"YOU'RE—**NOT**—GOING TO TIBET!" Chris stood at the side of the bed and sobbed, wiping away tears with his hands as they streamed down his face. Olivia, half-asleep, sat up slowly in bed and wondered if she was dreaming. She turned her head and glanced over at the face of the clock... 3:12am. "Something *very* bad will happen to you," he screamed. "You'll *die* or end up in a Chinese prison! You won't even be able to receive letters! You know how outspoken you are—which you cannot do in Tibet (China)! You and your academic freedom!" Olivia knew he would never travel beyond the confines of the USA, much less Tibet or a third world country like Nepal because he repeatedly reminded her of that. The only time he traveled was to play in annual golf tournaments in Florida, Nevada, and California. But a meltdown over her going to Tibet in the middle of the night? For a couple of minutes, Olivia was in such a stupor of disbelief that her mind went blank. Chris's tears continued. He sat down on the edge of the bed, head hanging down and shoulders heaving. She heard him whisper over and over again, "This isn't going to work. This isn't going to work. This isn't going to work."

Finally—scattered thoughts began to flash in Olivia's mind: "Is this what watching Fox News does to someone?" It was Chris's routine to grab the black television remote first thing in the morning and turn on Fox News as if he was feeding an addiction, captivated by the Fox's News anchor babes—perfectly made-up, clad in tight miniskirts that showed off more than gorgeous, toned legs. Interestingly, the rise of those skirts seemed to be in perfect congruence with the rise in their network ratings. Oh, and their cleavage-revealing, low-cut blouses! Chris thought that cleavage was "beautiful," reminding Olivia on occasion that she was the most "covered up woman" he'd ever met. But—back to reality—back to what was unfolding in front of Olivia's eyes.

She wasn't dreaming. "This isn't a dream," she thought. "I'm not dreaming. This is for real." She couldn't do now what she did in the morning when she saw Chris reach for that all-so-important remote. She couldn't roll her eyes with an excuse to fly out of the room and land in the kitchen for a cup of Starbucks' Keurig coffee—black.

Thirty years prior, Olivia and Chris met during their undergraduate university days. She had spotted him in their dormitory cafeteria one day as he sat with his hippie-type friends—tall, lean, blonde, handsome. "Why am I attracted to good looking men who are over 6 feet tall?" she thought. "Do I need to place a gorgeous package on my dresser and look at it every day, wondering if there is anything inside? Shouldn't I care about what's inside?" But they were soon inseparable for three years, traveling to see each other when separated during university summer breaks, sometimes in Malibu, Grosse Pointe, or Las Vegas. Regardless of where they were, however, they never missed *Star Trek* at 4pm, laying on the bed next to each other, her head on his right shoulder. He was always amused that she was a serious, National Honor Society student, never neglecting her studies. More often than not, when he finished his mechanic's job at the end of the day and walked through the door, he found her sitting on his bed with her books, studying or doing homework. For him, studying wasn't his modus operandi although he was a registered university student. Receiving semester grades meant photoshopping a fake report card for his mother. "How can you do that?" Olivia would ask in disbelief.

Yes, Olivia left him at times. She temporarily moved out-of-state to complete her student teaching for a semester, always believing they were devoted to each other. Did she ever not see a hint of his self-centeredness? One afternoon he agreed to take her to Baskin Robbins on the back of his Harley-Davidson motorcycle for her favorite rocky road ice cream; however, once she was happily eating it, he insisted that she hop back on his motorcycle because he didn't want to wait for her. Because Olivia had no choice in the matter, she was back on his Harley, covered head to toe in wind-blown, melted chocolate ice cream. Like so many things in life, the thing she loved was gone in a flash. She screamed, "STOP." Why wouldn't he stop? Is it surprising that she had an exhaust pipe burn—turned scar—on her left calf?

One fall morning, awakening in the apartment that she shared with five girlfriends, Olivia felt the need to see Chris. Those were the days of no cell phones, and Chris didn't have a main telephone line. She pulled on her stiff Levi jeans and a short-sleeved striped blouse, forgot about coffee or eating breakfast, and drove her yellow, black-trimmed Camaro until she reached the large dirt parking lot behind his basement studio apartment. However, stepping out of the car seemed different this time. She could see from a distance the upper part of the white wooden door to the entrance of his basement apartment, accessed after descending four concrete steps. Once at the bottom of the steps she noticed his set of keys hanging with a key still in the door lock. "Strange," she thought. "He would never do that." She quietly pulled the key out, turned the door knob and entered, which placed her in the kitchen facing an old, white, gas burner stove, but with an open entrance to his bedroom to the left. Nothing was in the bedroom but a double bed—without a headboard—shoved against the wall with a television facing it in the far right corner of the room, which was mounted to the back wall. On that wall was a door that led to the remaining unfinished basement of the house, which included a framed-in bathroom without sheetrock on the walls—a toilet, sink, and shower that was functional.

As Olivia stood at the entrance to the bedroom, the scene in front of her seared into her psyche like a red-hot branding iron—leaving an indelible mark. Her trusted boyfriend and fiancé was asleep in his double bed next to another woman who immediately awakened and pulled the sheet up over her head, hiding her face. There was no escaping for her as she hid underneath the sheet, trapped between the wall and Chris. Olivia froze as she felt a wave of numbing paralysis sweep over her. Then her knees buckled, and she went straight down to the floor, collapsing in a heap. Next to her laid a pair of worn, casual, brown, closed-toed shoes, much smaller than Olivia's size 9½. "Size 6… yes, they're probably a size 6," she thought. In the meantime, Chris, with a startled but disgusted look on his face, quickly grabbed the white sheet covering him with his left hand and lifted it enough that he could hop out of bed onto his right foot. He seemed to stagger before he planted himself in front of Olivia, looking down at her—speechless. His new puppy, Jackson, bounced in—a white, fluffy ball-of-fur, half Golden Retriever, half mutt. Olivia seemed to feel a sense of relief at seeing him because she pushed herself up off of the floor and grabbed Jackson, clutching him in her arms as she scurried out the door.

Olivia could not remember getting into her car and driving, much less recall how she arrived at her apartment. She was in a time warp. By then, shock gave rise to tears as she held Jackson close to her chest. Trisha, one of her roommates, saw Olivia coming and, suspecting that something was very wrong, ran to the medicine cabinet and handed Olivia one of her prescription sedatives with a glass of water. Olivia didn't need to tell Trisha, through her tears and now sobs, "He was in bed with another woman." She simply swallowed the capsule and took a gulp of water, without hesitation. No *Physicians' Desk Reference* this time. No looking up what this drug was with its contraindications. She then made a beeline for the bedroom and collapsed on her bed with Jackson looking on, obviously trying to comfort her as he snuggled close. Talking to Jackson, as if he understood every word, she moaned, "I'm going to die. This must be what dying feels like." She could feel her eyes starting to swell as her face flooded with tears.

A few minutes transpired before Chris walked through

Olivia's bedroom door. He spotted a chair and slowly pulled it up to the side of her twin bed, its length against the wall and pushed into the corner of the room. Stoically, he sat there, leaning forward with his chin in his calloused hands, supported by an elbow on each knee. Trisha momentarily appeared at the door as a protectress, her eyes glaring, sending daggers to Chris. As Olivia cried, Chris remained speechless—not one word—not an explanation—not an apology—nothing. The only sound was the sound of Olivia's staccato-like sobs. Chris didn't seem remorseful—but certainly wasn't happy that he got caught. Many years later, someone in a similar situation would remind Olivia of this same lack of remorse. Bill Clinton! "Oh, Hillary, we will forever be bonded in sisterhood," Olivia would one day say. "We are both women who have been lied to and cheated on!" After a few minutes, Chris reached for Jackson and left. Was that why he was there—to get Jackson?

Olivia couldn't talk to Chris about what had happened but she decided to see a counselor at the university. At the time she was a 21-year-old who did not have a repertoire of coping skills or tools. She was a Christian who had learned how to feel bona fide guilt, and she searched outwardly for answers and relief to her suffering, rather than inwardly. The counselor was a middle-aged man with deep, penetrating brown eyes. He listened quietly with an empathetic expression on his face, suggesting to Olivia that he wasn't listening to an everyday, typical story. Olivia told him that she had been sitting in the Student Union Building looking at the shoes on young women's feet as they walked by. "Perhaps I'll see her shoes, and I'll know who she is." Her counselor felt compassion for Olivia; after all, she was a serious student but something this unexpected left Olivia wondering if she would be able to crack open a book, much less comprehend and learn academic material.

Of course, there had to be a final blow. A couple of days later Chris's upstairs neighbor, Dewey, telephoned Olivia saying that he couldn't wait to meet with and talk to her about what had happened between she and Chris. Sensing his sincerity, she didn't hesitate to meet him in his backyard while Chris was at work. Stuttering, he told her that the mystery woman with the sheet over her head was not an isolated woman. There were other women, and there was one occasion when Olivia missed—by seconds—running into one of those women driving out of Chris's driveway. Dewey nervously anticipated that he might one day witness an awkward, and possibly explosive, encounter between two women. F-L-A-S-H. The bobby pin! Olivia suddenly remembered a large, three-inch gold bobby pin that she found underneath one of the pillows on Chris's bed several months ago. She completely dismissed it. How could she have been in such denial that she would ignore an obvious piece of evidence and not confront him? Were there other clues? One night she saw a straw decorative bird with a note on his door but he annoyingly said that it was from the girl in the upstairs apartment. Perhaps Olivia was a bit suspicious but wasn't concerned that Chris would be interested in her. Regardless, the ***trust*** between them was irreparably gone. And because Olivia believed that trust was the foundation of a relationship, it was over. In this respect,

Olivia was not Hillary Clinton.Chris pursued Olivia, almost to the point of stalking. He would telephone her or show up on her apartment doorstep. She refused to talk to him and refused to see him. If she was dating someone, Chris would investigate, finding out who he was, his address, and his telephone number. Chris would then telephone him, asking to speak to Olivia. "She doesn't want to talk to you," Olivia would hear him say; however, after several weeks, Chris convinced Olivia that she should have dinner with him at an exclusive restaurant that required a half-hour drive up a majestic canyon, lined with pine trees. "Perhaps we can finally end this," she thought. During dinner, the conversation was light—more like superficial chitchat. But soon, dinner was over. Tears came to Chris's eyes. "Marry me. Please marry me. I can't live without you," he begged. So much of the pain she had experienced weeks before was gone—but there was an indescribable emptiness and a feeling of residual pain, as she muttered, "I can't." She still found it impossible to expound or talk about what had happened between them weeks before. I-m-p-o-s-s-i-b-l-e.

Olivia went on with her life, completing her Master of Science (MS) Degree and teaching in the public school system. She married a year and a half later; of course, he was nothing less than handsome, thin, and over six feet tall; however, the marriage seemed to loom over her like a death sentence—a mistake to begin with. She should have realized her demise when she vomited for hours the night before the wedding. The more obvious omen, however, was lowering her wedding dress over her head backwards and pulling the zipper up the front instead of the back. It was apparent that she was turned around in more than one way. Even a witness to the wedding ceremony commented that Olivia looked "peaked" before she said, "I do." Perhaps this was called "going from the frying pan into the fire." Perhaps being 23 years old didn't necessarily mean it was time to get married.

The fact is—Olivia chose to marry a man she thought she could trust rather than a man she loved, divorcing 12 years later after bailing out on her marriage counselor twice, saying, "I can't go through with this." The last time she walked through his office door, he said, "I knew you'd be back. If you would have ever been in love with this man, there would have been a 50–50 chance of rekindling that love, but there was nothing to rekindle." Perhaps she was back because she had just been released from an 11-day hospital stay with pneumonia. Perhaps she realized that she was so unhappily married and depressed that her immune system had shut down, and she became seriously ill. Perhaps she stared at the IV drip in her arm long enough to realize that there had to be another way out. She had heard about the "love triangle," which depicted the three sides of a relationship: intimacy, passion, and commitment. Sometimes people only wanted one or two of those components, and if a couple wanted different components there was a conflict of needs. Olivia wanted all of them. Unfortunately, she had commitment. That was it. Ironically, that was the one thing she didn't have with Chris. Yet, paradoxically, during that time and for the next 30 years she wondered if she had made the right decision about Chris. He had been the love of her life. She often thought, "Why didn't I talk to him? Why didn't we discuss what had happened? I saw a counselor. Why didn't I take Chris with me to see the counselor? Could we have worked it out?" And almost as fast as a wish made while rubbing Aladdin's Lamp, Chris was back in her life again—30 years later.

It was July. Olivia dreamed about Chris's mother, Ann, whom she had met on a couple of occasions. Olivia was not close to her but remembered her as being quiet and stoic, but sophisticated. With her best sterling silver flatware, Ann served lunch for them one day on their patio, overlooking the Pacific Ocean. "She must have liked you," Chris would later say. "She wouldn't do that for everyone." But, the dream. Jung would ask, was it relevant? Was Chris's mother reaching out to her? Perhaps. Olivia had discovered over the years that she received relevant, accurate, reliable, and sometimes predictive information through dreams. She trusted them. She e-mailed Chris: "Are you okay? I just wanted to touch base with you before I leave for the Himalayas. With what I'll be doing near Everest I might not come back. LOL Surprisingly, I had a dream about you a few nights ago and your mom was in it. Dreams aren't meaningless... mine aren't, anyway. Olivia." Chris immediately responded to Olivia's e-mail. Sure enough, his mother had recently died. Chris had also divorced his second wife after discovering that her many trips to California included an affair with another man. He had been single for a few years. He included his phone number in his e-mail and asked Olivia to: "Call me when you have a chance."

November. Four months passed. Olivia, absorbed in her daily, but quiet routine, didn't give much thought to Chris or their e-mail correspondence. But then, one day, she had a layover at the airport nearest to Chris's home, several hundred miles away. She remembered that she had entered and saved his phone number in her cell phone. Almost as if she was on autopilot, she scrolled to his name and called his number. He didn't answer so she nervously left a message that she was at the airport and thought she'd finally give him a call. She hung up but immediately her phone rang, which she answered on the first ring. "Couldn't get the phone out of my pocket fast enough," she heard him say, "and I had to put on my glasses to see who had called." Olivia guessed that he had a flip phone, and she was right. Why do rich men have flip phones?

Upon hearing Chris's voice, Olivia was unexpectedly hit by a tidal wave of emotion. She heard him say, "Let me know ahead of time the next time you're here so we can at least sit down and have a beer." She never saw him drink beer or any alcohol when they had been together during college, and Olivia wasn't a beer drinker, but a coffee drinker—so wasn't that rather odd that he would say that? However, they ended their brief telephone conversation, and Olivia boarded her plane, thinking, "Oh, my gosh. Could it be that Cupid really does shoot people with an arrow? Is that what this is? Have I been shot? What else can explain what I'm feeling right now?" She was love struck—or do you call it lovesick? For the next two days Olivia couldn't eat or sleep, laying around as if half alive. What happened?

> If one comes across a person who has been shot by an arrow, One does not spend time wondering about where the arrow came from, or the caste of the individual who shot it, or analyzing what type of wood the shaft is made of, or the manner in which the arrowhead was fashioned.

Rather, one should focus on immediately pulling out the arrow.
Buddha, *Majjhima Nikaya Sutta* No. 63

The logical words of the Buddha. Olivia needed to pull out the arrow. She was no better off than a fish from the Pacific Ocean, now stuck and immobilized in a pot of emotional glue.

As an aside—who *was* this Buddha? Olivia first heard of Buddha, known as the "Historical Buddha" or the "Fully Awakened One," when she was a child. She knew he was a real man—not a myth or a legend—who sat under a Bodhi tree over 2,500 years ago until he reached Enlightenment. Enlightenment, defined in general terms as "being brought into the light," is the spiritual goal of many systems of belief—clarity of perception in which truth can be comprehended through a conviction of both mind and heart. She believed that Enlightenment simply meant that Buddha had developed a realization about life's meaning without her understanding the depth and breadth of his discovery. Buddha (meaning "one who is intuitive, awakened or enlightened") was known by several names including Shakyamuni ("the sage of the kingdom of Sakya"), Tathagata ("the one who has come thus"), and his birth name, Siddhartha ("he who has accomplished his aim") of the Gautama clan. She had an appreciation for his Tibetan name, Song Gyay, because the Tibetan language is powerful and beautiful, enriched with meaning. "Song" can mean to awaken but it can also mean to purify—to eliminate jealousy, hatred and anger. Gyay means to develop, expand or perfect, such as in expanded love and compassion.

Buddha sought the highest insight into the nature of the human condition through analysis and meditation, driven by his conviction that not to be enlightened is to suffer. However, he admonished us not to rely on his testimonial of Enlightenment but, rather, to be our own master and discover the truth for ourselves through our own understanding. His words, "Be a lamp unto yourself," emphasized that knowledge is acquired through self-exertion and self-development and not from external sources. "I have shown you the way to liberation, now you must take it for yourself," he said. A "finger pointing at the moon," symbolic of Buddha's message, conveys to us that truth can only come from personal experience.

We all possess, within ourselves, what Buddha discovered in himself. We all have the same potential to free ourselves from suffering. Sogyal Rinpoche (1994) reminds us that the name "Buddha" has deep meaning: a person, **any** person, who has completely awakened from ignorance and opened to his or her vast potential of wisdom. A Buddha is also one who has brought a final end to suffering and frustration and discovered a lasting and deathless happiness and peace. The Buddha never presented himself as a savior, god, or deity nor did he seek fame, recognition, adulation or worship from others. One day a Brahmin, named Drona, asked Buddha if he was a god, a nature spirit, or a human. Buddha's response was, "No." Drona then asked, "If you are neither divine nor nonhuman nor human, what are you?" Buddha replied, "I am awake." That sounded good to Olivia. It was what she was looking for—an end to suffering. Wake up! Everything else was secondary to inner peace.

Olivia dug through file folders in her black, metal, four-drawer filing cabinet and found a 30-year-old black and white Polaroid picture that Chris had taken of her hugging Jackson. After a bit of photoshopping, she e-mailed a copy of it to him. "Great memory of the two of you," he said. "Jackson was the best dog I ever had. I miss him." They exchanged pictures of each other. He sent her a picture of a stunning, golden sunset that he took from his sunroom after Olivia told him that she was a sunset watcher. How thoughtful. But—within a few days, Olivia knew that she needed to set Chris straight about their past. She wrote a treatise about the counselor she had seen. She told him about

Dewey's disclosure to her about the other women Chris was seeing and how Dewey lived in anxious suspense, worried that Olivia would run into one of them. She also told him that she wasn't the emotional person she had been many years ago because her meditation practice had changed that. Chris responded, "I thought you were the one. I guess I had too much ego. I never was that smart. I've always been more of a sledge-hammer than a thinker… I'd like to think one can make up for some of the bad shit done in life. I don't want to get deep but sometimes I wonder how it would have turned out. I don't remember all the screwing around I was doing. That's because I tend to think about the good times—not the crazy ones. I've done some bad things over the years but maybe not that bad because people still talk to me. I've never expected to get a do over although I prayed for it a couple of times. I gave up praying a long time ago. It didn't work so I just try to learn from the mistakes I continue to make." Chris had changed. Olivia was convinced.

Chris was struggling with a laundry list of health issues. The most immediate problem seemed to be physical pain from an accident that broke bones and required several surgeries. Consequently, he was in the process of selling his business and retiring. Olivia mailed him a book she had published a couple of years previously that had to do with alternative approaches to healing (Wilson, 2011). "Wow," he said, "I knew you were smart but had no idea you were so heady. You sound like a true academic." She suspected that Chris had a prescription medicine addiction, not only to narcotic pain medication, which he heavily relied upon in order to keep up his golf game, but sleep medication, known as long-acting Benzodiazepines. He was a die-hard medical model junkie and knew nothing about preventative health measures—nor did he want to know. He preferred to focus on diagnosis, catching a disease before it killed him, and relied heavily on worshipped physicians who were in bed with the pharmaceutical companies—physicians who received perks for the prescriptions they wrote and the pills that they pushed. Chris also scrutinized—and shared with Olivia—the results of his medical reports from excessive procedures, obsessing about his annual colonoscopy and removal of polyps as if he had a chronic case of hypochondriasis. He had a Russian roulette approach to health as he continued to pull the lifestyle trigger.

Not that a colonoscopy wasn't beneficial. Olivia's endeared maternal grandmother died from colon cancer in 1978. No one loved junk food more than her grandmother. Heaven for her was baking a chocolate cake from scratch with chocolate icing and waiting for Olivia to take her to Dairy Queen for a vanilla swirl soft ice cream cone. When her lower bowel perforated it was the beginning of the end. As paramedics arrived in an ambulance and lifted her onto a stretcher to transport her to the hospital emergency room, she grabbed at her cherished gold, flower-engraved clasp bracelet that she always wore on her right wrist. It wasn't easy to get on and off because a small metal guard button needed to be pushed first, and in attempting to do so she broke her thumbnail vertically in half. She was rushed into emergency surgery. Following the surgery, Olivia, two thousand miles away, across the country, telephoned the surgeon and asked, "How is my grandmother? Does she at least have a 50–50 chance of making it?" The surgeon replied, "Your grandmother has less than a 1% chance of living until tomorrow."

At the funeral home, Olivia gasped at the sight of her grandmother's broken thumbnail and complained to the funeral director that it hadn't been fixed and manicured. Her grandmother's contagious laughter had been silenced. She laid there in her prized turquoise, full-length formal dress with gold braid trim that she had purchased for Olivia's wedding reception. The gold bracelet that she always wore was noticeably missing. It was days later when her grandmother's neighbor, Kae, from her senior citizen high-rise apartment building, handed the gold bracelet to Olivia. "This was your grandmother's dying wish... that I give this bracelet to you. I saw her trying to take it off of her wrist when the paramedics were putting her on the stretcher. It's how she broke her nail." Years later, Olivia's mother was wearing a similar looking bracelet, and Olivia's father confronted Olivia, asking her why she had her grandmother's gold bracelet. Olivia quickly replied, "Kae gave it to me," and told him the story. He was speechless, but he believed her—perhaps because it explained the grossly broken thumbnail that no one seemed to forget.

It was no surprise that Olivia was reaching out to Chris in an attempt to improve his health because she had done that for hundreds of people over the years, beginning with the university health classes she taught while completing her Doctor of Philosophy Degree (PhD). She required that her students write daily health journals and was gripped by the depth of their honesty, candor, and suffering, particularly when they disclosed what they would **not** disclose to their physicians and therapists. She read hundreds—if not thousands—of daily accounts that described the human condition, including anxiety, depression, attempted murder, suicide ideation and suicide attempts, rape, date rape, death, substance abuse addiction, terminal illness, road rage, stress, financial distress, loss of relationships, dysfunctional relationships, anorexia, and bulimia. She delved beyond shallow observations. As she read their accounts she was inside their hearts and wearing their shoes as a witness to their suffering. She experienced an awakening of her own heart and a growing compassion, a wish that others would not suffer—an aspect of bodhicitta. This also became a double-edged sword for Olivia. Her big, compassionate heart—vulnerable and exposed—risked being filleted open, time and time again, especially when she saw suffering.

Olivia later taught group psychotherapy and completed a Postdoctoral Fellowship in Clinical Psychology, practicing for a short time as a Marriage and Family Therapist (MFT) but began to feel disillusioned with Western psychology when she recognized that its therapeutic approaches could make people worse—instead of better. Western psychology was scratching the surface compared to what the Tibetans had known for centuries. How could Olivia possibly continue to practice in a Western system where there were over 100 different therapeutic models, many of which contradicted each other and none that had been empirically tested to determine if they produced a positive outcome? Anyone who truly adheres to the Hippocratic Oath, "First, do no harm," will simply be motivated to search elsewhere for answers to the nature of human suffering and how to best approach it.

Chris and Olivia corresponded again about his mom. He believed that if his mom was watching him, it was probably because she was, according to him, "PISSED. She was that way a lot. I do miss her though." He especially missed visiting her at her assisted living facility for cocktail hour at 4:00pm.

"Why would your mom be pissed at you?" Olivia asked.

"Drink too much, party too much, generally irresponsible. All good things rolled up in one lovable package. Women love being pissed at me. I'm an easy target."

Olivia didn't see the red flag. But how thoughtful that he would ask when a good time to call her would be, rather than attempt to call only when it was convenient for him. Laughing, she wrote, "Any time, except when I am watching *Dancing with the Stars* on Monday night."

The phone calls began, on a regular basis. And then one night—of course, when she was watching *Dancing with the Stars,* Chris telephoned. She told him that she was watching *Dancing with the Stars* so he immediately turned it on his TV. He saw Cheryl Burke on the screen dancing and exclaimed, slurring his words, "She's a dead ringer for you!" He was drunk. Yes, years ago, when she and Chris had been together, Olivia had short hair, like Cheryl. Then he said, "Remember when we were in college, and your car was sliding around in the snow because you didn't have snow tires—so I put some tires on your car?"

Olivia slowly stammered, "I—think—so."

"And then remember how I wasn't around on the weekends for a while?"

"I think I remember."

Chris was silent for a few seconds and then continued, "I was in jail on the weekends. I stole those tires."

"You did WHAT?" Olivia screamed.

Chris murmured, "I love you," and hung up the phone.

Olivia forgot about the snow tires because she wondered if she had heard correctly: "I love you." She clung to those words—words that were bigger than a fish hook. He had never been expressive. She had only heard him say "I love you" a couple of times over the years, and he never addressed her with endearing words such as honey, babe, baby. She knew when he missed her because he would take the initiative to see her, often with great difficulty, but he never said, "I miss you." As she continued to watch *Dancing with the Stars*, she realized that they had to see each other. She found herself penning the following on a piece of notebook paper:

To Chris

The protective wall stood steadfast and stoic,
Dismissing whispers and pleas from heart
Until the wall could bear it no longer—
Crumbling one day in weary defeat,
Allowing the window of my heart to open.

I love you..........
I have always loved you.
I never stopped loving you.
My life was incomplete without you.
Memories—like echoes—faded into emptiness.

I love you completely—just the way you are.
There is nothing about you I want to change.
You are smart enough.
You have purpose enough.
You are everything enough.

I love you..........
I have always loved you.
I never stopped loving you.
The mirage—the dream—is on the horizon.
The sunset waits for us.
Olivia

"I'm sorry." Chris apologized for telephoning Olivia while in a drunken state after downing half a dozen shots of Woodford Reserve—on the rocks. One of his friends had died. A lot of his friends had died, most of them from cancer, because they smoked cigarettes. How can people have blithe regard of the fact that smoking cigarettes is the leading cause of premature death? Addiction.

Chris and Olivia decided to meet in Florida three months later, after he played in an annual golf tournament. But once he arrived in Florida, a week before Olivia's arrival, he was a wreck, having anxiety attacks about the anticipated outcome of seeing each other. Telephoning her one night, she could hear a song playing in the background. Patsy Cline was singing, "Crazy—Crazy—I'm crazy for feelin' so lonely. I'm crazy for feelin' so blue." It really is true that country western songs are about cryin', lyin' or dyin'. Chris was at a bar, drunk again and depressed, afraid that Olivia would see him and reject him. But, Patsy wasn't helping the situation. She was now singing "*I Fall to Pieces* every time I see you again." He asked, "Am I going to be a can you kick down the road?" Olivia replied, "Are you going to get cold feet and not meet me?" Some of Chris's golfing buddies thought it was preposterous that he would be meeting an old girlfriend after 30 years! One of them speculated, "She probably wears no makeup and Birkenstocks!" By that time, Patsy's singing was progressing from moderate to severe depression: "I've been so wrong—for so long." Olivia would later discover that Chris would never once ask her what music she wanted to listen to although Olivia was quite the connoisseur of upbeat, world music. He simply wouldn't listen to it.

However, Olivia arrived in Florida, and Chris knocked on her door the next afternoon. She greeted him with a hug that seemed to surprise him but it also seemed as though time had stood still. He was as handsome as ever, looked younger than his actual age and was wearing a black In-N-Out Burger T-shirt and a pair of Ralph Lauren khaki Bermuda shorts. Olivia would later smile about his mix of labels—Ralph Lauren always among them. They spent three days at an ocean resort, as if they had never been apart. They had a lot of catching up to do and a lot of years to talk about. He talked more than when he was younger, and he focused on politics. Some might call him a silver spoon Republican whereas Olivia had no political affiliation whatsoever nor was she interested in politics. She had concluded that watching American politicians was more like watching men play in their sandbox. He commented, "I thought about becoming a politician but I didn't have the fire in the belly that you have to have." They enjoyed a dinner cruise, watched the sunset paint the horizon in splashes of gold, yellow, and various shades of orange as dolphins danced in the ocean alongside the boat. A marriage ceremony took place within feet of them as they shared a bottle of Olivia's favorite Shiraz red wine. Chris had also been drinking his favorite Woodford Reserve, and what most people called a double, he called a single, even arguing with the bartender, "I said a double, not a single." Olivia stopped at one glass of wine because of her low tolerance for alcohol. "You're a cheap date!" Chris exclaimed, as they laughed. They dined at several wonderful nearby restaurants during the next couple of days. The crab cakes. They reminded her of the yummy Maryland crab cakes that her maternal grandmother would mix up for her and fry in her black cast-iron frying pan.

Chris and Olivia met a month later in Las Vegas. Her Vegas friend, Liz, loaned Olivia her white Mercedes Benz in order to pick up Chris at McCarran Airport. There he was—standing next to the curb waiting for her with his golf clubs, wearing a rare smile on his face. She didn't know if he would be able to travel to Las Vegas because he had to appear in front of a judge in court in order to get permission to travel out-of-state. Another disclosure bomb had been dropped on her that week when he told her over the phone, "Olivia, I'm on probation." For the previous six months, Chris had been on a one-year probation for a DUI that also involved assaulting a police officer. He was also proud of the fact that it took not one—not two—but three police officers to subdue him and pin him to the ground—in order to handcuff him—and without a stun gun. The terms of his probation included that he could not go near alcohol, much less consume it; however, Chris knew how to beat the system. He simply didn't drink alcohol after 9:00pm at night in case he was called to pass a breathalyzer test in the morning. Alcohol shows up in the breath because it gets absorbed from the mouth, throat, stomach, and intestines into the bloodstream. It is not digested upon absorption or chemically changed in the bloodstream, and as the blood goes through the lungs, a physiologically predictable amount of the alcohol will move across the lung membranes and into the lungs themselves. Once in contact with the air in the lungs, it evaporates and is exhaled. The concentration of the alcohol in the air within the lungs is directly related to the concentration of the alcohol in the blood.

Chris was assigned one of five colors by his detested female probation officer whenever he met with her, and a daily 5am phone call would announce which one of the colors needed to appear within the hour at the probation office. Some colors were randomly selected more frequently than others. Olivia learned that Chris had already completed court ordered classes pertaining to alcohol and had paid someone to sign off on completed community service hours; however, the Shiraz wine they drank together in Florida the previous month threw a wrench in Chris's manipulative master plan. He got caught via a blood test—not a breathalyzer test—that probation required of him when he returned home from Florida. He was in violation of his probation, which meant incarceration. Of course, Chris hired a big-gun attorney to fight the test results. His best friend, Roy, was in court with him in case Chris was handcuffed and taken to jail in which case Roy would telephone Olivia to break the news. After a long, suspenseful Perry Mason-like saga, Chris's attorney won his argument in court, and poof, Chris was on his way to Las Vegas. In dismay, Olivia telephoned her brother. He blurted, "Assaulting a police officer! He should be in the big house!" And why wasn't he in the big house? Because he had money, and he could "buy" his way out of trouble over and over again. Olivia knew it would be a protracted six months before Chris was off probation if he didn't end up in jail first. She suddenly had visions of traveling to visit him in jail, seeing him handcuffed and outfitted in a two-piece, orange prison scrub set uniform. They would sit facing each other at an outdoor picnic table, discussing which book he was reading.

A dark cloud had moved in. They spent the next week hanging out at the Fremont Street Golden Nugget Hotel while he played in yet another golf tournament. It didn't matter that they were on the 23rd VIP floor with complimentary coffee, peanuts, and M&Ms. The week was long and rather unbearable for Olivia, given the casino noise downstairs and the ding-ding-ding of Diamond Double slot machines. On the contrary, she loved the silence of solitude, enhanced by the harmonic sound of birds singing outside. They did leave Fremont Street a couple of times, dining at the rotating Top of the World Restaurant at the Stratosphere for magnificent views of Las Vegas while a professional photographer took pictures of them. They also saw Faith Hill and Garth Brooks in concert at the magnificent Venetian Hotel where Olivia posed for a picture in front of a large Buddha statue. But back at the hotel, Chris refused to watch *Dancing with the Stars* with her, choosing to meet his buddies downstairs in the lounge for a beer. The best Olivia could do now that she knew Chris was on probation was to set an example and refuse to drink herself because he wasn't about to give it up—even with jail staring him in the face. In his opinion, every VIP in his little town would drink and drive. He simply was unlucky and got caught—now the victim. He was angry that anyone, especially a "pot-smoking, alcoholic judge," would tell him not to drink. Olivia tried to reason with him. He didn't appreciate that probation was a gift in lieu of him going to jail. His attorney had really pulled a rabbit out of a hat on that one.

By the River

For months, Chris had wanted Olivia to visit him at his home in order to meet his friends and family. She finally agreed, and he purchased a plane ticket for her to arrive the following month. For Olivia, the day came soon enough because she was aware that their relationship had evolved to the point where they would both be making serious decisions that wouldn't involve the purchase of a plane ticket every month. Chris picked her up at the airport in his new, white BMW SUV and drove her to his home at the outskirts of a little rural town. A long, newly-asphalted driveway led to the house, which sat yards in front of a river, lined with lush, green trees. It was breathtaking. The interior of the house was well decorated, albeit more suited for a bachelor with framed pictures of cars on the walls and a large moose head hanging in the study. The unused sunroom, with a wall of windows, faced the river. Olivia viewed it as the perfect meditation room—the kind of meditation room one would see in a magazine or in pictures. From that room, there was a view of the river, which seemed to constantly change in color and appearance, especially in the morning. She loved to walk down to its bank and sit in meditation, occasionally spotting a deer or several of them in a group. One day she selected the NOTES icon on her phone and wrote:

> A moving river… the perfect metaphor for our lives—always moving, impermanent, each day bringing change. Today is a little murky but does it matter as long I can sit in stillness?

The animals seemed to be curious about Olivia's presence; one squirrel sat on a tree trunk and watched as if joining her in meditation rather than in anticipation of her next move, which was nothing—just sitting. Olivia wanted Chris to learn to meditate because she knew it would help him with his health problems, including pain and insomnia. He would also be able to sit with her both inside and outside of the house. She selected a maroon, organic cotton, and oversized zafu and zabuton for him from a mail order magazine. Unfortunately, he wasn't interested. It was easier for him to pop pills from an array of bottles that were lying around the house with multiple bottles of the same prescription. One day she courageously asked, "Is it okay if we put these away in the medicine cabinet?" And if he was sitting, it was in the front of the television watching old-time movies. His favorite movie was *Gentlemen Prefer Blondes,* with blonde sex symbol Marilyn Monroe singing, *Diamonds are a Girl's Best Friend,* which Olivia appreciated as much as Fox News. "Diamonds are *not* a girl's best friend," she insisted, as she rolled her eyes and headed for the kitchen again—for more Starbucks' Keurig coffee—black.

Escape

The idiosyncrasies! Olivia could not have assessed the idiosyncrasies of this little town in two weeks. It took a month to realize that the social activity, as far as Chris's life was concerned, was the bar scene. Olivia had never been in a bar, much less hung out in one on Thursday, Friday, and Saturday nights. She didn't even know what "bar food" was, which caused a lot of laughter among he and his friends. However, Chris and Olivia joined his friends frequently for what seemed to be trite, idle talk, often at a restaurant for breakfast. Surprisingly, the waitress would stand and listen catatonically to their conversation, and after she took their order and delivered their food, she would join in the conversation with everyone sitting at the table. Everyone thrived on gossip, knowing the everyday business of every man, woman, and child in town. In fact, Chris eagerly awaited the arrival of his cleaning lady, Jody, on Saturday morning because she would fervently—with a zealousness—update him on the town gossip as they stood in the kitchen sipping coffee. There was even a juicy rumor circulating about Olivia: "She looks like a Kardashian!"

As Olivia listened to Jody divulge the community health updates, she always felt sorrow for the many who were ill because of their lifestyle habits—smoking and drinking. Sadly, one of Chris's closest friends, Drew, was in a local hospice dying from lung cancer—100 pounds lighter, skin and bones, and in and out of a coma—but that kind of suffering didn't seem to deter people from their lifestyle habits. Chris would visit Drew while Olivia waited in the SUV, and Chris would always return badly shaken with tears in his eyes. Impending death felt comfortable to Olivia. She had taught a university Death and Dying course, was a trained hospice volunteer, and Elisabeth Kübler-Ross, MD, Psychiatrist, considered a world revolutionist on the topic of death and dying, became one of Olivia's heroines. During that time, Olivia exhausted the research literature on the topic of death and clearly understood the process of dying; however, she came to believe that the West had only scratched the surface on this topic when compared to the profound knowledge of the Tibetans, as found in *The Tibetan Book of the Dead*. Yes, it seemed normative that dying of cancer was the way life went down in Chris's little town. The way you live is the way you die. Fortunately, Chris didn't smoke because he had a slight case of asthma, which also meant that he was still alive.

The inevitable day came when Chris and Olivia attended Drew's Roman Catholic funeral. Olivia joined in the ritualistic service, not only in reciting prayers but holding a hymnbook and singing songs with the congregation. She had attended catechism classes with her friends when she was ten years old, had studied Catholicism and Protestant religions for years, and completed a graduate course *Deism: The Rise of Religious Skepticism*; however, despite this knowledge, she wasn't bigoted. She truly believed in different strokes for different folks and always appreciated the words of Henry David Thoreau (Thoreau, 2004, p. 372): "If a man loses pace with his companions, perhaps it is because he hears a different drummer. Let him step to the music which he hears, however measured, or far away." Chris, however, would not participate in the funeral service, although he had been raised in the Catholic Church. This nonparticipation was so glaringly apparent that he might as well have been an altar boy on strike at the Vatican. Olivia began to suspect that he had not only grown to be anti-religious but that he felt uncomfortable with any and all things that were spiritual in nature. In fact, one day as Chris left the house to play golf, he asked Olivia if she would sort through his deceased mother's personal belongings and discard what was unimportant.

Although more than a year had passed since the death of Chris's mother, he still had not opened the cardboard box that contained her prized possessions. As Olivia lifted the flaps to the box, one of the first things she noticed was a silver rosary, with light blue glass beads, among family pictures. She then realized that she was not the one who should be sorting through these belongings. She would tell Chris that the items in the box were important to his mother, and if he didn't want to keep them, they should be given to his son or another family member. Olivia noticed a framed picture that was lying face down on the floor. She picked it up, turned it over, and saw that it was a print of a Buddha sitting in full lotus position. She gasped and carried it up the stairs, that night asking Chris if she could hang it on a wall. He didn't seem to mind that she removed a framed print of a spotted giraffe off of the bathroom wall in order to replace it with a framed print of a Buddha.

Olivia had also noticed another old, framed print with Chinese writing whose meaning she knew she had to investigate. Apparently, the writing was about the vidya elder Vimalakirti who obtained the power over birth and transcended the three lower realms. Vimalakirti's wife was standing in the print, as he demonstrated the dharma through his everyday life as a layperson. He was known to debate non-dual theory with Manjushri, the Buddha of Wisdom, and the latter replied with silence. In the whole country of China at the time, there is no other match to Manjushri other than him. There was a dharma phrase written by the Emperor Qianlong of the Qing dynasty. (Dharma refers to doctrine, law, way of higher truths, teaching, or discipline. The general concept forms a basis for philosophies, beliefs, and practices originating in India; Hinduism, Buddhism, Jainism, and Sikhism retain the centrality of dharma in their teachings.) Olivia was ecstatic that Chris's mother would have an appreciation for sacred pieces of art; however, the significance of it meant nothing to Chris, expressing to his son that the print might have some monetary value. Regardless, Olivia would never ask a man to drive a nail for her. She found a hammer and a nail and hung it the next day on a wall in what would be a perfect meditation room overlooking the river.

As Olivia was hammering, her cursory glance at the open arched television room revealed a cardboard box sitting on the floor. It was the box in which she had mailed her book, seven months prior. Appearing to be empty, she picked it up to place in the recycle bin in the garage but there was a rattle. There it was—the pewter sun and moon pendant on a sterling silver chain that she had included with her book for Chris. The pendant was special to her because it was one of her Guru's insignia. The pendant, or any sacred object, simply does not belong on the floor; in fact, if sacred text touches the floor, a Buddhist will immediately touch it to the top of his head. She carried the chain and pendant to her traveling jewelry case, which contained a mala and gau, and placed it there. She didn't mention it to Chris because she didn't think he would notice or care. There was a jewelry box sitting on his bedroom dresser, which included watches and cuff links, but the chain and pendant she had mailed to him had been on the floor for seven months. With chagrin, she later noticed the bodhi seed mala that she had brought to Chris, still sitting on a shelf in a mala bag, now thinking that he probably would never remove the mala from the bag to look at it, much less use it or place it in a sacred space. But, according to Chris, there was no place sacred in the house except his bottom dresser drawer where he stashed thousands of dollars in cash—bail money, he called it—in case he ever needed to get bailed out of jail. Olivia didn't need to be Sigmund Freud to conclude that his fear of going to jail was his fear of getting caught driving under the influence (DUI), which was now one of the reasons for his probation.

That was one of the things Olivia loved about Nepal. She had seen Nepalese policemen combing the streets, stopping people who were driving vehicles to see if they had been drinking. There was a zero tolerance policy, which meant no drinking and driving whatsoever, with no legal limits as in the United States—limits that people, especially Chris, were always trying to beat.

Olivia scurried off from Chris's home after five weeks to visit family; however, she had gotten a few things down during those few weeks. Besides being a meat and potatoes man, Chris liked unhealthy white bread, which had to be buttered and sprinkled with salt. He refused to use paper napkins. The napkins set at the table had to be cloth napkins. And no one could mess around with his 11-ounce box of York Peppermint Patties in the refrigerator. Chris told her that when she left, the hummingbirds also left. She wondered if he just didn't feed them. She had desperately wanted a red, glass hummingbird feeder, and Chris relented. He took her shopping at a hardware store where she selected the only glass feeder on display—among an array of plastic ones—and later hung it on the back deck of the house. Every couple of days she would bring it into the kitchen and fill it with her mixture of sugar water, which kept several hummingbirds coming and going. She loved to photograph them while they vibrated, suspended in the air; each one of them had different personalities and distinctive markings. Her favorite hummingbird was a small female that had a black head and red neck with a circle around it as though she were wearing a dainty necklace. In the meantime, Chris had sent her another plane ticket, and she returned a month later for another visit.

But something was wrong. She would find Chris reading a book in the middle of the night in the living room, wrapped in a blanket in his leather La-Z-Boy chair. One night she staggered out and tried to climb in the chair next to him. He angrily snapped, "Go back to bed!" Perplexed, Olivia decided to retreat to the bathtub, instead. She was the first person to use his sunken, white marble Jacuzzi bathtub, drawing hot water while watching bubbles rise from the shower gel she poured under the faucet. She rarely saw a bathtub in the East and relished every minute that she could soak in *any* bathtub, especially at night when she could light candles. That's what she would do now. Submerged in temporary, blissful oblivion, she watched the flickering lights of candles dance on the long vanity mirror on the wall in front of her. She wondered if Chris couldn't sleep because he was weaning himself off of the sleeping pills that she wanted out of his life—a mix with alcohol that could be lethal. That he might not awaken one morning was a real fear.

Nearly an hour later, Olivia staggered back to bed in the dark, and as usual, had no problems falling asleep. She could sleep like a rock—anywhere, any time, any place—one of the benefits of her meditation practice after experiencing years of anxiety-related sleep disturbances. Olivia knew the research literature in regard to the indisputable benefits of meditation, including Davidson's neuroscience brain plasticity research, but here again, the West was scratching the surface in knowledge compared to what the Buddha—the Great Psychologist—discovered and what the Tibetans practiced as they sat in meditation for a thousand years, isolated from the rest of the world.

It wasn't long before Chris's 3:12am "You're not going to Tibet" meltdown, which Olivia believed could have been the onset of a nervous breakdown—or was it a psychotic break? In all of the years that she had known Chris, she had never seen him cry—not once. Yes, she had seen tears in his eyes when they were in college and he begged her to marry him and recently, after he saw his friend in hospice care, but cry—never. He reminded Olivia that she was always leaving him, and then, in a manipulative, veiled kind of threat, told her that there was a local, single woman (later to be known as Barb) who might be better suited for him. In fact, her boyfriend of 15 years had just kicked her out of their house, she was homeless, and of course, it was her boyfriend's fault—one hundred percent. She certainly knew how to play on Chris's sympathies because he identified with the downtrodden, which made him feel needed and important. His male ego was flashing its neon lights. Barb, who was "waiting in the wings," would also drive Chris home from the local bars.

Undeniably, the mention of another woman could have triggered quite a reaction from Olivia, given their history, but Olivia calmly and flatly told him, "I'm not going to be a barmaid bimbo." The bar scene was *not* her thing. More than one glass of wine once a month—or was it once a year—was also *not* her thing. Was this why he asked her to visit him in this little town where the mortality rate from cancer was the highest in the state—to see if she could embrace the bar scene way of life and support his obsession with alcohol? Olivia was draped in a long, strappy, black cotton Natori nightgown as she sat cross-legged on the bed next to Chris. They talked as he continued to cry. For the *first* time, they talked about his problem with alcohol, and he *acknowledged* that it was a problem. The reality was—he was an alcoholic, and alcohol was more important to him than Olivia. As was the nature of any addiction, it would always trump her. Olivia had progressively seen that Chris drank *a lot* of alcohol—Kentucky straight bourbon whiskey—on the rocks--42.2% alcohol by volume or 90.4 US Proof. No wonder he wanted to purchase a liquor store. But on that particular night, perhaps because of his unstable, erratic behavior and incessant crying, she became astutely aware of his arsenal of loaded guns throughout the house. It is one reason why she did not raise her voice or shed a tear. She wouldn't do anything that would escalate his emotional state that persisted for more than two hours. There were pistols in drawers with magazines and ammunition. There were rifles in an unlocked gun case near the front door, and a loaded shotgun was propped up next to the bedroom door within six feet of them. Joe Biden, the "buy a shotgun," advocate would be pleased. But to fire two blasts of a double barrel shotgun outside on the balcony to deter invaders?

Chris had once offered to remove all of his guns from the house by giving them to his son, knowing how Olivia felt about the hotly debated interpretation of the Second Amendment by SCOTUS that provides US citizens with the right to bear arms, immune from reasonable regulation. Olivia simply did not agree with the gun advocacy argument "guns don't kill people—people kill people" when mass shootings in America had become an ethical outrage and moral disgrace. Teaching gun safety to children, as an antidote, demonstrated its futility when researchers reported findings that even when children were taught not to touch a gun, in a room with a two-way mirror, every child touched and handled a gun that was hidden in a toy box! Bottom line—Olivia wouldn't shoot someone, not even in self-defense. She would never want the karmic consequences of shooting or harming someone. In such a situation she would rather be shot. Friends of Olivia's from around the world often questioned her, in disbelief, about the guns and mass shootings in America. One of her European friends said, "America needs to once again come under British rule so Americans will need a license in order to carry a vegetable peeler in public."

Because of the fact that Chris never followed through on removing his stockpile of guns from the house, Olivia was now in a situation where she was intuitively thinking, with a sense of urgency, "You need to get out of here." Alcohol, prescription drugs, nervous breakdowns, and loaded guns don't mix, especially where Olivia was in a situation where she could not be controlled. Characteristic of domestic violence. Olivia believed that Nicole Simpson was murdered for no other reason than that she could no longer be controlled. Olivia also believed that Denise Brown would be telling her right now to get the hell out of Dodge. Coincidentally, no sooner had that thought entered her mind, Chris mentioned that he was sitting outside on the back deck and saw a shell casing from one of his guns. It struck him that Olivia would get upset if he shot an animal in front of her. "Yes," Olivia said. "But you don't have to be a Buddhist to believe in not killing animals. Remember what your great American writer James Oliver Curwood said, 'The greatest thrill is not to kill but to let live.'" Chris was speechless.

It was now 5am. The telephone rang. Yellow. Yellows had to go to the probation office for a breathalyzer test, and Chris was a yellow. Still crying, he went to the bathroom, grabbed a washcloth, placed it under cold running water, and held it over his eyes. "My eyes are so red, they'll think I've been drinking." He was nothing short of a wreck. Olivia was hurt, and according to Western standards, would have been justified in reacting with anger. Why would he fly her out to see him on a vacation just to tell her in the middle of the night that their relationship wasn't going to work? Couldn't he have informed her of that in an e-mail or over the phone? A therapist probably would recommend that Olivia get angry with him in order to "create emotional" distance between them, viewed as a healthy and necessary step in the bereavement process. Olivia looked over at the bookshelf where she had placed framed pictures of the two of them. He was kissing her in one picture. Another picture showed them ready to board a dinner cruise boat, a dolphin popping out of the water in the background. And there was also the black and white picture of her hugging white, fluffy Jackson over 30 years ago. No, she wouldn't pick them up and throw them against the wall, shattering the glass into a million pieces. Even Pema Chodron would have at least picked up a rock and thrown it at him; however, Pema took that action in response to her husband leaving her *before* she became a Buddhist nun. From a Buddhist perspective, anger is one of the three poisons (ignorance, attachment, and aversion/anger) from which all other negativity and non-virtuous actions arise. One outburst of anger can instantly destroy eons of accumulated virtuous merit. Therefore, this abysmal negative emotion—anger—was one place where Olivia was determined not to go even if she was hitched to a team of horses, and they tried to drag her there. Chris did appreciate the fact that she wasn't hysterical, without as much as an "oh me, oh my, oh dear" Hardy Har Har line. When she assured him, "I am going to handle this with dignity," he cried even more, thanking her over and over again as he hustled out the door. It was a 30 minute drive to the probation office where he would stand in line with other "yellow" parolees to blow into a breathalyzer—a test he had taken dozens of times during the past six months.

That very day, Chris was playing in an annual golf tournament to honor another one of his friends who had died an untimely death. Olivia was with Chris once when he visited his gravesite where he left a golf ball and a beer glass in lieu of flowers. This golf event was not included in his usual Tuesday–Thursday 18 rounds of golf, which meant at least four hours of play before he and his friends got together to drink a few rounds. The entire Golf and Country Club atmosphere meant drinking alcohol—the way that a Cineplex movie meant popcorn and a football game meant hot dogs. Chris had asked Olivia to join him at the country club at 5:00pm for a golf tournament dinner celebration—as if nothing had happened between them—however, she wanted to be gone. The "fight or flight response" had kicked in, and Olivia was not going to fight. It would take everything she had to "flight" right over the border to Alaska—or *anywhere* but there—within the day. She had to pack, ship a kitchen appliance, and find transportation. "Why can't I think?" she asked herself, shaking inside.

Olivia had monkey mind, and the monkey was swinging from one thought to another. Or worse, she had a raging elephant mind that needed to be trained, referred to in ancient Pali text and used in Tibetan Buddhism: When a wild elephant is captured it is tied to a post with a strong rope, which enrages the elephant as he screams, tramples, and pulls against the rope for days until he realizes that he is not going to escape. At this point, the elephant settles down. He can be fed and handled with safety, the post and rope are not needed, and the elephant can be trained in order to be useful. The wild elephant is analogous to our wildly active mind, the rope is mindfulness, and the post is the object of meditation—breathing. The tamed elephant that emerges from this process is a well-trained, concentrated mind that can pierce the layers of illusion that obscure reality. We realize the damage that an untamed elephant incurs when running wild, just as we do damage not only to ourselves but to others when our untamed mind runs wild. Olivia observed that her mind was running wild like an untamed elephant but there was no time to sit, no time to focus on the breath now. The most she could do at the moment was try to concentrate on what was in front of her face and what she needed to do.

"What did Chris do with my dresses that were hanging in the closet?" She was in a time crunch—as though a time bomb was ticking, ready to go off. "He cannot know I'm leaving. He cannot come home before I get out of here." She started making phone calls. There were no taxis to the airport—or anywhere, for that matter—and in checking flights, she couldn't fly out of the nearest airport for two days. After 30 minutes and no quick solutions, she remembered Meg, a friend she met years ago at a Lake Geneva meditation retreat. She lived only an hour south. Olivia telephoned her, "Meg, I need to get out of here." Olivia explained the situation, embarrassed that she would BE in such a situation. "I need to get out of here without him knowing because he might try to stop me. He's not emotionally stable right now." Without hesitating, Meg agreed to pick her up at 4:00pm. In the meantime, Chris had called about dinner because he wanted to introduce her to some "important" people. That's what Olivia's credentials did for Chris. He could use them to impress people—political animal style. "You know, Chris, I might be there and I might not. After last night, I'm not feeling well, but I'll see you later." She was then back on the phone trying to ensure that a scheduled delivery would arrive by the time she left with Meg.

Olivia drove Chris's black Lexus to town and found the local hardware store where she could ship her kitchen blender; however, she blinked and got lost, trapped in a maze. She had no choice but to telephone Chris while he was ready to tee off, in order to give her directions back to the house. Olivia truly did have a missing template in her brain when it came to sense of direction, believing she was certainly born that way. Finding her way back to the house was a relief, followed by the task of packing while not being able to think straight. She unplugged the essential oils diffuser that she had purchased and emptied the water out of it in order to pack it in her suitcase, then carefully wrapped about a dozen bottles of essential oils that she had hoped would help Chris. She might as well have been Florence Nightingale doting over him with a bottle of lavender as he lay critically wounded on the battlefield. She was grateful that under ordinary circumstances she did not have to endure scattered, fragmented, all-over-the-board thinking. Finally, suitcases were packed, zipped up, and lined up at the front door. "Oh, no," she said aloud. She saw from one of the front windows that Chris's son was working on his car in one of the garages. "How can I get out of here without him seeing me?" she thought. Olivia paced the foyer wood floor, looking out the window for Meg. Suddenly, Olivia remembered the bodhi seed mala beads that she had given to Chris that were lying on a bookshelf. She couldn't reconcile leaving them there with his "bail money." She knew that someone else could use and appreciate them. She had no idea who—but someone. She ran back to the bedroom, grabbed the mala bag with beads off the shelf, and ran back to the foyer, unzipping and zipping up a side zipper to her smallest roll-on suitcase—safely tucking them inside. She had also brought him a case of Costco Kirkland brand soap, the only soap he used because of the way it lathered. She would gladly leave him the bubbly soap—but not the mala.

It was 4:00pm—precisely—Meg pulled into the driveway. The delivery truck was right behind her. Meg jumped out of her car and ran to accept the package from the deliveryman as Olivia flew out the front door, pulling wheeled suitcases and quickly loading them in the trunk of the car before Chris's son noticed. Surely he would telephone Chris if he saw that Olivia was leaving. Meg and Olivia hurriedly got into the front seat of what was now a getaway car and sped out the driveway. They breathed a sigh of relief, not believing that their plan had been orchestrated so perfectly. They decided to have dinner at a Mexican restaurant near Meg's home, and just as Olivia started to dive into the cheese enchiladas she had ordered, her iPhone started ringing. It stopped ringing… then rang again… and then again. Olivia wouldn't answer but Chris had left messages, "You can imagine my surprise when I came home and found you weren't here. I do want to know where you are." Of course, Olivia wouldn't disclose her location. He had been to Meg's home the previous year. Olivia didn't want him showing up at the door during the two days that she had to wait for her flight back to her home. It was going to be a long and painful two days as Olivia began to analyze and reanalyze what had happened between them, clinging to time-delineated past events that were over. She was living in the past, which was a memory. But regardless, she needed to get a grip, as in the logical words of the Buddha:

> Lift up yourself by yourself;
> Examine yourself by yourself.
> Thus self-protected and attentive
> You will live joyfully, mendicant.
> For self is the master of self;
> Self is the refuge of self.
> Therefore tame yourself,
> Like a merchant tames a noble horse.
> The Buddha, *The Dhammapada* 25:20–22

Part II

Training for Tibet

Olivia had reached the point where temporary Band-Aids—a hug from a friend, well-meaning advice, self-help books, ice cream, Mexican food, a trip to Sam's Club, and inspirational quotations—weren't very helpful. She couldn't remember when she had been in more pain, but now understood why the Buddha delineated different kinds of suffering as dukkha (Sanskrit). She was experiencing all three of them—1) the pain of pain (suffering of birth, illness, old age, and death); 2) the pain of alteration (suffering caused by the failure of happy moments to last); and 3) the pain of formation (a subtle form of suffering arising as a reaction to qualities of conditioned things such as the five aggregates (shandkhas): 1) form; 2) feeling; 3) perception; 4) mental formation; and 5) consciousness as a basis for understanding and achieving liberation from suffering and factors constituting the human mind.

Olivia's primary meditation practices were shinay and Lojong meditation. The term shinyata (Sanskrit) it is translated into shinay (Tibetan). Shin Nay is two words put in to one. Shi means shiwa that means peaceful, the peacefulness, and the quietness that is shiwa. Nay means naypa. Naypa is not moving just being there, remaining sitting so remaining in peace or being at peace. However, Olivia found that she needed a support for her elephant raging mind and the easiest support was to focus on her breath to a count. As she sat on Meg's basement floor, the first inhalation and exhalation of her breath was "1." She couldn't concentrate on "1" so she tried again and then again. Finally, she was able to proceed to "2" on her next breath and, subsequently, to "10." She settled her mind enough that she could proceed to follow the breath without a count. Then she was able to rest in shinay, which was like going on a mental vacation, sitting in the present moment in naturalness without the pain of the past nor worry about the future—freeing the clouds of obscurations in order to see mind directly.

Six weeks until Tibet, Olivia's recovery heart rate was poor. "Oh, my gosh, I could go into cardiac arrest at Mt. Everest Base Camp or circumambulating (the act of moving around a sacred object, found in many religions) Mt. Kailash," Olivia thought. She was forced to face the inevitable: "How can I train and get ready for Tibet in six weeks? I need a personal trainer." Doreen was perfect. Olivia hired her and committed herself to working hard every single day. Each day the prescribed exercise was different: Olivia ran intervals one day, biked or hiked the next with different sets of exercises, many executed with t-bands or the blue Reebok balance ball that she found at Walmart. One day Olivia worked on upper body, alternating the next day to lower body, abs, yoga, and core strength. It was all so complicated that Olivia had to refer to pages and pages of exercise diagrams and instructions. And the diet and nutrition! "Oh my gosh, I'm starving. I feel as though I am starving all of the time."

Olivia began her training program with a lemon juice cleanse of squeezed lemon, distilled water, and organic maple syrup… no sugar, no coffee, no junk food! She ate an apple every day, protein before bed, and drank LOTS of distilled or reverse osmosis water! She saw a physician in order to get a prescription of Diamox (Acetazolamide) for altitude sickness, which can be unpredictable, and she needed to purchase a list of other items: i.e. Ahnu hiking boots, odorless Incredisocks, toe warmers, hand warmers, canned oxygen, which even came in flavors; headlamp, power bars, trail mix, vitamins, probiotics, power adapters, and a battery back-up. She had learned from past experience that learning to pack properly was vitally important, which included knowing what supplies you could and could not obtain in the country one was visiting. For example, prior to Olivia's first trip to Nepal, she packed a large suitcase full of bottled water because she had heard about the need to drink *only* bottled water in

Nepal; however, bottled water is the one thing that can be easily obtained there.

Shopping at Lululemon became routine: four pairs of cropped pants, and four pairs of long pants, six of which had side pockets for Olivia's iPhone so she could listen to music with her Skullcandy earbuds while she exercised. She purchased two sport bags, a running jacket, four short-sleeved shirts, four long-sleeved shirts that covered the hands with a thumb insert, a running hat, gloves, three sports bras and a yoga top. "OMG, will it ever end?" Olivia thought. "And why do I continually put these yoga pants on backwards or inside out? Can't I see that the drawstring is in the front, inside the pant rather than on the outside?"

Soon, Olivia could run several miles. When Doreen evaluated her on a weekly basis, Olivia could progressively run on the treadmill longer without shortness of breath, stay in a plank for a longer period of time, do "real" push-ups, and endure wall sits. Olivia's resting heart rate decreased, and her recovery heart rate soon fell into normal range. Doreen told her, "I won't have you ready for Tibet but this will make an impact." Impact it was... of the Americans who went to Tibet with her, Olivia probably felt the least amount of distress. She wasn't gasping for breath and didn't need oxygen. She didn't get sick with crushing headaches nor did she have insomnia. Her heart rate was never elevated, and she wasn't at the back when the pack was hiking except one day on the stairs of the Potala Palace. The training paid off, and Olivia felt and looked great, 20 pounds lighter.

Even though Olivia and Chris had not been in communication for weeks, the last time they talked she promised him that she would telephone him before boarding her Cathay Pacific international flight in Los Angeles for Kathmandu. She didn't forget—nor did he. He was sitting in his white SUV in front of a title company, waiting for her call. "I know that Tibet would be too difficult for you because of the high altitude but you could meet me afterwards in Kathmandu when I arrive there in a month," Olivia said. She was surprised when Chris replied, "I'll think about it." Did he really say that he was considering coming to see her in Nepal—a third world country? She couldn't believe what she had just heard. Perhaps there was hope, after all, and there was good news. He was off probation even if that didn't mean much. There was a mountain of obstacles that appeared to overshadow their relationship but she remembered the words of one her teachers, "See the potential of a relationship." A feeling of hope floated in, and Olivia grabbed it and clung to it, now living in the fantasy of the future. She observed the feeling of hope, however, and asked herself, "Where did that hope come from? Where is it now? Where will it be tomorrow?" If a feeling could be that unpredictable and undependable—if a feeling can suddenly appear and then disappear, vanishing into thin air—how real is it? It isn't.

Olivia decided, however, that she would make strong wishes for her relationship with Chris throughout her travels in Tibet. Yes, she believed in the power of wishes, and if anything could help to remove the obstacles in their relationships, wishes could. After all, wishes are part of our legacy. As children, we learn to place our wish, written on a small piece of paper, in a wishing jar. We make a wish before we toss a coin into a water fountain full of coins, where others had also made wishes. We learn to wish upon a star (Washington and Harline, 1940):

> When you wish upon a star
> Makes no difference who you are
> When you wish upon a star
> Your dreams come true.

The childhood heroine in Walt Disney's 1950 production of *Cinderella* (David, Hoffman, and Livingston, 1949) expressed her belief in the song *A Dream Is a Wish Your Heart Makes*:

When you're fast asleep
In dreams you lose you heartaches.
Whatever you wish for, you keep.
Have faith in your dreams and someday
Your rainbow will come smiling thru.
No matter how your heart is grieving
If you keep on believing
the dream that you wish will come true.

We make a wish before we blow out lit candles on our birthday cake, usually one candle for each year of our life. In the early 17th century, the custom began of making a silent wish with a partner, each grasping an end of a chicken or turkey wishbone (furcula bone) (called a merrythought until 1860) and then pulling until the wishbone snapped; the wish coming true for the person who ended up with the largest section of the broken wishbone. We make New Year's Resolutions, which are wishes that we will accomplish certain goals.

As Olivia traveled the world, she found that making wishes was more prevalent than what we might think. For example, the King of Naga, Anavatapta, made a wish that non-virtuous deeds would be rinsed away from those who touched or drank from the water of the Ganges River. The 4th century iron pillar of New Delhi is the oldest structure at the Qutb Minar Complex and stands in the courtyard of the Quwwatu'l-Islam mosque. An iron fence was placed around it to prevent people from touching it because at one time they would stand with their back to the pillar, wrap their arms backwards around the pillar, clasp their hands, and make a wish, believing it would come true. In the Emperor's Courtyard at Fatehpur Sikri, Uttar Pradesh, India at the tomb of Sufi Saint Sheikh Salim Chisti, which lies inside a white marble mausoleum (mazar), one offers prayers and then ties up to three different threads to the lattice windows in order to have one's wishes fulfilled. At the magnificent Swaminarayan

Akshardham in New Delhi, India, visitors pay respect and make wishes before a large white marble replica of Bhagwan Swaminarayn's holy feet (charanarvind), bearing the 16 sacred signs of God. They also pray for the fulfillment of wishes as they perform abhishek of the murti of Neelkanth Vami, pouring waters of river Ganga. In Greenwich (southeast London, England), it is necessary to stand up to the line of the Prime Meridian (another version to rise above it, to one leg in the Western Hemisphere, and the second in the East) and make a wish. Mahatma Gandhi included the word wish in what would become a timeless quote: "Be the change you wish to see in the world."

Olivia first met His Holiness the 17th Gyalwa Karmapa, Trinley Thaye Dorje when he visited the USA in 2003 and he gave her the name Karma Rinchen Lhama (Precious Goddess). He was only about 22 years of age at the time but she instantly recognized that he was beyond extraordinary. He was polished, refined, and had an impressive command of the English language, explaining to the audience in English when the translator struggled to make the translation from Tibetan to English. Being in his energy field was a never forgotten experience.

His Holiness once stated that wishing for candy is not meaningful as compared to wishing that all sentient beings will accumulate merit and never be met by obstacles. He explained that wishes have no form and because they are an act of the mind, *wishes can dissolve a bad mental state* and shape the mind in a pure way. "The more we wish good things continually, the more free will be the state of our mind—more perfected, more free. When we wish deep from the bottom of our heart, it shapes the perspective of mind... Harmony, peace, and understanding are most important for a community so we must always make wishes that there will be harmony. The greatest gift you can give me is harmony. You will have fulfilled my wish that helps me fulfill your wishes" (Trinley Thaye Dorje, 2009).

How did making strong wishes become relevant to Olivia? How did she come to believe that they could be a relevant tool for others? They became relevant when she saw that making wishes are very much a part of Buddhist practice. In Shantideva's *The Bodhicharyavatara* (2012, p. 34) he said that even the wish to soothe the headache of a living being can bring boundless merit:

> No need to speak, then, of the wish
> To drive away the endless pain
> Of each and every living being,
> Bringing them unbounded excellence.

She also saw the positive outcome of her wishes. On pilgrimages in 2005 and 2008 to Nepal, Bhutan, and India she made strong wishes at every powerful, sacred, and holy place that she visited. A pilgrimage involves visiting places that are sacred to a particular Buddha or places that have been blessed with the presence of great yogis and sages. When a site is sacred for both of those reasons, it is a powerful source of inspiration for spiritual practice and, thus, has attracted great yogis and sages for meditation and inner spiritual realization that leads to liberation and enlightenment. More importantly, Enlightened beings have made wishes that individuals will find peace and accumulate positive merit when visiting these places. It is also said that the spiritual progress made in one month at these sacred sites would take a year elsewhere. Olivia experienced sitting in the same cave near Bodhgaya, India, where the Buddha meditated for six years after departing from his Palace in southern Nepal, renouncing worldly life. She had also visited other caves, such as the Namkading Cave in Tibet, where the great Tibetan yogi, Milarepa, meditated for 20 years.

It's not about me but we; however, we humans have a strong misconception about self that is imprinted in us like an innate instinct (Rinchen, 2015). When a larger-than-life "I" is strongly present, which Westerners are encouraged to develop, there becomes a strong distinction between self and others. In Western psychology, this is defined as a normal developmental process called individuation, and we are extolled for becoming independent and autonomous; however, encouraging this misconception gives rise to strong attachment to self and everything associated with it and, thus, aversion to that, which is considered to be "other" or hostile. From a position of "me" and "mine" comes clinging to "my happiness" and the "happiness of those associated with me" and an attitude of fear and repugnance arises towards anyone or anything that threatens that happiness (Richen, 2015). Unfortunately, we then act out of ignorance.

Olivia believed that *we* rather than *me* was a beautiful concept. "I am one," she would say, "but they are many." Thus, she wasn't motivated to make strong wishes at powerful places for herself but rather for others—especially those with challenges that seemed to be insurmountable:

> disease, illness, infertility, hopelessness, loss, and despair. Bodhicitta is the entrance to and the motivation behind the Bodhisattva Way of Life, to seek enlightenment not for oneself but for the benefit of all beings.

After the completion of Olivia's first trip to Bhutan, Nepal, and India, she looked forward to making wishes again during her next journey in 2010–2011 to new holy sites. His Holiness the 17th Karmapa, Trinley Thaye Dorje addressed the importance of this when he requested that we make wishes for others: "Think of yourselves as, let's say, an ambassador, an ambassador for all sentient beings, and since they cannot come, and since most of them do not have an opportunity to make wishes at such sacred places—it doesn't matter whether they are Buddhist or not—they can be strangers also, but whatever, you all are here with this very precious existence and this precious opportunity to do something incredible and that is, for their sake, to make wishes, to make prayers for their happiness. Basically, it is a logical thing. If everyone else is happy, naturally you are happy. It's a wonderful logic so therefore, based mainly on compassion—genuine compassion—make wishes. In front of the Stupa, in front of the Buddha statue, in front of Bodhi Tree, and whatever other sacred places you might visit, Nalanda, Vulture's Peak, all those sacred places—wherever you are going—even if you can just have five minutes to make wishes, that itself is a lot. It is something that of the 8 billion population of sentient beings, this is an opportunity that they wouldn't have in their lifetime, so make wishes. We make wishes. You have to know that wishes **do** work and aspirations **do** work" (Dorje, 2007).

Thousands gather every winter at Monlam for a week in order to recite wish fulfilling prayers at Bodhgaya, the principal pilgrimage site for Buddhists of all traditions because it is where the historical Buddha Shakyamuni reached enlightenment while sitting under the Bodhi tree. Bodhgaya is also the place where all Buddhas of the past attained enlightenment and where all Buddhas of the future will attain enlightenment. It is recorded in one of the Vinaya Sutras, that the historical Buddha Shakyamuni said that future Buddhists, who were not able to meet with him, should gather in one of the four great places of pilgrimage: 1) Lumbini, where the Buddha was born; 2) Bodhgaya, where he attained enlightenment; 3) Sarnarth, the deer park where he taught for the first time, turning the Wheel of the Dharma; and 4) Kushinagar, where he passed into Parinivana. From among the four great places of pilgrimage, all of which Olivia had visited, Bodhgaya seemed to be the most powerful. Thus, Olivia decided to attend Kagyu Monlam where many prayers are recited, particularly the "King of Aspiration Prayers" or "Samantabhadra Wishing Prayer." The prayer comes from a collection of sutras (the preserved teachings of the Buddha Shakyamuni), which contains a great number of aspiration prayers, "There are countless beings, as limitless as the very confines of the endless sky. Whatever their karma and afflictions may be, may my wishing prayers encompass them all."

Olivia asked her students and friends to write their wishes on a piece of paper that she would carry with her throughout her pilgrimage. At the holy sites she visited, she made strong wishes that their wishes would come to fruition. She also asked them to focus on their written wishes during the week that she was at Monlam in Bodhgaya. Making wishes was becoming automatic, and Olivia found that it kept her in a positive mindset. She remembered being in a computer room after Monlam when a wonderful young man found an electrical charger that would charge her cell phone. As Olivia sat, waiting for her phone to charge, she became aware that there were four computers in the room, and none of them were functioning. A young European woman moved from computer to computer, and not one of them would start up. Finally, with a deep sigh, she asked Olivia, "What do we do?" Olivia didn't do any of the routine things she normally did when her computer didn't work, such as unplugging it from its electrical outlet and then plugging it in again. Instead, she said, "Make strong wishes." They looked at each other and started to laugh, realizing that they had been making so many strong wishes that it was becoming modus operandi!

Making wishes is a step beyond intention, a concept that had become popular in the West. For years Olivia talked about the power of intention and how essential it is that we set a positive intention in order to manifest a desired outcome. Dr. Wayne Dyer wrote *The Power of Intention* (2005). Jonathan Goldman spoke of the formula Frequency + Intention = Healing (2002). Intention is the process of creating, or bringing into existence, that which we desire; however, although important, intention does not, in and of itself, require an action, which can cause difficulty in its comprehension. Some of this difficulty lies in the fact that the words "intent" and "intention" have also been imbued with a negative connotation. How many times have we heard a suspicious person say, "What is your intention?" On the contrary, making a wish has a positive connotation.

We have also heard about "The Secret" although not a secret, but rather, the ancient "Universal Law of Attraction" (Hicks, 2006), based on the teachings of Abraham. This law basically states, "That which is like unto itself, is drawn." We attract everything that shows up in our life experience because the Law of Attraction is responding to the thoughts we are offering. Every thought, feeling, word, and action carries a vibration and because it attracts other like vibrations, it is crucial that we are aware of the vibrations that we emit. For example, a woman was trying to decide on a location for the purchase of a home and an important criterion was how long it would take to get to the nearest hospital via an ambulance. Olivia responded, "You don't want to be sending *that* wish out to the universe!" The woman hadn't realized that she was planting a negative seed thought for a "quick" ambulance ride to the hospital. This is what many of us do if we are not aware of our thoughts. We sometimes make a wish that we actually do not want to manifest, not realizing the second universal law, "The Science of Deliberate Creation." This law states, "That which I give thought to, and that which I believe or expect—is." Essentially, we get what we are thinking about whether we want it or not. In this respect, The Science of Deliberate Creation is more applicable to making wishes than the Universal Law of Attraction.

Tibet from Nepal

Olivia met her group that was traveling with her to Tibet—11 other Americans—in Kathmandu, Nepal, a country full of memories, some of them adrenalin-producing. The first time she traveled to Nepal in 2005 it was in the middle of a civil war but during a 30-day Maoist-guerilla cease-fire. In 2010, after she deplaned from the Tara Air, Air de Havilland, Canada DHC-6, Twin Otter airplane at Lamidanda Airport it then crashed in the mountains five minutes after taking off again, killing all passengers on board: 19 Bhutanese and 3 flight personnel. At the time, Olivia's group wasn't even aware of the crash because they were traveling by Jeep to Maritika Caves in the Mt. Everest region where Olivia had another near death experience, sleeping at night in freezing temperatures in a wrongly pitched summer tent that should have been a winter tent. She actually reached the point where she wondered how long her body would lie in the tent the next day before someone discovered that she had died.

This was her first experience with camping—getting in her tent without tracking in dirt, zipping it open and zipping it shut before she crawled into not one but two sleeping bags on the ground, stuffing her sage green satin pillowcase into the mummy hood before zipping them shut and then zipping them open so she could trek to a hole-in-the-ground tent bathroom in the middle of the night. Fitting into the sleeping bags was arduous because she was also wrapped in an ankle-length black Eileen Fisher fleece coat over her black and white zebra print flannel pajamas. Her stainless steel Starbucks tumbler and Brighton black and brown suitcase, covered in a clear plastic zipped case *and* on silver, spoked wheels—laid next to her. The suitcase was embarrassingly ridiculous because anyone "in the know" carried a backpack. As she tried to sleep, she learned to identify animals by the way they were breathing around her tent: cows, dogs, and a huge boar that was known to destroy tents, looking for food. Olivia was alone with the tents during the day when the boar attacked as she stood screaming, "Help!" No one responded. "Doesn't one person understand the English word HELP?" Of course not. She was just a dramatic American woman standing in the middle of a field having a "terrible, horrible, no good, very bad day."

It wasn't surprising, then, that the first night Olivia scuffled in the dark for the outdoor bathroom, she stepped into a large pile of cow dung. She couldn't wait to tell Chatna, one of the Nepalese guides:

"This cow dung all over the place is a public health problem, and it needs to be removed."

Totally shocked, he replied, "I grew up with cow dung. We use it for everything, even cooking."

"Please, no more… don't tell me more," as she waved her hand.

Chatna looked exasperated; however, with his bare hands, he picked up and removed all of the cow dung around Olivia's tent, carrying it into a nearby field.

"And what about the wild boar?" she asked.

"If he comes back, just hit him in the nose."

No running water. No shower for days. When Olivia asked Chatna where the shower was, he handed her a 10-pack package of Wet Ones. He also had to pull off her hiking boots with a struggle, hoping he wouldn't have to cut them off. The boots were too small, not allowing room for her swollen feet. However, at least Olivia brought hiking boots. Chatna shared with her that he once had to give his slippers to a young woman who had only brought a pair of high-heeled shoes to trek in. "Was she an American?" Olivia asked. "Sounds like an American to me."

Perhaps this is why Chatna decided to pitch a tent next to Olivia. Perhaps she needed close supervision. Years later, just prior to the Gorkha earthquake, Chatna asked Olivia to join him for breakfast. Laughing, she asked, "We're still friends? Am I the most difficult client you've ever had?" Chatna replied laughing, "Not the most difficult but certainly the most different." Fortunately, the experience broke her in and prepared her for even greater adventures.

Regardless, there was always something intense about being in Nepal with its spontaneous, unexpected occurrences, mixed in with the pure magic and joy of being there. As Olivia and her friends sat on the dirt ground of the Lamidanda airport waiting for their return flight to Kathmandu, a Chinese woman was complaining about the delay. The sun was intense, and she feared a sunburn. "If the plane is going to be late, why don't they just tell us so we can go and sit elsewhere—in the shade?" Olivia looked at her and said, "Because we are in Nepal, and they operate on Buddha time here. Whenever means whenever. The plane will be here—whenever." It took years for Olivia to settle into that. She remembered the first time that she visited Nepal in 2005, clutching her computer as though it were a life-long baby blanket. A taxi driver had offered to take her to New Orleans Cafe, the only place in town at the time with Wi-Fi. She had exactly 60 minutes to get her "work" done; however, the driver didn't any more know where New Orleans Cafe was than the man in the moon, driving around and around in circles on a one-way street. Her one-hour window period of time dissipated, and Olivia began to cry. Never before had she seen a badly shaken taxi driver, a witness to seeing someone cry because she couldn't get her all so important "work" done. Years later, Olivia shook her head and laughed about the "Western neurosis" she once had, the result of first world stress that affects one's mental health. First world vs. third world stress would become one of her favorite topics of discussion, and she grew to appreciate the third world stress of mere inconveniences.

It was now 2014, and Olivia had arrived in Kathmandu a week earlier than her group, eager to visit the country she had grown to love prior to departing for Tibet. She slowly met members of her group for breakfast at another hotel as they arrived. Rob had spent five months planning their itinerary and going through a necessary approval process with the Chinese government. They were individually scrutinized, and Rob told Olivia that she could not indicate that she was a writer or she might not be approved to enter the country; thus, Olivia listed only "teacher" as her profession. The process wasn't easy because the Chinese wanted to dictate, which often didn't include an authentic experience of Tibetan culture. The group was especially enthused about the five days they would spend on legendary Mt. Kailash, located in a remote and inhospitable area of the Tibetan Himalayas, a sacred place for four religions: Bön, Hinduism, Jainism, and Buddhism, known to Tibetan Buddhists as Kangri Rinpoche; "Precious Snow Mountain." It is the home of the Buddha Demchok (also known as Demchog or Chakrasamvara), Supreme Bliss, and an important Yidam in the Kagyu Buddhist tradition. There are also sites associated with Padmasambhava (Guru Rinpoche) and Milarepa, who ensued a winning competition on Mt. Kailash. It is also considered to be the abode of Lord Shiva, and for many eastern countries the holiest place on Earth.

Every year, thousands of individuals make a pilgrimage to Mt. Kailash, following a tradition going back thousands of years; however, following the political and border disturbances across the Chinese-Indian boundary, pilgrimage was stopped from 1954 to 1978. To think that pilgrimages were stopped for thousands of pilgrims for nearly 25 years is unfathomable. The Mt. Kailash journey is arduous, and one of the primary reasons why Olivia hired Doreen, a professional trainer. Out of respect, no one has attempted to climb Mt. Kailash and thus, it remains unconquered; however, walking around the holy mountain—a part of its official park—is done on foot, pony, or yak, taking some three days of trekking starting from a height of around 15,000 feet. Some pilgrims believe that the entire walk around Kailash should be made in a single day, which is not an easy task. A person in good physical condition walking fast would take perhaps 15 hours to complete the 32-mile trek. Some of the devout do accomplish this feat, little daunted by the uneven terrain, altitude sickness, and harsh conditions faced in the process. Other devoted pilgrims venture a much more demanding regimen, performing body-length prostrations over the entire length of the circumambulation: The pilgrim bends down, kneels, prostrates full-length, makes a mark with his fingers, rises to his knees, prays, and then crawls forward on hands and knees to the mark made by his/her fingers before repeating the process. It requires at least four weeks of physical endurance to perform the circumambulation while following this regimen.

Soon, the group ecstatically boarded a China Air flight to Gonggar Airport, 39 miles southwest of Lhasa, Tibet, at an elevation of 11,700 feet. Upon disembarking, they were met with a procedural delay at the airport. An airport agent in Kathmandu had kept one of their two original group visas, required for entry into China; thus, with only one group visa, they were denied entry. In disbelief, they sat in the hallway on the floor while a two-hour debate ensued between their group leader, Rob, and Chinese officials. Officials were perplexed as to how to proceed because this had never happened before—an unprecedented event—but Rob was told that they would probably be sent back to Nepal and fined. This was the best example of lack of critical thinking skills that Olivia had witnessed among the Chinese, which happens when people respond to what they are told to do and don't have to think for themselves. Rob was busy on the phone with a Nepal tourist guide, wondering if the guide could find their original visa at the Kathmandu airport and bring it to them but that would mean hours and a very expensive last minute plane ticket. Rob also suggested that Chinese officials simply make a copy of their single original visa, which they were unwilling to do. During this time Olivia could think of nothing else to do but chant the mantra of Green Tara: OM TARA TU TARE SOHA. Finally, a 3-Star General arrived and suggested that they make a copy of the single group visa that was in their possession. Of course, he thought it was his idea. Bingo! They were in!

They were warmly greeted by their Tibetan guide, Sam, donning a navy blue ball cap. He placed a white (symbolizing purity and compassion), traditional 2x5 silk khata scarf around each one of their necks as they boarded the bus. Khatas are usually seen in the colors of the five Buddha families (red, green, blue, gold, and white) but white is more commonly seen (sometimes gold) and are not only presented to arriving and departing guests but worn or presented at many ceremonial occasions, including births, weddings, funerals, and graduations. Once loaded on the tour bus, the group departed for a 30-minute ride to their hotel in Lhasa, via the Lhasa Airport Expressway, connecting the Gonggar Airport to Lhasa. It was the first expressway built in Tibet, opening in 2011. They traveled over a bridge prior to entering the Galashan Tunnel, drilled into a mountain, the entrance built of white and red brick, similar in style to the Potala Palace. What was striking was the accelerated building by the Chinese. Olivia had never seen so many large, gold cranes, typical of mass construction, but yet the open spaces were beautiful, full of willow trees that reminded her of her favorite quaking aspen trees, leaves rustling in the wind. They don't allow the willow trees to grow very tall, but keep cutting them down so that they can use the branches to stick in the ground and start new trees. Later, Olivia would notice that the river valleys were huge groves of new, young willow trees, which presumably are intended to protect against soil erosion from rain and winter snows.

The Chinese changed their travel itinerary! They received word that the Chinese had removed Mt. Kailash from their schedule because the mountain was being closed due to weather.

The group could not believe it. For some, it was their primary reason for being in Tibet. After five months of planning and preparation, how could the Chinese do this? Olivia now took seriously what a friend of hers, Bola, had told her in Kathmandu when they met one day for lunch. Bola had just returned from Mt. Kailash with a group and told Olivia that the mountain was going to be closed because of a terrorist threat from the Muslim Brotherhood. It had nothing to do with weather. Olivia never could grasp the many ongoing political situations in China; most of them were isolated and had nothing to do with each other.

Once checked into their hotel, the plan was to rest and acclimatize to the high altitude, which means that more red blood cells need to be created for better oxygen transport. Interestingly, just last year, in 2014, important research findings were reported in the journal, *Nature,* that explained how Tibetans have adapted to the hypoxic environment of the high-altitude Tibetan plateau. A hypoxia pathway gene, EPAS1, was found in the DNA of extinct Denisovans, a poorly misunderstood human relative more closely related to Neanderthals than modern people. The gene, found in Tibetans, has been found very rarely in Han Chinese, Mongolians, and Sherpas, who are related to Tibetans, and no trace of the gene has been found outside East Asia. Denisovans were only discovered recently from fossils from Siberia, dating back approximately 50,000 years ago; however, we now know that this genetic variant, EPAS1, helps survival and adaptation to unique environments by affecting the amount of oxygen the blood can carry. When the body is exposed to the low oxygen levels encountered at high elevations, EPAS1 tells other genes in the body to become active, stimulating a response that includes the production of extra red blood cells.

The next morning, Olivia and her group were en route to the Jokhang Temple. The Jokhang ("House of the Buddha") Temple is located on Bharkhor Square in Lhasa. For the majority of Tibetans it is the most sacred and important temple in Tibet, partially because the great Buddhist Master, Atisha, taught there in the 11th century. It is in some regards pan-sectarian, but is controlled by the Gelug school, one of the four schools of Buddhism. The temple's architectural style is a mixture of Indian vihara, Chinese Tang Dynasty, and Nepalese design. It was built during the reign of King Songtsän Gampo, probably in 642, and with the Potala Palace, it is a UNESCO World Heritage Site. According to tradition, the temple was built for the two brides of the King Songtsän Gampo: Princess Wencheng of the Chinese Tang dynasty and Princess Bhrikuti of Nepal. Both wives brought important Buddhist statues and images with them to Tibet as part of their dowries. They wanted a temple built to house them, particularly the large standing child Buddha that Princess Bhrikuti brought from Nepal, which remains to this day in the Jokhang. Many Nepalese artists worked to construct this temple.

That the original building of the Jokhang has remained standing (additions have been constructed) throughout a turbulent history is beyond belief. It was sacked in 1966 by the Chinese Red Guards and thousands of artifacts were burned and destroyed. When told that 400 statues remain out of thousands, one realizes the magnitude of the Chinese invasion. Devoted Buddhist practitioners can always be seen doing full prostrations in front of the Jokhang Temple. Prostrations are done to purify one's defilements and negative karma. It is believed that as long as humans suffer from delusions, we are creating bad karma—intentionally and unintentionally—all the time. To counteract our bad actions, one thing we can do is to engage in wholesome spiritual practices, such as reciting mantras, making offerings, or doing prostrations.

In the case of making prostrations, it is believed that we can both purify some of our negativities and generate and accumulate merit, and we can multiply these benefits by doing more prostrations. This is why in Tibet there is a long history of pilgrims prostrating with devotion, respect, and compassion for all sentient beings. They walk and prostrate for long distances, sometimes for many hundreds of miles—purifying negative past and present karma and creating positive merit—with the final destination of their journey usually being a very holy site, like the Jokhang Temple. They had witnessed this en route to Lhasa, passing a family on the road, two members pushing a wagon with provisions while the other three family members prostrated at the side of the road, prostrating to the Jokhang. They wore long, thick leather aprons and used blocks on their hands to protect them when they fell onto the road after taking three steps and clapping the blocks together three times in the air while saying a mantra. Simply put: for a Buddhist practitioner, purifying negative karma and accumulating merit is the name of the game.

Tibetan Buddhist practitioners usually prostrate three times upon entering a temple or the shrine room of a monastery, nunnery, or dharma center. When they attend a teaching, they prostrate when the teacher enters and leaves the room. However, practitioners may engage in a regular prostration practice, often as a preparation—*ngondro*—for a long retreat. Like many Tibetan Buddhist practices, prostrations can be done in a variety of ways, and there is not really a "wrong" way to do them if you have in your heart and mind a sincere motivation to rid yourself of wrong-thinking and negativities. There are three basic styles:

- *Gyangchag*—Full body prostration. In Tibetan the *gyang* refers to "reaching out" and *chag* is prostration.
- *Kumchag*—Partial prostration, refers to prostrating from the knees. In Tibetan, *kum* refers to contracting your body, as opposed to reaching out.
- Symbolic prostration, with just the hand motions, done standing or sitting, often if there is not room to do a full body prostration, or if it is simply not practical for any reason.

Each style includes the same basic hand motions at the beginning, of joining the hands and touching them to three places, although practitioners sometimes also touch their foreheads:

- *Ku*—Crown of your head (Body)—to purify the negative karma caused by actions of the body and aspiring to all the good qualities of Buddha's body.
- *Sung*—Mouth or throat (Speech)—to purify the negative karma caused by our speech and aspiring to all the good qualities of Buddha's speech.
- *Thuk*—Heart (Mind)—to purify the negative karma caused by our minds and aspiring to all the good qualities of Buddha's mind.

Olivia and her friends walked past many prostrating pilgrims. She enjoyed videotaping a little Tibetan boy who was tenaciously trying to learn how to do prostrations all by himself without an adult coaching or encouraging him. He didn't appear to be more than two years of age, well dressed in a long-sleeved gray shirt, yellow down vest, and tan corduroy pants. He struggled to stand up on his feet, leaning forward, flashing the NYPD New York lettering across the seat of his pants. Upon walking through the courtyard of the Jokhang and prior to entering the shrine hall, they watched monks debating in the gray rock floor courtyard with potted juniper trees, an enactment not normally offered to the public, especially at the Jokhang.

Olivia had never seen a Tibetan monk debate, which involve two parties: a defender (damchawa), who answers, and a questioner (riklampa). She videotaped four different pairs of monks as they walked around the courtyard and made punctuated, vigorous gestures, which enlivened the ambience of the occasion. Each gesture had a meaning as the debater presented his case with subtlety. Some of the gestures (said to have symbolic value) made during the debates are: clapping after each question; holding the right hand and stretching the left hand forward and striking the left palm with the right palm; clapping hands loudly to stress the power and decisiveness of the defender's arguments denoting his self-assurance; in case of a wrong answer presented by the defender, the opponent gestures three circles with his hand around the defender's head followed by loud screaming to unnerve the defender; an opponent's mistake is demonstrated by wrapping his upper robe around his waist; loud clapping and intense verbal exchange is common; and the approach is to trap the defender into a wrong line of argument. Each time a new question is asked, the teacher strikes his outstretched left palm with his right palm. When a question is answered correctly, it is acknowledged by the teacher bringing the back of his right hand to his left palm. When the defender wins the debate he makes an allegorical dig at the questioner by questioning his basic wisdom as a Buddhist (Dreyfus, 2001).

The Jokhang Temple is comprised of an entrance porch, courtyard, and Buddhist hall surrounded by accommodation for monks and storehouses on all four sides. The buildings are constructed of wood and stone and are outstanding examples of Tibetan Buddhist style, with influences from China, India, and Nepal. They house over 3,000 images of Buddha and other deities and historical figures along with many other treasures and manuscripts. Exquisite mural paintings depicting religious and historical scenes and thangka paintings of deities cover the walls. Thangka is a Nepalese art form exported to Tibet in the 6th century after Princess Bhrikuti of Nepal, daughter of King Lichchavi, married Songtsän Gampo. Entering the Shrine Hall meant that Olivia could not take photographs but she will always hold the memory of what she saw, never forgetting the feeling of sacredness and awe at standing on such an ancient, holy site. Because Shrine Halls are usually dark inside, there are always light bulbs hanging, but even when light bulbs hang outside of the Shrine Hall, they do create some problems with photography.

The oldest Lama lived in a room upstairs in the Jokhang. When Olivia and her group of friends passed by his open door, the Lama, in his maroon robe, was sitting on a soft chair, covered in a peach-colored fabric that was positioned between his bed and a table. Above the bed were three windows with peach colored-curtains pulled to each side, allowing the sun to warm and illuminate the room. The table was cluttered with porcelain cups, a plastic water bottle, offering bowls, and two thermos bottles, one presumably full of hot water and the other, yak butter tea, made from tea leaves, yak butter, and salt. On the bed sat an old, beige telephone that appeared to include an answering machine. There were cloth bags and clear plastic bags that contained articles, possibly food. The Lama held a sacred text in his right hand and a bodhi seed mala in his left palm. He began to point at Olivia with his left forefinger, speaking in Tibetan to her guide, Sam.

Sam told Olivia that the Lama wanted to give her a blessing, which she was more than thrilled to hear. She approached and knelt down in front of this very special man, bowing her head with her hands folded at her heart in gassho. The Lama didn't have a shaven head but was completely bald, his skin deeply wrinkled. Olivia surmised that he was in his 80s. He wore metal wire-rimmed gold glasses, the nosepiece fitting snuggly near the tip, rather than the bridge, of his nose. He proceeded to give Olivia a very lengthy blessing, spoken in Tibetan, which Olivia didn't understand; however, she didn't need to understand the words because she could feel the power of the blessing. He then blessed everyone in the group, one by one. Olivia left this magical moment, but interestingly, as she exited the entrance to the Jokhang Temple, she turned to one of her friends and said, "I'm letting go of my relationship with Chris. He's not good for me." At the time, Olivia didn't make the connection that perhaps her change of heart had something to do with the blessing she had just received. In essence, the causes and conditions involved in meeting this Lama had come together and gave rise to an effect. The Law of Karma, the Law of Cause and Effect, is not as difficult to understand as some might believe. When a seed is planted, the result will come to fruition via causes and conditions: i.e., soil, light, temperature, rainfall. Our life is truly a manifestation of our karma, which we create. We *are* our karma. And if you want an idea of what your next life will look like, look at what you're doing now.

The group proceeded to the Bharkhor, an area of narrow streets and a public square located around Jokhang Temple in Lhasa. It remains a popular devotional circumambulation for pilgrims and locals, which Buddhists always execute in a clockwise direction. The walk is about .62 miles long and encircles the entire Jokhang, the former seat of the State Oracle in Lhasa called the Muru Nyingba Monastery, and a number of nobles' houses including Tromzikhang and Jamkhang. It has been the site of many demonstrations, and on Sunday, May 27, 2012, two men set themselves on fire (self-immolation). One of the men died and the other survived with injuries. Because of these events and the need for added security, metal detectors are now positioned at the entrance of the Bharkhor. Olivia had to adjust to the security measures; in fact, a Chinese policeman was with them day and night, the entire duration of their trip throughout Tibet. He not only observed their activity but reported to Chinese officials at the end of every day, and although he was a Buddhist, Olivia learned to accept that his first allegiance was to the Chinese. After all, it was his job.

Seeing the beyond-magnificent Potala Palace for the first time is jaw dropping. Built in the 7th century, it was the chief residence of the Dalai Lamas until the Chinese invasion in 1959 when the XIV Dalai Lama fled to India. It was constructed by the 5th Dalai Lama in 1645. The building measures 1,637 feet east-west and 1,148 feet north-south, with sloping stone walls averaging nearly 10 feet in thickness and more than 16 feet at the base, and with copper poured into the foundations to help proof it against earthquakes. This is difficult to believe but there are thirteen stories of buildings containing over 1,000 rooms, 10,000 shrines and about 200,000 statues. To the west and higher up the mountain the Red Palace contains the gilded burial stupas of the past Dalai Lamas. The Palace soars 384 feet on top of Marpo Ri, the "Red Hill," rising more than 1,000 feet above the valley floor. The Palace is now a museum and a UNESCO World Heritage Site.

Walking up the hundreds of steps to the Potala Palace was the one day that Olivia struggled with the high altitude, and she was behind everyone, gasping for breath. She realized the impact of the altitude when all of her black, Precise V7 liquid pens exploded, and heard that many computer hard drives don't survive. However, once the ascent was made she was fortunately over the hump. She'll never forget the roped-off stairways that were only used by the Dalai Lamas, the exquisite stupas where previous Dalai Lamas were entombed, and the bedroom of the 14th Dalai Lama, including a sitting area where he studied. There was a gift shop where stamped books of the Potala Palace could be purchased along with huge, white khatas with a red design of the Palace. Olivia purchased two khatas. Because she had a weakness for books she tried to avoid them because of weight travel restrictions, a nemesis for Olivia. On the descent from the Palace, Olivia felt much better and followed behind two professional photographers. When one of them climbed into a moat and lay down on his back in order to shoot pictures, Olivia did the same. When another photographer walked into a field of lavender and white daisies to shoot pictures of the Palace grounds through the flowers, Olivia did the same. She learned a few things about photography and, as a result, snapped some excellent pictures of the Potala Palace that she will always cherish.

A couple of miles outside of Lhasa, the group visited Sera Monastery, named for the wild, blooming roses or raspberry shrubs surrounding it, and founded in 1419 by Jamchen Chojey of Sakya Yeshe of Zel Gungtang (1355–1435), a disciple of Je Tsongkhapa. It is known as one of the "great three" Gelug university monasteries, and also known for its debate sessions. During the 1959 revolt in Lhasa, Sera monastery suffered severe damage, with its colleges destroyed and hundreds of monks killed. After the Dalai Lama took asylum in India, many of the monks of Sera who survived the attack moved to Bylakuppe in Mysore, India. The group visited Sera very briefly because of this massacre—sometimes the feeling of bloodshed was still too great to bear. As they departed, Olivia noticed the many hermitages in the foothills of the Pubuchok Mountain, also known as Tatipu Hill, surrounding Sera. Apparently, there are 19 of them, including four nunneries.

Ganden was the original monastery of the Gelug order, founded in 1409 by Je Tsongkhapa ("The man from Tsongkha," 1357–1419), usually meaning "the Man from Onion Valley." Garden Monastery was traditionally considered to be the seat of Gelug administrative and political power, located at the top of Wangbur Mountain, Tagtse County, 22 miles northeast from the Potala Palace in Lhasa, at an altitude of 14,108 feet. As their bus climbed upwards to the monastery on an asphalt road with many winding, hairpin turns, the hills were covered with mustard-colored wild shrubs. Upon arriving, the first thing they saw was juniper branches burning in a chorten, and a lot of construction underway.

Je Tsongkhapa, was considered an emanation of Manjushri, the Buddha of Wisdom, and was one of the foremost authorities on Tibetan Buddhism. He was a great scholar and a prolific writer, addressing emptiness as the teaching that no *dharma* ("thing") has an existence of its own, but always comes into existence in dependence on other *dharmas*. He received lineage transmissions from all of the schools of Buddhism, focusing most on the Kadampa teachings of Atisha. He was extolled by the 8th Gyalwa Karmapa, Mikyo Dorje, in his poem *In Praise of the Incomparable Tsong Khapa* (Newland, 2008):

When the teachings of the Sakya, Kagyue,
And Nyingma sects in Tibet were declining,
You, O Tsong Khapa, revived Buddha's Doctrine,
Hence I sing this praise to you of Ganden Mountain.

Drepung Monastery (another of the "great three" Gelug monasteries) was founded in 1416 by Tsongkhapa's disciple Jamyang Choeje. At one time considered the largest monastery in the world, housing up to 10,000 monks, there are now only about 300 monks in residence because of population capping enforced by the Chinese government. It is heart-wrenching and difficult to fathom that these monks are actually prisoners in their own monastery. We did enjoy taking pictures with the head Lama in residence who was beaming with joy at our presence. Drepung was the home of the Dalai Lamas before the Potala Palace was built in the 17th century. Resembling a heap of white rice from a distance, it was dubbed "Monastery of the Collecting-Rice" (Drepung Gompa) in Tibetan. Drepung is especially known as the site of the annual Shoton Festival, with its dramatic unfurling of a giant thangka painting on the hillside.

Olivia might well have seen her largest butter lamp at Drepung, burning over 40 wicks, attended full time by a nun, wearing an earloop mask and using a silver metal scooper and metal pitcher to manage the melting yak butter. She also attended a puja with about 15 monks; thus, they were soon engulfed in a sea of vibrations—a symphony of chanting mantras, crashing cymbals, thumping drums, blowing of long horns (*ra-dong*) and oboes (*ja-ling*), and occasionally the blowing of a conch seashell, sounding much like the deep, sustained note of a trumpet. There were unforgettable thangka paintings hanging and the most detailed, intricate artwork painted on wooden doors and walls. Drepung monastery was shut down by Chinese authorities on March 14, 2008, after monk-led protests against Chinese rule turned violent and businesses, shops, and vehicles were looted and torched. The People's Republic of China claims that 22 people were killed in the riots but Tibetan sources put the figure much higher. The *International Herald Tribune* reported that the monastery reopened in 2013 after being closed for five years. Since the 1950s, Drepung Monastery, along with Ganden and Sera, have lost much of their independence and spiritual credibility in the eyes of Tibetans since they operate under the close watch of the Chinese security services.

Most of the monasteries included gift shops where Olivia and her group purchased amulets, jewelry, and khatas but they shopped until they dropped at the Tibetan markets, always bartering for the best price possible. Olivia found a coral mala, earrings, and a coral belt to wear with one of her chupas (Tibetan dress) that she bought from a dressmaker at Boudhanath Stupa in Kathmandu. She purchased gold khatas, pieces of 7th century armor, worn for protection and several Tibetan brass and silver alloy antique astrological melong amulets, showing the Nine Palaces, Eight Trigrams, and 12 animals of the zodiac, believed to ward off negativity and protect one from unfavorable planetary alignments. A melong with a suspension hole or ring at the top allows it to hang from the body on a string, often seen attached to a belt hoop at the waist.

Yak meat, even yak tongue, was featured on the menu in every restaurant. Olivia felt revulsion at the thought of eating yak—a stately, long-haired bovid found throughout the Himalayan region. She had developed a fascination and love for this animal nearly ten years ago when she first spotted one in Bhutan, marveling not only at their long, shaggy hair, long horns [19 to 39 inches in length for a male (yak) and 11 to 25 inches in a female (dri)], and long eyelashes, but their powerful stature—their presence. They were heavily built with a short neck, pronounced hump and rounded shoulders, with sturdy legs, strong and athletic, resembling the American bison. The yak (male) is a herd animal, the male weighing 770 to 1,280 pounds and the dri (female) weighing 496 to 562 pounds. They cannot live below an altitude of 10,000 feet and have one more rib than a cow; however, they bellow, squeal, honk, growl, whimper, snort, and have far more vocalizations than your average cow, and appear to never lose their sense of goofy calf-ness. They do seem to have a sense of owning the road as cows do in this part of the world, where cows are considered holy.

When not loaded with goods to transport, yak scramble across the hillsides like mountain goats, fling themselves in dust wallows, and wander up to strangers like inquisitive puppies. They are a gentle animal, and there are no accounts of one being aggressive except when trying to protect its young. They wander at will past bedroom windows, across fields, and into campsites, with no one seeming too concerned that a 1,000-pound animal is on the loose. It is prudent to feel comfortable around them, however, in case you're sharing a 4-foot-wide trail with a train of yaks loaded with mounds of propane canisters, flour, rice sacks, and other commercial goods, as you're about 2,000 feet above the helicopters flying below the clouds you're walking in. The yak doesn't mind, nor does it get spooked, but ambles past like another trekker, the train being led by the most intelligent yak in the group. He wears a bigger bell around his neck, which sounds noticeably different from the bells worn by the rest of the herd. Olivia loved the gentle sounding of their bells as they grazed among the mountainside eating grass roots, herbs, and wild flowers. She even captured the sound on recordings.

When Olivia talked to a yak herder, the yak formed a circle around him in a defensive posture, ready to protect their herder, much like arctic musk ox will circle their calves to protect against wolves. One of Olivia's most thrilling moments was riding a white, long-haired yak (dri) at Yamdrok Lake. The dri (female) was adorned with a decorative, red-feathered headdress, a 3-inch-wide burgundy and white braided rein worn around her neck, and a blanket, saddle, and stirrups. As Olivia mounted her she couldn't help but notice her broad forehead, eyes set wide apart. "Jackie O," Olivia thought. "I should name you Jackie O." Only a few days prior, Olivia had taken pictures of a much larger, dark brown yak (male) standing in a huge puddle of water on the road to Ganden Monastery. He weighed well over 1,500 pounds.

The three main sights at Ganden Monastery are the Serdung, which contains the tomb of Tsongkhapa, the Tsokchen Assembly Hall and the Ngam Cho Khang, the chapel where Tsongkhapa traditionally taught. The monastery houses artifacts which belonged to Tsongkhapa, and Tsongkhapa's preserved body was entombed there in a silver and gold encrusted tomb by his disciples in 1419; however, in 1959 Ganden was destroyed and in 1966 the Red Guard artillery unbelievably dragged artillery up a very large mountain in order to shell it (before there were roads to the monastery) at which time monks had to dismantle the remains of Je Tsongkhapa. His mummified body was burned but his skull and some ashes were saved from the fire. Rebuilding has been continuing since the 1980s. What Olivia remembers the most is that the red-painted lhakang in the center is the reconstruction of Ganden's sanctum sanctorum containing Tsongkhapa's reliquaries; however, what once housed about 6,000 monks now houses less than 200—again, prisoners in their own monastery. Circumambulating pilgrims on the lower kora will encounter Je Tsongkhapa's original meditation cave. Set in a hillside of scrubby juniper bushes, the cave now contains five self-arising rock carvings on the wall. Tsongkhapa is the largest central image.

Disneyland. Olivia couldn't help but feel that the Chinese were trying to turn Tibet into a Disneyland. She did everything she could to avoid taking pictures of the Chinese flag, a red field charged in the canton (upper corner nearest the flagpole) with five golden stars. The design features one large gold star, with four smaller gold stars in a semicircle set off towards the fly (the side farthest from the flagpole). The red represents the

Communist revolution; the five stars and their relationship represent the unity of the Chinese people under the leadership of the Communist Party of China (CPC). The Chinese flag is flown everywhere and is seen on everything, including cow dung. One afternoon when she looked out of their bus window she counted 14 Chinese flags. Overdone. So Overdone! It was then that she noticed the massive black ink tattoo that the Chinese had branded on the inside of Sam's forearm: a six-inch black ink tattoo of a double-handled sword driven through a heart, symbolizing that he had driven a sword through the heart of China in his allegiance to the Dalai Lama. The glaring tattoo, signifying betrayal, placed him and thousands of other Tibetans on China's "black list," meaning that they can never leave Tibet. Olivia was in shock. The Nazis had branded Jews with numbers but nothing like this. The Chinese had also taken away Sam's Tibetan name and given him a new name, believing that this would destroy his Tibetan heritage.

Sam's grandfather was a great Sakya Buddhist Master, and Sam's only child, a son, was recognized to be his reincarnation; thus, his son escaped from Tibet at the age of five, never to return. Sam's wife died shortly thereafter. To this day, Olivia cannot reach Sam or communicate with him. This kind of censorship is not realized until one is actually in China; i.e., the first morning that Olivia was in Lhasa, she tried to connect to the Internet for over an hour, only to discover that Facebook, Twitter, and e-mail were blocked. She was off the grid, in a Communist country. Olivia observed every day what this did to the people living there. Because they were told what to think and what to do by the Communist Chinese, they lacked critical thinking skills. They didn't have the ability to think out of the box, but then, doing so would mean torture or death.

Olivia knew that the wishes she had planned to make throughout Tibet for her relationship with Chris were not going to happen. Somehow she felt that the Lama in the Jokhang Temple, through the power of his clairvoyance, was eager to give her a blessing because he was able to take a complete read on her. And with that powerful blessing a seed must have been awakened within her because there came a clarity—as if obscurations and clouds of confusion were transformed into a discriminating wisdom. It was time to let go of her attachment and clinging to Chris. Letting go—a phrase heard so often but so difficult to do. She needed to heed the admonishment of the Buddha—to take a close look at the cause of her suffering—her desire that had given rise to not only attachment but clinging and craving, an afflictive feeling that causes suffering. It wasn't Chris who was causing her suffering but, rather, her craving! Perhaps this is what the 8th century Buddhist Master, Shantideva, meant when he said, "We shrink from suffering but love its causes" (Shantideva, 1979). Wasn't it Veronica A. Shoffstall who wrote in her well-known poem that futures do have a way of falling down in mid-flight [because of the impermanence of them]? We do need to plant our own garden… rather than wait for someone to bring us flowers.

Olivia found large, square, heavy cotton prayer flags at Swayambhunath Stupa in Kathmandu in order to hang at Mt. Everest Base Camp. There are two kinds of prayer flags: horizontal ones, called *Lung ta* (Wylie: *rlung-rta*, meaning "Wind Horse") in Tibetan, and vertical ones, called *Darchor* (Wylie: *dar-lcog*, meaning "flagstaff"). *Lung ta* (horizontal) prayer flags are of square or rectangular shape, and are connected along their top edges to a long string or thread. They are commonly hung on a diagonal line from high to low between two objects (e.g., a rock and the top of a pole) in high places such as the tops of temples, monasteries, stupas, and mountain passes. *Darchor* (vertical) prayer flags are usually large single rectangles attached to poles along their vertical edge. Darchor are commonly planted in the ground, mountains, cairns, and on rooftops, and are iconographically and symbolically related to the *Dhvaja*. Traditionally, prayer flags come in sets of five: one in each of five colors. The five colors are arranged from left to right in a specific order: blue, white, red, green, and yellow, representing the five elements and the Five Pure Lights. Different elements are associated with different colors for specific traditions, purposes, and sadhana. Blue symbolizes the sky and space, white symbolizes the air and wind, red symbolizes fire, green symbolizes water, and yellow symbolizes earth. According to Traditional Tibetan medicine, health, and harmony are produced through the balance of the five elements.

There are many different images and mantras that are wood-block printed on prayer flags. The prayer flags that Olivia found at Swayambhu had a printed image of Green Tara in the center of each flag, surrounded by prayers and mantras written in Tibetan—prayers not to gods but prayers and mantras to be blown by the wind to spread good will, peace, strength, compassion and wisdom into all pervading space, benefitting all sentient beings; however, the image of the wind horse printed in the center of the prayer flag is also commonly seen. "The term wind horse refers to the fact that the flags blow in the wind, or 'ride' the wind, whereby the power of the sacred images and invocations printed on them are dispersed into the world at large, benefitting many levels of beings and the natural environment. The virtue accrued from the act of raising prayer flags then carries on into the life of the person(s) offering them, and to those whom they dedicate the merit of such an offering. This is possible because of the total interdependence of all mind, life, and phenomena. Through such ritualistic gesture, joined with wholesome, magnanimous intention, that web of interdependence (tendril, Tib.) can be accessed and influenced" (Warren, 2014). Because the symbols and mantras on prayer flags are sacred, they should be treated with respect. They should not be placed on the ground although they can fall to the ground and should not be used on clothing. When old prayer flags are replaced with new prayer flags on the Tibetan New Year, they should be burned rather than simply discarded.

With a black Sharpie magic marker Olivia wrote Aubrey Sacco on one flag, a young, extraordinary Colorado woman who disappeared in Nepal in 2010 while hiking solo in popular Langtang National Park, just north of Kathmandu. The names of each family member and an 86-year-old friend were also written on a flag, which she then took a picture of in order to share with all of them; however, the prayer flag that had been designated for Chris surprisingly remained blank. She rolled up the flags and placed them on the bus, to be hung the next day at Everest Base Camp. They were within a couple of hours of driving distance to Base Camp and stayed at the Everest Snow Leopard Guest House for the night; however, it was cold, without heat in the room. Olivia shared a solution that she discovered while in college. She told everyone to get out their hair blow dryers, turn them on, and let them run all night. It worked. Olivia and her roommate had two blow dryers running, which created so much heat in the room that Olivia had to get up in the middle of the night to turn one of them off. They slept in their clothes they were going to wear the next day to Base Camp in order to save time; however, one of her friends accidentally spilled a thermos full of hot water on Olivia at breakfast so blow dryers once again came in handy!

Frantic messages had been received by some members of the group about an avalanche at Annapurna. Family members, praying that they were alive, didn't realize the geographical distance between Mt. Everest and Annapurna, a collection of mountains in the Himalayas. For most people, the Himalayas are the Himalayas, and that is exactly where they were. Frankly, Olivia didn't know how far away Annapurna was from their location (less than 200 miles) although rescue efforts were underway. Three days prior, on October 14, 2014, a snowstorm and series of avalanches occurred on and around Annapurna and Dhaulagiri in the Manang and Mustang Districts of Nepal within the Himalaya range. Apparently, the storm arose from Cyclone

Hudhud and was the worst in a decade with almost 5 feet, 11 inches of snow falling within 12 hours. Electric power, cell phone service, and Internet connections failed in the Manang District, hampering relief efforts. Trekkers in the area at the time of the storm consisted of citizens from several countries including 78 from New Zealand. Twenty-one trekkers and guides from Nepal, Slovakia, and Germany were rescued on October 15 after the avalanche the previous day. When search and rescue operations ceased on October 19, up to 400 people had been rescued from various areas including Thorong La, the Manang, and Mustang areas and the Tukuche Base Camp of Mustang. The storms resulted in the deaths of at least 43 people. Among the dead were 21 trekkers from several countries walking the "Annapurna Circuit" and several local Nepali mountain guides, cooks, and yak herders. Up to 50 people were estimated to be missing with 175 reported to have injuries such as severe frostbite. Olivia had lived through a history of "near misses." This snowstorm missed them but it was a sobering thought as they prepared to depart for Mt. Everest Base Camp, realizing that there was no system in place at the time to inform trekkers of weather conditions en route. Because of that fact, there had just been the greatest trekking disaster and loss of lives in the history of Nepal.

There it was at a distance in front of them. Mt. Everest. As they approached in the bus, it was a sight that left Olivia transfixed. This was the Mt. Everest they had heard about all of their lives—the lofty pinnacle rising to 29,035-feet—the highest mountain in the world—when in 1953, New Zealander Edmund Hillary and Nepal's Sherpa Tenzing Norgay became the first climbers to reach its summit. However, this landmark triumph is also riddled with the tragic realization that Mt. Everest was the mountain where so many have died, some still frozen and buried there. Olivia couldn't help but remember, with great sadness, that less than six months earlier, in April 2014, an avalanche on Mount Everest, just above Base Camp in the Khumbu Ice Fall, killed 16

Nepalese sherpa mountain guides, the worst recorded single accident in the mountain's history. The rest of the climbing season was cancelled as the sherpas understandably demanded better compensation, pay, and conditions. Before that incident, the deadliest single-day toll was from an accident in May 1996, when eight climbers disappeared when a huge storm hit. Their tragic story was chronicled in Jon Krakauer's bestselling book *Into Thin Air*. The deadliest *year* on Everest was also in 1996, when 15 people died. Another 12 climbers were killed in 2006. Until the late 1970s, only a handful of climbers reached the top of Mt. Everest each year. The number topped 100 in 1993, 300 by 2004, and more than 500 by 2012. In 2013, 658 climbers reached the summit of Everest, according to the Himalayan Database; thus, more than 4,000 climbers have summited Everest since 1953, but again, hundreds have died attempting to reach the peak.

Little did Olivia know that in approximately six months, another natural disaster would hit Everest—the April 25, 2015 Gorkha earthquake and subsequent aftershocks, causing a large avalanche to sweep down the southwest side of the mountain, killing at least 18 climbers, including American Google engineer, Dan Fredinburg. Most of the more than 1,000 climbers, including 400 foreigners, were at Base Camp when it was partially buried by the devastating avalanche. Over 60 people were injured, mostly from falling rock and ice. Rescue attempts were made by an Indian Army mountaineering team before a helicopter arrived, despite bad weather, to transport the most seriously injured.

En route to Mt. Everest, Olivia and her group of friends passed herds of sheep. The dirt road was so rugged and full of holes that at one point in time the driver was forced to stop the bus. Several of the women eagerly got off the bus and wandered to pick up rocks, filling holes on the road in order that they could continue. One of the women was seriously ill; however, she was dispersing the cremains of her deceased son, which he had requested prior to his death. At one point, she stopped breathing.

The bus driver stopped the bus, and nearly everyone was out of their seat. The atmosphere grew from tourist excitement to suspenseful concern. Sam insisted that we return her to the hotel. He was not only praying that she wouldn't die while repeating a stream of mantras—he also drew it to our attention that he was the one responsible for her welfare. After 30 minutes of fervent discussion, Sam realized, much to his chagrin, that there was no turning back for her, even if she died in the process; after all, she had travelled thousands of miles from America. Paradoxically, we were supportive of her wish to continue to Base Camp. It was a triumph to the human spirit to see her rise to the task of dispersing her son's cremains on her own and without assistance. It was a tradition to leave items "behind" at Everest, symbolic of closing a door in order to embrace a new beginning. One of the women left her wedding ring under a rock; thus, because Olivia knew that people had special, symbolic, and ritualistic things to do at Everest, including herself in the hanging of prayer flags, she stuck to herself, respecting everyone's need for privacy.

Olivia had trekked uphill in the snow to Base Camp by herself, the wind growing stronger by the minute. Once there, it was difficult for her to stand, much less hang a string of prayer flags that were now wrapped around her body. A young Chinese male guide saw her plight and rushed to her assistance, securing the strings at both ends of the row of flags. Olivia thanked him as he replied with a slight bow in gassho, hands folded at his heart. The wind was blowing so loudly that she needed to raise her voice to thank him; a young woman rushed over to her and told her not to speak loudly or it might "anger the gods." Olivia was thrilled about the strong wind, however, because it meant that the prayers on the flags were being carried. She trekked back to the bus, through snow and slush, and although the sun was shining, a storm came shortly thereafter. The weather was inviting just long enough for them to get in and out of Base Camp, which demonstrates how quickly the weather really can change at Everest.

As Olivia boarded the bus, she glanced back at Mt. Everest and the Everest group of mountains to gaze at them one last time. To the right of Everest sat the peaks of Nuptse at 25,791 feet and Lhotse, the fourth highest peak in the world at 27,940 feet. (The third highest mountain peak in the world—Kanchenjunga at 26,169 feet—was not in the Everest group, but in Nepal.) She suspected that she might spend years learning the names of 104 mountain peaks in Nepal but knew the 5th–8th highest mountains peaks on earth: Makalu (27,766 ft.), Cho Oyu (26,906 ft.), Dhaulagiri I (26,795 ft.), and Manaslu (26,759 ft.). The tenth highest mountain peak is Annapurna I at 26,545 feet. Within a minute of departure, the bus got stuck driving out but everyone got off the bus and let the bus driver do his magic! He then drove them directly to Rongbuk monastery, ranked in 2011 at the top of CNN's "Great Places to be a Recluse!"

Rongbuk, the monastery with the highest elevation in the world, lies near the base of the north side of Mt. Everest, usually visited by those who climb Mt. Everest. Hermitage meditation caves dot the cliff walls all around the monastery complex, and up and down the valley. Rongbuk is of the Nyingma (meaning "ancient") tradition, the oldest of the four major schools of Tibetan Buddhism, and is the only monastery where Olivia has seen both monks and nuns in residence. Prior to entering the monastery Olivia was surprised to see a huge, white satellite disk sitting near a large, round, terraced chorten containing a reliquary. She was always prepared to climb a long, wooden ladder at the entrance of a monastery. In this case, it entered the dirt courtyard area where mountain goats ran loose. In the main Shrine Hall, four monks were doing a puja, sounding symbols and long horns (*ra-dong*). One of the Anis (nun) led Olivia up some very steep stairs to the Padmasambhava Chapel with a gorgeous, gold statue of Padmasambhava (Guru Rinpoche). Just outside of the door entrance were two tables of burning butter lamps; once inside the chapel a beautiful altar in front of Guru Rinpoche displayed more burning butter lamps and silver offering bowls, filled with water. From there, Olivia walked out onto the rooftop for a spectacular view of the mountains. Whereas there were hundreds of monks and nuns in residence prior to the Chinese invasion, at present there are only about 20 of them. Of course, like all of the important monasteries in Tibet, Rongbuk was left in ruins by the Chinese invasion that Olivia refused to refer to as "the cultural revolution." Even Sam had to refer to the Chinese invasion as "the cultural revolution" over and over and over again. "It was the Chinese invasion," Olivia would state. Renovation work at Rongbuk began in 1983; thus, the newer murals are the result of this work.

Tashi brought Olivia to tears. Earlier they had been sitting alone on the bus, Tashi in the driver's seat and Olivia two rows behind him on the left. Their group had been instructed not to mention the Dalai Lama's name in Tibet because it could put them and others in danger. They had heard stories about Tibetans being tortured or killed for saying the Dalai Lama's name or having a picture of him in their possession. Olivia's guide, Sam, was astounded that Olivia had gotten through the customs inspection at the airport with her *Lonely Planet Tibet* book because the forward had been written by the Dalai Lama. Because of this, Lonely Planet books are confiscated by Chinese Immigration; thus, Sam advised Olivia to have the book on her physical body when she departed from China. Olivia carefully hid it in the inside pocket of her down vest, which was a good thing because her suitcases were searched by border security officials. Tashi turned around and looked at Olivia and asked, "Dalai Lama?" Olivia was surprised that he would mention the Dalai Lama to her, and for a moment she didn't know how to respond. "I love the Dalai Lama," she said. He then got out of his seat, walked over to her and showed her his cell phone screen where he had pulled up a picture of the Dalai Lama. He then took his phone with the picture and placed it over his heart, holding it there with both hands. It was the only time on the trip that Olivia cried, recognizing his devotion to the Dalai Lama to the extent that he would risk his life and that of his family.

Butter lamps. Olivia had sent an e-mail to dozens of her students about her plan to light butter lamps the following month. "I will be lighting butter lamps after you retire to bed on Saturday. The lamps will burn continuously throughout the night and the next day, radiating your prayers and aspiration. The reason why I decided to do this is because I have always made butter lamp offerings when I have been in Nepal, Bhutan, and India. Some of these offerings have been as a result of individual requests from family and friends; however, I am receiving even more requests now, to the point where I am having to record them. Therefore, I am going to light 108 (very auspicious number) butter lamps. I will say a prayer and will make strong wishes as I read and think of your request and light your candle(s). It is important that you make strong wishes as you retire Saturday night and throughout the next day. This is not an exercise for negative people or negative thoughts. Our collective karma will be very powerful."

Olivia went on to explain, "Offerings at a Buddhist monastery are a traditional means of accumulating merit, and purifying illness and obstacles. A prayer request (for example, for a relative who is ill, for someone who has passed away, for a business venture, for safe travel, or simply for a friend's good health and long life) typically accompanies the offering. In the Buddhist tradition, butter lamps symbolize the clarity of wisdom and this offering of light creates harmony and brings joy to the mind. In general, making these offerings is a wonderful way to accumulate merit, while promoting success, prosperity, longevity, and world peace. In the Avatamsaka sutra it says, 'Offering Lamps can dispel all darknesses.' All of our emotional sufferings come from darkness. In the Sutra of Giving, it says, 'Those who offer lamps, will possess the pure heavenly eyes and clear wisdom in the future.'" Olivia saw huge butter lamps throughout Tibet that took her breath away. Some of them were three feet in diameter and had dozens of burning wicks in them that required constant attention from a nun or a monk. She not only took many pictures of them but also videotaped them, flames dancing. Throughout the monasteries she lit butter lamps but not a single one for Chris. Her relationship with him had become an exercise in letting go rather than an exercise in an inappropriate wish. Perhaps it is wise to evaluate our motivation and intention in the wishes we make. No wonder there is the expression, "Be careful what you wish for."

Olivia learned that the great Master Atisha wrote a butter lamp prayer that he recited as he visited butter lamp houses in central Tibet with approximately 18 of his disciples. The prayer was said in Tibetan with the wish: May this benefit all sentient beings, including our parents of this life, and throughout all rebirths. The mantra for fulfilling wishes is TADYA THĀ PANCHA.

Sixty-two miles from Lhasa is the stunning Yamdrok Lake, 42 miles in length, one of the three largest of four sacred lakes in Tibet. (The other lakes are Lhamo La-tso, Namtso and Manasarovar.) All of these lakes are considered to be divinatory. Olivia was mesmerized when she saw the lake, surrounded by many snow-capped mountains and fed by numerous small streams. Its crystal clear water acted like a mirror under an eternal blue sky. As the sun reflected from the waters at different depths, its colors changed, giving it an opulent, mysterious appearance, often compared to the finest jade, which is why the lake has often been referred to as Jade Lake. Olivia didn't know if she would ever again capture such a magical moment. At a distance she saw a couple posing for wedding pictures with a photographer. She was happy for them that their relationship had worked, and they wanted to be together, which only reminded her that her relationship with Chris was over—truly over. The pain was still there at times, appearing unexpectedly, as if mourning the loss of what was hoped for—the dreams—albeit fantasies—that would not come to fruition—a perfect example that expectation causes disappointment and suffering.

Lakes are considered sacred by the Tibetan people, because they are the dwelling places of protective deities and, therefore, invested with special spiritual powers and, thus, a powerful pilgrimage destination. Yamdrok Lake is considered sacred, as one of the four "Great Wrathful Lakes," guarded by the goddess Dorje Gegkyi Tso. The lake is revered as a talisman and is said to be part of the life-spirit of Tibet. It is said that if the largest lake in southern Tibet dries, Tibet will no longer be habitable. Yes, Olivia, thought, this is the perfect place to think of Chris and make wishes for him. Wasn't it Seneca (4BC–65AD) who said, "To wish well is part of becoming well"? She walked down to the shore of this holy lake filled with termas, picked up a stick, and wrote in the sand her signature sign-off: MUCH love. When traveling with a group it is often difficult to find a time and place to meditate but this was a perfect opportunity for her to sit and practice the meditation of giving and taking (tonglen, Tib.). Frankly, it helped when she focused on the suffering of others and forgot about herself. According to Kalu Rinpoche (1994, p. 140):

> Visualize that while breathing in, you take away all the sufferings from all sentient beings, removing confusion, lack of clarity, and so on. This suffering is transformed into a kind of smoky black light that is absorbed through your right nostril into your heart center. While absorbing this suffering, think, "I have completely absorbed all the pain and suffering of sentient beings into myself, freeing them so they can have all the happiness that they could desire." Then, while breathing out, imagine that a white light leaves from the pure intention of your heartfelt prayer and carries with it all your goodnesses and pleasures, carrying these to benefit all the

> other sentient beings. This simple practice of giving and receiving is very powerful; it is considered to be an important part of development along the path to liberation. It not only benefits all beings by its efforts at purifying their suffering, but it also helps to eradicate the massive amounts of negative accumulations of the practitioner. Its practice will definitely strengthen your bodhisattva intention.

Afterwards, Olivia remained sitting and wished for Chris's happiness. She couldn't wish for their relationship. She couldn't wish that they would be deliriously happy together—for once. She couldn't wish that he would meet her in Kathmandu in a couple of weeks. The more she thought about it, he wouldn't like Kathmandu. He would be annoyed at the community dogs that barked all night. He would be disgusted at seeing garbage strewn everywhere, especially on the streets. He would have an anxiety attack riding on the merging, chaotic five lanes of traffic. He would hate the pollution but would refuse to wear an earloop mask. He wouldn't drink instant Nescafe coffee, eat white rice, or eat Nepalese, spicy food, which would limit his selection of food. He would miss his ice cube refrigerator. He wouldn't like the height of the shower head in the shower, the way the toilet flushed, or the plumbing problems in general; e.g., no hot water today! He wouldn't even like the tiny rolls of coarse toilet paper. If he had to use an outdoor squat toilet, never equipped with toilet paper, he'd be on the next plane back to the USA. He expected and enjoyed the modern conveniences of elevators, escalators, and banking without the use of ATM machines that had annoying daily withdrawal limits and transaction fees.

Electricity in developing countries such as Nepal commonly involves load shedding. When the supplying company receives more demand for electrical power than it is generating, or transmission or installed capacity can deliver, the company has to resort to rationing available electricity to its customers. In Nepal, a load-shedding schedule is published according to when one of seven population groups will receive power during the day. However, even when utilizing power when it is scheduled to be available, outages are common and undependable. Olivia remembered being in Nepal in January 2011 when only one hour of electricity was rationed each day. It was especially problematic for her because she had a Hewlett-Packard laptop with a very short battery life. Charging all of her electrical devices in an hour was a challenge and meant that the day's activity had to be planned around when electricity would be available because she had to attend to charging. Carrying a small flashlight became a necessity, and although candles were plentifully lit, Olivia saw them as a fire hazard. This unpredictability and lack of electricity is what would be the end-all to Chris being in Nepal if he survived seeing the dire poverty. He couldn't stand to witness poverty and wasn't motivated to understand it, much less feel compassion for people living in unfortunate circumstances.

If Chris did come to Kathmandu, he wouldn't last long, and he would be disgusted with Olivia for suggesting that he meet her in this third world country that she had grown to love. He *would* like the Everest, Gorkha, and Nepal Ice beer, however, and he loved mountains. If anything, he would be in awe of the Himalayas—their indescribable majestic beauty and powerful energy—forever making the Rocky Mountains of the USA the Rocky Baby Hills. Studies show the Himalayas continue to grow to stupendous heights. Some parts of the Himalayas are rising about 0.4 inches (1 cm) every year, due to the ongoing collision between the Indian and Eurasian tectonic plates. But did it matter now? Chris and Barb—the woman more "suited" for him—were now a couple. She had even moved in with him. Chris wanted to keep this a secret from Olivia but Chris's best friend, Roy, had recently become another Dewey—an informant for Olivia, not willing to lie or cover up for Chris.

Olivia thought about her friend, Linda, whose husband

divorced her for a younger woman after 30 years of marriage. Linda consulted one of her Buddhist teachers, and he replied, "Visualize Green Tara over your head, say her mantra, OM TARE TU TARE SOHA, and wish for your husband's happiness as far away from you as possible." Olivia thought, "Should I wish for Chris's happiness as far away from me as possible when he couldn't be farther away from me?" She decided to leave out the "as far away as possible." Thus, after reflection upon what she could or could not wish for, she simply wished for his happiness. After all, Buddhists are taught that when someone harms you, the best antidote is to wish for his/her happiness.

The Buddha not only understood that space contained and held information, he also experienced it directly. For him, mass appeared as energy—and with that, all objects, things, and bodies can manifest as light forms. In the same way, he perceived thoughts and feelings as energy. His Holiness the 16th Gyalwa Karmapa was often referred to as the "wish-fulfilling jewel," which is a sign of highly realized Lamas. The time difference between the wish and its fulfillment shrinks. When no separation between inner and outer is experienced (duality), space is information; and the thought impulses reach the "speed of light," because they do not have to work through the hard-as-concrete concepts of finitely existing realities (Seifert, K., 2007). Thus, wishes can move across space. Not only does the wind carry prayers, mantras, and wishes written on prayer flags but the energy inherent in wishes is boundless and not contained.

One of the most compelling examples of sending wishes across space is found in the story of Gampopa after he heard about the great yogi, Jetsun Milarepa, a lineage holder in the Tibetan Buddhist Karma Kagyu tradition. It is well-known that at the age of 44, Milarepa began meditating in caves, reaching enlightenment in one lifetime and disappearing into a rainbow at his death. Gampopa decided to seek out Milarepa with a grueling pace; however, after he walked many miles he came to the center of a great plain and sat down upon a rock, overcome by hunger and exhaustion. He fainted, fell from the rock, and remained unconscious for half a day. When he regained consciousness, he was in agonizing pain and unable to move. No one passed by to help him as he lay without food or water for two long days and two long nights. On the third day, feeling impending death, Gampopa spoke these words with a strong wish through parched cracked lips and with tears streaming down his dusty face: "If I cannot see the Jetsun in this life, then in the three bardos after my death I will look only to him as my sole refuge. I swear I will be born near him in the next life, and that my mind will then be united with his." Then he lay back and wept, awaiting his death. Soon, however, a Kadampa monk who was also going to visit Jetsun Milarepa came upon Gampopa who was lying by the side of the road. The monk gave Gampopa some water and food, and Gampopa's strength returned. Invigorated, he and the monk continued their journey. [NOTE: Gampopa's devotion to Milarepa, his teacher, as Milarepa's devotion to his teacher, Marpa, are perfect examples of the Kagyupa deep devotion to teacher, the extent to which Olivia has not seen elsewhere. Some believe that Milarepa's tearing down bricks walls and building them up again was a lesson in impermanence; however, Milarepa persisted with Marpa's instructions because of deep devotion to his teacher.]

Meanwhile, Jetsun Milarepa was teaching the Dharma at Joyful Fortune Peak. In the midst of the discourse, he would sometimes stop and remain silent for a while, and then suddenly laugh. One of his female disciples asked him why he would suddenly become silent and then burst into laughter. "Because now, my son, the monk from U, has arrived at Dingri. There he fainted and fell and lay in great pain beside a rock. In his agony he cried out to me for help, in tears and with great faith and sincerity. I felt pity for him, and in my samadhi I sent him blessings, whereupon help quickly came to him. Seeing that, I felt very moved and joyful, and laughed out loud." As he told this story, tears welled up in Milarepa's eyes (Stewart, 1994).

Olivia was captured by the beauty of the gorgeous Heavenly Namtso Lake sitting at an elevation of 15,479 feet. White, snow-covered mountains painted the horizon as a backdrop that seemed to mirror the white-capped waves on the turquoise surface of the lake. The shore was spotted with yak, including auspicious white yaks who are spared from physical labor and carrying loads. The remains of yak horns, rock formations, and mani rocks were scattered. They had spent the night at a guest-house within walking distance of the lake, awakening early to finish breakfast and visit the Tasha Doi monastery there. It appeared to be more like a chapel but with a delightful Lama who gave a short blessing to everyone in the group. It was a bitterly cold, windy day; thus, Olivia was unable to sit on the shore of the lake as she did at Yamdrok Lake.

Drigung Thil Monastery, 75 miles northeast of Lhasa, was founded in 1179 by Jigten Sumgön (1143–1217), the founder of the Drikung Kagyu tradition. It sits on the south slope of a long mountain ridge in such a way that it reminded Olivia of Tiger's Nest in Bhutan. She knew they would have some hiking to do and that is probably why the parking lot was packed with motorcycles—parked against each other, covered with blankets. Vehicles would have difficulty with the ascent. Visiting Drigung was memorable to Olivia because she had never been given two khatas by anyone; thus, when the resident Lama put two khatas around her neck, one with blessing knots tied throughout, it was special. Those khatas remain her most appreciated items—of all of the things she received or purchased in Tibet. As of 2015 there were about 250 resident monks at Drigung.

Drigung has been the main seat of the Drikung Kagyu tradition of Tibetan Buddhism. In its early years the monastery played an important role in both religion and politics, but it was destroyed in 1290 by Mongol troops under the direction of a rival sect. The monastery was rebuilt but was primarily a center of meditative studies, which included meditation caves. The monastery was destroyed after 1959 during the Chinese invasion, looted of almost all its collection of statues, stupas, thangkas, manuscripts and other objects apart from a few small statues that the monks managed to hide. Reconstruction began in 1989 but it is still undergoing construction, which Olivia observed. She turned a large red prayer wheel with gold mantras and then climbed 13 narrow concrete steps to its left in order to reach the upper level of the monastery. There, she watched three men raise buckets of large, square, rectangular beige rocks with a crane up to the upper ledge where she stood. Apparently they were going to construct a wall but she was hoping that they wouldn't fall 200 feet to the ground in the process. Behind them and to the right sat a large white, smoke-blackened chorten, and from that vantage point, there was a breathtaking, panoramic view overlooking the Sorong Valley.

The Tsuglakhang shrine room holds many statues and stupas, including a central statue of Jigten Sumgön made of gold and copper and filled with rare jewels and relics. The image of Jigten Sumgön stands beside a large figure of the Guru Rinpoche, and a chorten in the hall holds Jigten Sumgön's remains. It was the first time Olivia had ever seen exquisite long horns (*ra-dong*) roped to columns in the assembly hall and the most gorgeous, large, green ritual drums, hanging from their artistically decorated wooden frames. Regardless of which monastery they were visiting, however, Olivia was intrigued with taking pictures of butter lamps, prayer wheels, windows, and doors. Whenever she saw an open door she always wished that all beings will open their door to the world. And when she saw a closed door, she wished to open it!

Olivia was an incurable lifelong learner and always wanted to know the meaning of symbols and artistic detail; i.e., two birds together, facing each other, represent wisdom and compassion—inseparable. The most common Tibetan symbols seen, however, were the eight auspicious signs that symbolize the eight-fold path of Buddhist practice, commonly found on numerous decorative objects, walls, wall hangings in temples, wooden furniture, metalwork, carpets, silk brocade, jewelry, paper, and used as good luck symbols.

1) Parasol: The canopy symbolizes preservation and protection of the dharma against suffering and sorrow. The parasol is an ancient emblem of wealth and status, patterned after the decorative canopies which have been traditionally used to protect and cover royalty. The parasol can also be viewed as a sort of axis mundi, a symbolic tree of life, and can be likened to the sacred Bodhi tree.

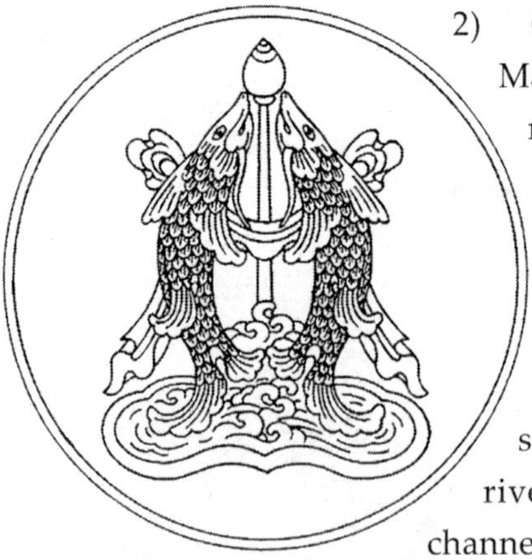

2) Golden Fishes (Suvarna Matsya): A pair of golden fishes represent joy, freedom, and fearlessness. In Vedic (Hindu) tradition, the fish is the first incarnation of the god Vishnu, two fishes together symbolized the sacred Ganges and Yamuna rivers, and later, the twin channels of ida and pingala, through which pranic energy moves through the body.

3) Vase: The treasure vase is filled with precious and sacred things, yet no matter how much is taken out, it is always full. It represents the teachings of the Buddha, which remained a bountiful treasure no matter how many teachings he gave to others. It also symbolizes long life and prosperity.

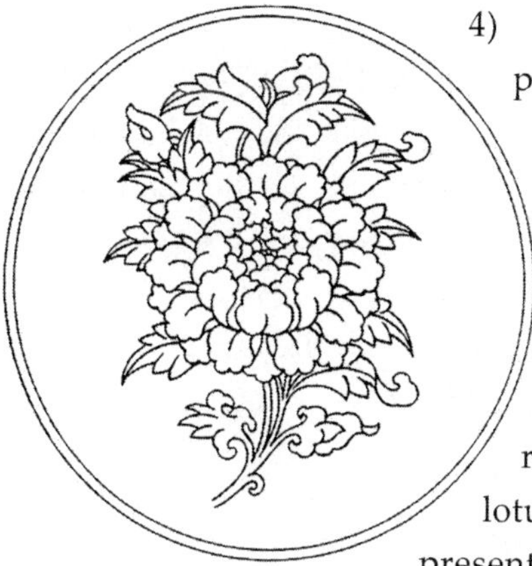

4) Lotus (Padme): An eight-petaled lotus used in Buddhist mandalas symbolizes cosmic harmony, a thousand-petaled lotus, spiritual illumination. A bud symbolizes potential. The well-known Buddhist mantra, "Om mane padme," refers to the "jewel in the lotus," the spark of enlightenment present in every living being. The lotus symbol in Buddhism is of course drawn from thousands of years of use in Vedic religion, where it symbolizes purity, illumination, and unfolding potential. As in Egyptian symbolism, the lotus is observed to rise from a tiny seed in the mud to unfold into a ray of beauty as it reaches the sunlit surface, making it a natural emblem of growth and transformation. The thousand-petaled lotus is the emblem of the highest spiritual attainment, the opening of the crown chakra at the top of the head that occurs when kundalini energy moves through the purified chakras. The lotus in both Hinduism and Buddhism serves as the seat of wisdom for

gods and illuminated beings. The earliest prayer beads were made from the dried seeds of the lotus.

Color symbolism in Buddhism: The lotus in Buddhism has numerous aspects according to its color and the numeration of its petals. An eight-petaled lotus represents the ashtamangals, or eight auspicious symbols that embody the eight principles of the Dharma (sacred law). A white lotus symbolizes purity and spiritual perfection. A red lotus, passion and love. A blue lotus bud is an emblem of intelligence and communication. A pink lotus is the emblem of transcendence.

5) Conch Shell (Shankha): The Conch represents the voice of the Buddha and the truth of the dharma. A white conch that coils to the right represents the sound of the Dharma reaching far and wide, awakening beings from ignorance.

6) The Endless Knot or Shrivatsa: The knot, also known as the "mystic dragon," is a symbol of eternity and unity. From ancient times, such knots were commonly found in decorations on fabric and on the exterior of buildings, under the common belief that the endless looping of the designs confused evil spirits and prevented

them from entering homes. The knot is called the dragon knot because it is believed to have evolved over time from images of protective nagas or dragons.

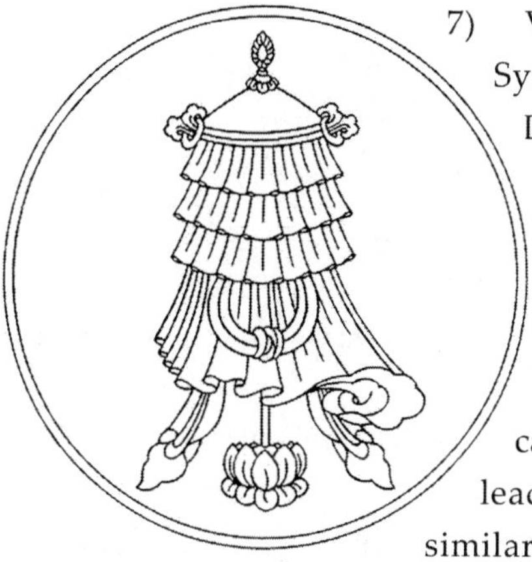

7) Victory Banner (Dhvaja): Symbolizes victory of the Dharma over fear, ignorance, and death. The banner is drawn from Hindu religious symbolism, and is shared with the Sikh and Jain religions, after the standards carried into battle by military leaders. The emblems have similar meanings in all of these faiths; that is, the victory of doctrine over ignorance and evil. In Tibetan Buddhism specifically, the banner symbolizes victory over the four Maras, or great illusions, which bar the way to illumination: emotional defilement, lust, passion, and the fear of death.

8) Dharma Wheel (Dharmachakra, Wheel of Law): The Dharma Wheel, resembling a wagon wheel with eight spokes, each representing one of the eight tenets of Buddhist belief. The circle symbolizes the completeness of the Dharma, the spokes represent the eightfold path leading to enlightenment: Right faith, right intention, right speech, right action, right livelihood, right endeavor, right mindfulness, and right

meditation. It is drawn from an Indian symbol, but instead of representing Samsara, or endless rebirth, it symbolizes overcoming obstacles. In Tibetan Buddhism the wheel is often seen flanked by deer, which refer to the deer park in which the Buddha is said to have given his first sermon.

As far as art, the four harmonious friends or four harmonious brothers became Olivia's favorite after she saw them throughout Bhutan, not only on the walls of Tibetan sacred buildings but in homes. The four friends represent one of the most universal and beloved of tales, originating from the Buddha himself and found in the *Vinayavastu*. The image of a bird, rabbit, and monkey standing on each other's shoulders on the back of a patient elephant portrays social and environmental harmony. The bird finds a seed and plants it. Then, the rabbit waters it, and the monkey fertilizes it. Once the seed sprouts and begins to grow, the elephant protects it. After some time, the small plant grows into a big, bounteous tree full of healthy fruit. By working cooperatively together and using their individual talents, the four friends are often able to reach and enjoy the fruit. Therefore, Olivia immediately noticed them throughout Tibet. Another version of the tale is that an elephant stands at the base, under a fruit tree carrying a monkey; a hare stands on top of the monkey, and a bird stands on top of the hare. The four animals were trying to find out who was the oldest. The elephant said that the tree was already fully grown when he was young, the monkey that the tree was small when he was young, the hare that he saw the tree as a sapling when he was young and the bird claimed that he had carried the seed from which the tree grew. Thus, the bird was recognized by the other animals as the oldest, and the four animals lived together in harmony, cooperatively helping each other to enjoy the fruits of the tree as the bird, standing at the top, would pick the fruit for them.

Samye Monastery is a living mandala that you can see and

feel, surrounded by a circular protective wall with a view of Yamdrok Lake. Samye was the first monastery built in Tibet in the 7th century, the land consecrated by Guru Rinpoche himself. Samye Monastery is laid out in the shape of a giant mandala, with the main temple representing the legendary Mount Meru in the center. Other buildings stand at the corners and cardinal points of the main temple, representing continents and other features of tantric Buddhist cosmology. Olivia remembers entering the courtyard and seeing a dirt ground instead of the usual rock laid floor and piles of juniper branches lying on the ground next to three white chortens lined up in a row next to each other. Sweet-smelling juniper branches were being burned as an offering. It was at here that Olivia had her first experience of seeing an animal get aggressive with someone. A goat wrapped one of its horns around the knee of a man standing next to her, nearly bringing him to the ground. The man absolutely could not free himself. Only when the man's wife started running away, out of fear, did the goat release the man to chase after her! Olivia had no idea what had transpired between this couple and the goat but was relieved that the goat had ignored her; however, beyond the spectacular experience of being in a living mandala, Olivia remembers the long rows of prayer wheels at Samye, which she turned many times.

Although all of the monasteries seen in Tibet were magnificent, Olivia looked most forward to visiting Tsurpu Monastery, 43 miles northwest of Lhasa at Tolung (*sTod-lung*) and 14,100 feet above sea level. Tsurpu is the Seat of the Karmapas, founded by the first Karmapa, Dusum-kyenpa (*Kar-ma Dus-gsum mkhyen-pa*) (1110–1193) in 1189. It was rebuilt in 1263 by the Second Karmapa, Karma Pakshi (*Kar-ma Pak-shi*) (1204–1283). A number of reliquary shrines of the previous Karmapas, deity shrines, monastic quarters for monks' residences, meditation halls, printing house, offices, and the Karmapa's summer residence are built around the main temple. Tsurpu was the home for two large libraries enshrining the sutras, tantras, instructions, collected works of all great masters of the four schools, Tibetan literature, and, most important of all, the writings of the all the Karmapas and their disciples. In 1959 there were nearly 1,000 monks at Tsurpu, but it was completely destroyed by the Chinese in 1966 and reconstructed in 1983.

At dusk, Olivia and her group arrived at Tsurpu, and were told they could sleep in a couple of monastery rooms despite much controversy. Initially, there was definitely a feeling of fear in the air as they were asked to leave because a Chinese official was arriving the next day. They couldn't believe it! They had traveled so far! Finally, they were told that they could stay the night but had to depart by noon the following day. They were disappointed, but somehow were learning to live with Chinese politics. They knew they would not have time to visit the nearby Sky Burial site where the dead are carried to the top of a mountain and left for vultures after the bodies are dismembered. Most people do not realize that for the ground of Tibet to be frozen most of the year makes being buried in the ground impossible; however, giving the body to hungry vultures is viewed as one last act of charity. Not all Tibetans are buried this way, but it is still quite common.

They settled into their rooms, and at this point, no one seemed to mind having four roommates. The outdoor, private bathroom facility was clean with a high, open window on the back wall facing north with a wonderful view of the Tsurpu River. Clean bathroom facilities were always appreciated; the worst one being at Tridum Nunnery and hot springs, which was shared by both men and women. They had to first walk down steps to get out of the building where four of them shared a sleeping room and then down many steps to the bathroom. Upon opening the door to a large toilet room there were six holes in the concrete floor. Invariably, when one walked in, more than one person was in the room. It didn't matter whether the person was of your gender or not and a little scary if it was pitch dark in the middle of the night.

Squatting was painful for Olivia because of previous knee injuries so she made a fist with both hands and placed a fist behind each knee which took some pressure off the knee. Carrying toilet tissue in pockets was essential because it was not provided.

The reason why they stopped at the Tridum hot springs and nunnery, which wasn't easy to access because they had to carry luggage over a narrow metal bridge and many steps, was to sit in the hot springs, famous for their medicinal properties. The springs are located in a narrow gorge at the confluence of two separate streams, and the entire valley is festooned with prayer flags. One of the women in the group, Jan, convinced Olivia that it would look strange if Olivia wore her swimming suit in the hot springs because everyone else was nude. It was true. Upon approaching the pools, carefully walking on wet, narrow paths of rocks, there was first a big pool for the men and then a pool for the women with a privacy wall separating them. Olivia was assured of complete privacy from Jan, who was already soaking in the hottest area of the springs, saying mantras. Olivia completely stripped down, only to look up and see several more than delighted men standing on top of the wall looking directly at her. She was standing, naked as a jaybird, in the middle of Tibet for an audience of smiling men. She must have frozen because Jan jumped out of the water, naked of course, and stood in front of Olivia, smiling and wildly waving her arms at the men. Of course, their attention was now directed at Jan as Olivia quickly slipped down into the water to join about a dozen other women, mostly Tibetans. The springs were wonderful; however, afterwards, Olivia realized that there were seriously ill people staying at the springs because she accidentally wandered into a room of bedridden people, thinking it was the on site restaurant. Yeshe Tsogyal, the wife of King Trisong Detsen and consort of

Guru Rinpoche, had strong connection with the small nunnery there, and Kandro-la, the resident spiritual leader of the nunnery is considered a reincarnation of Yeshe Tsogyal.

Although Olivia always requested a private room, when it was impossible, her roommates appreciated her. She could prepare for bed in a minute, hit the sack, and fall dead asleep. On the contrary, DiDi took at least a full two hours to get ready to go to sleep. She would sit in the dark with her flashlight under her blanket, trying to get organized. One night, awakening to the noise of crinkling paper, Olivia asked, "Are you eating candy?" DiDi was taking the wrapper off of a can of oxygen. DiDi carried around more stuff—trekking poles hanging from her backpack that was overflowing with everything imaginable. Olivia wondered how she could even walk and would point to the organizer purse hanging from around her neck and say, "Everything I need is right here."

Back to Tsurpu. After stowing their belongings in their rooms, they walked to the entrance of Tsurpu, supported by a red beam on either side and topped with a beam painted blue with white, gold, and green ornamental Tibetan paintings. At the top of each beam was a painted gold wheel with spokes, representing the Wheel of Dharma. Olivia sighed at the sight of one more red Chinese flag, centered and flying above the entrance. A light seemed to shine through the darkness onto the complex as they searched for a place to eat dinner. They were directed to an unkempt, one-story cinder-block looking house, in need of fresh, white paint. There was much debris in the yard—stacked cinder blocks, wood, and unidentifiable items that caused Olivia's heart to sink. After all, this was Tsurpu. They were able to sit and enjoy a meal in a traditional Tibetan kitchen although everyone had grown intolerant of seeing white rice every day. Traditional Tibetan momos, a type of steamed dumpling, with or without filling, eaten with different side sauces, were a favorite. French fries, called fried potatoes, were on every menu and frequently ordered by Olivia. Although no one in the group liked to drink the staple yak butter tea, made from tea leaves, yak butter, water, and salt, soft drinks were always available.

Interestingly, when they entered the kitchen, they saw no cows outside but when they exited, 40 minutes later, there were six cows standing there, facing the door as if waiting to greet them.

As they began their walk back to their rooms for the night, Olivia looked to the right and her heart was lifted. On top of a white painted rock and brick wall, with a two-foot maroon stripe at the top that was dotted evenly with white blocks, flew the Karmapa's blue and gold dream flag. His Holiness the 16th Gyalwa Karmapa, Rangjung Rigpe Dorje saw this flag in a dream. He called it Namkhyen Gyaldar, meaning "Victorious Flag of the Buddha's Wisdom" and announced, "Wherever this banner is flown, the Dharma will flourish." The flag also flew at another one of the entrances at Tsurpu... by itself—without a Chinese flag. However, officials in the gift shop at Tsurpu were promoting and selling a "new" dream flag that was similar in design to the traditional dream flag but it did not include the color gold. Olivia asked the officials why the image of the dream flag was being changed. No one knew why. Why was a word that the Chinese did not understand. They took orders.

The next morning they knew they had little time to accomplish what they had planned at Tsurpu and certainly would not have time to trek to the Sky Burial Cemetery. Hurriedly, five of them entered the entrance to Tsurpu, a 3,200 sq. foot complex. Of course, every monastery has prayer wheels; they saw a long row of solid gold prayer wheels mounted on a maroon-painted brick and rock wall alongside ascending steps. Seeing a wall didn't mean an ordinary wall—some of them were 13 feet in width. What appeared to be an attractive and newly constructed administrative office was near the entrance of the grounds, appearing to be administrative, not because of the Tibetan design and deer on either side of the Wheel of Dharma centered on the roof of the building but because there were so many vehicles parked in front. There was a mountain in back, and upon looking to the right, it was clear that the complex was built in a valley facing south, surrounded by sloping mountainsides, dotted with colorful, wild flowers. The sky was incredibly clear and deep blue in color. A green stupa was near the base of one mountain, and higher up the mountain one could see a white complex and individual complexes where the Karmapas had lived. Much higher up on the hill was another white complex, a three-year retreat center.

The five of them walked through some narrow corridors, always lined with concrete steps and freshly painted gold and maroon painted walls. And then they came to the main Shrine Hall, which was breathtaking. The roof was adorned with the typical deer facing the Wheel of Dharma and gold banners on either side; below, hung a gold banner with auspicious signs painted in blue; a railing laid below and more brown fabric hanging at either side, halfway down a maroon-painted brick and cinder-block wall, and above the entrance door. On either side of the brown fabric there were a brown and white emblem and two white deer facing the Wheel of Dharma above the door. A very large mountain goat sat noticeably on a shelf that was built into the maroon-painted wall at the entrance behind a chorten that was covered in black soot from burning juniper offerings. A large, white marble statue of a lion stood on either side of the steps to the entrance.

It was clear that steps led upwards to the main Shrine Hall. The prayer wheels at the entrance of the Shrine Hall were gorgeous and beyond anything Olivia had ever seen. They were covered in artwork, framed in red box wooden squares. Once inside, the main hall was breathtaking with beautiful fabrics. The statues were unbelievable, some of them appearing to be dozens of feet tall. They were whisked away to view the massive 43-foot-tall, gold statue known as the Great Buddha Statue, the Buddha Shakyamuni, with an artistic mandala above his head. The statue is not normally viewed by Westerners because of its sacredness, containing many precious and rare relics. Tsurpu enshrined many rare and historical relics, many well-preserved, either inside statues, stupas, shrine boxes, or publicly displayed shrines. Great reliquary blessings and images from the time of Buddha and Nagarjuna through the Karmapas are enshrined at Tsurpu, including the relics of the historical Buddha Shakyamuni. Clay statues hand-made of the most renowned Indian master Nagarjuna, relics from Naropa, Marpa, Milarepa, Gampopa, the Karmapas, and many other great enlightened masters remain enshrined at Tsurpu.

Olivia carried a plastic bag full of yak butter in order to make offerings at some of the huge butter lamps, some with more than 30 wicks burning. She saw pictures of the 16th Karmapa not only on the wall but on altars, one picture draped with a gold khata. At the front, in the courtyard paved with gray rock, was a pillar, surrounded by a red metal fence. Olivia always noticed the large brown cooking pots in the courtyards, some of them six feet in diameter, used to cook for thousands of monks. One of the highlights of Tsurpu was seeing the Karmapa's handprint high on a maroon cinder block wall, painted gold with a gold khata hanging above it. Olivia loved telling stories about the Karmapas. When one of the women in the group was hosting her mock radio show on the bus she identified who could sing or play musical instruments for her show. Two of the women, Billie Woods and Deborah Schmidt, were professional musicians who later cut the remarkable CD: Suite Journey, *Tibet Land of Our Tears,* which included yak bells for the song *Yak Butter Blues* that Olivia mailed to them from Nepal. As far as what Olivia could contribute to the talent show—"And Olivia can talk about the Karmapa!"

Yes, Olivia loved to tell stories about His Holiness the 16th Gyalwa Karmapa, Rangjung Rigpe Dorje. She developed a special connection to him years earlier after she began practicing with a Nyingmapa sangha of the Nyingma Buddhist tradition because she knew of no Kagyupas in the area. After several months of practice, she was pressured to join the Nyingma tradition. One night Olivia thought she would join the Nyingmapas for the sake of convenience; however, when she fell asleep that night, she saw the 16th Karmapa in a dream, with his hand raised to his Black Crown, the depiction that would allow Olivia to easily recognize him. The dream actually terrified her at the time, and she promised the Karmapa that she would never leave the Karma Kagyu lineage. Months later, the 17th Karmapa, Trinley Thaye Dorje, personally told her not to mix the methods of different schools because it would be like trying to go up stream with one foot in one boat and the other foot in another boat.

The 16th Gyalwa Karmapa was known as the "King of the Yogis" because yogis would come down from the mountains and ask the Karmapa to teach them to meditate. Legend tells of one yogi who was attacked by a wild dog, but as soon as the yogi said the mantra "Karmapa Chenno" ("power of all the Buddha's work through us"), the dog retreated. Many amazing stories are told about the Karmapa beyond the physical miracles he performed, such as leaving footprints on stone and a footprint in the water in a lake in Tibet, which remains to this day.

The Karmapa loved birds and always had a zoo of them, referring to canaries as Bodhisattvas. He would communicate with them and teach them to meditate. When his birds died, they would sit in the peaceful glow of meditation on their perch for three days and then they would fall to the bottom of their cage. One of the best-known bird stories about the Karmapa had to do with a time when he was in a bird store in Nepal with Lama Ole Nydahl. According to Lama Ole, the Karmapa started to tell the bird shop owner what each one of the birds was thinking, and one of the birds wasn't at all fond of its owner. The bird shop owner became so upset by this information—that the birds actually had thoughts and feelings—that he exclaimed to the Karmapa, "Take them. Take them all." Of course, the Karmapa was more than happy to add these birds to his aviary. The Karmapa's "all-knowingness" is found in countless stories; therefore, when monks or other people were in the presence of the Karmapa they would watch their thinking, knowing that the Karmapa knew their every thought. Sherab Gyaltsen Rinpoche, a highly respected Lama in the Kagyu lineage, ordained by the Karmapa when he was 15 years old, once said of the Karmapa, "His ability to know things is unobstructed" (Sherab Gyaltsen Rinpoche, 2007, p. 39).

Sherab Gyaltsen Rinpoche also explained that one of the main activities of the Karmapa was to find incarnations. When people would come to the Karmapa looking for the incarnation (tulku) of their former teacher who had died, the Karmapa would tell them exactly where the incarnation was born, the name of the father and mother, and the exact birth date of the child. He was one of the few who could find tulkus; it was one of his special activities. Nearly all Kagyu and Nyingma tulkus were found by the Karmapa, in addition to some Gelug and Sakya tulkus; however, the most amazing account of the Karmapa had to do with the events preceding his own death in 1981, which the Very Venerable Kalu Rinpoche believed was a fulfillment of a prophecy made by Guru Rinpoche in response to a question raised by Yeshe Tsogyal (Kalu, 1986).

Yeshe Tsogyal was a Tibetan princess who lived in the 7th century. She had a miraculous birth, fled from persecution to self-exile and made untold sacrifices to a selfless end. She performed miraculous, Christ-like deeds such as resurrecting the dead, healing the sick, feeding the multitude, making a gift of her body to the needy and attaining Buddhahood in a body of light (Dowman, 1996). She is an example to all women and demonstrates that Buddhism did not discriminate against women (or anyone, for that matter). Women were able to stand on an even playing field with men, void of patriarchal power plays that grow from greed and fear. Nonetheless, Yeshe Tsogyal asked Guru Rinpoche what could be done to help beings in the dark ages that she foresaw (the Kalpa of Great Conflict, the Kalpa of Weapons, and the Kalpa of Famine). Guru Rinpoche answered, "In order to help eliminate intense sufferings in that dark time, make supplications to one whom in the future will bear the name Karmapa. Sincere supplications and devotion to that being will bring about harmony" (Kalu, 1986, p. 155).

Centuries later, in 1981, when His Holiness the 16th Gyalwa Karmapa lay in the hospital near Chicago, Kalu Rinpoche witnessed that His Holiness had undergone many operations and blood transfusions. Every day the doctors discovered symptoms of a new disease, only to find that the symptoms were gone the next day and replaced by another disease, as if all the diseases in the world were finding room in his body. For two months His Holiness ingested no solid food. Finally, his doctors gave up hope, saying it was impossible for him to live, and life support systems should be disconnected. The Karmapa responded, "No, I am going to live. Leave them in place." Astonishing his doctors, he did live, remaining not only at ease but humorous, playful, and smiling, as if he were rejoicing at everything his body suffered.

Kalu Rinpoche knew that the Karmapa had voluntarily submitted to this suffering to help minimize the coming pains of war, disease, and famine, and in this way he was working to avert those terrible kalpas. His death was an unforgettable inspiration and an example that enlightenment for the sake of others can actually be achieved (Kalu, 1986, pp. 155–156). When the enlightened mind (consciousness) of the Karmapa left its physical shell, his body remained in gentle meditation for three days, during which time the heart center remained very warm and the skin supple. This was witnessed and attested to by the doctors and medical staff despite all the other clinical symptoms of death. Only after three such days did the usual manifestations of death appear.

Even more profound than the death of the Karmapa were his life and his teachings. Hannah Nydahl reminisced how the Karmapa had a way of "throwing us in the water and we simply had to swim" (Nydahl, H., 2008, p. 21). His "skillful, direct and non-conceptual style of teaching always taught the essence, not so many detailed things. This is what he wanted to transmit and what he wanted us to use and realize" (p. 20). "We also had several meetings with him where he would just look, not say anything, and just rested in space. I don't know how much time passed and then he blessed us without saying anything. This blessing pervades all our activity. It is our root, our source" (Nydahl, H. 2008, p. 25).

As the seat of the Sakya (or Sakyapa) school of Tibetan Buddhism, Sakya Monastery was founded in 1073, by Konchok Gyelpo (1034–1102). Its powerful abbots governed Tibet during the 13th and the 14th centuries under the overlordship of the Mongol Yuan dynasty after the downfall of the Tibetan Empire until they were eclipsed by the rise of the new Kagyu and Gelug schools of Tibetan Buddhism. Although most of the buildings were destroyed during the Chinese Invasion, the great library of Sakya remains on shelves along the walls of the great hall of the Lhakhang Chen-po. In 2003, a huge library of as many as 84,000 scrolls were found sealed up in a wall 197 feet long and 33 feet high at Sakya Monastery. It is expected that most of them will prove to be Buddhist scriptures although they may well also include works of literature, history, philosophy, astronomy, mathematics and art. They are thought to have remained untouched for hundreds of years; thus, Sakya has the largest library in the world, and when a teaching needs to be given, the sacred text simply slides out from the wall, and a khata is placed over it, hanging. Olivia had to see it to believe it. There were actually several texts protruding from their stack on the wall with a khata draped over them. Preserved also are many volumes written in gold letters; the pages are six feet long by eighteen inches in breadth. In the margin of each page are illuminations, and the first four volumes have in them pictures of the thousand Buddhas. These books are bound in iron. They were prepared under orders of the Emperor Kublai Khan, and presented to the Phagpa Lama on his second visit to Beijing.

There are several reasons why Olivia will never forget Sakya beyond being mesmerized by the library. As Olivia proceeded to the Shrine Hall, an elderly Tibetan woman ran up to Olivia, threw her arms around her and clung to her, hugging her and talking ecstatically in Tibetan, which Olivia did not understand. This encounter—or reunion—continued for several minutes, which several people noticed. One of the women in the group wished she could have recorded it or at least taken photographs of it but it occurred spontaneously and unexpectedly. Truly, it was one of those encounters of recognition that does happen among Buddhists from time to time, recognizing that we have known each other and had relationships with each other in previous lives.

There is also preserved in this temple a white conch shell with whirls turning from left to right [in Tibetan, *Ya chyü dungkar*], a present from Kublai to Phagpa. It is only blown by the Lamas when the request is accompanied by a present of seven ounces of silver; but to blow it, or have it blown, is held to be an act of great merit. Olivia requested that one of the Lamas blow the conch shell for her father who was recovering from surgery for cancer. As he held the shell with a red cloth and blew it, the sound was penetrating, and it proved to be one of the things she remembered the most about Tibet. Olivia was touched when Sam asked the Lama to give him a blessing, and the Lama replied, "Only unless you give me a blessing first."

Everything at Sakya was gorgeous—the statues, the art, the massive butter lamps, the entrance doors, framed in fabric... all of it was simply breathtaking and certainly constituted one of the most elegant monasteries in Tibet. Fortunately, in most instances, whenever Olivia asked for permission to take photographs she was not refused, which often infuriated professional photographers who were not given such permission. On one occasion, a Chinese photographer was livid that Olivia was taking photographs at the Sakya Monastery where he was denied permission. When he got angry at Olivia one of her friends wanted to seek assistance from the police but Olivia wanted to walk away from the conflict because she felt it was inappropriate in such a sacred place.

Outside in the massive courtyard with a floor of gray rock, and near a low row of prayer wheels, Olivia saw the largest bell and dorje in existence, although the handle of the bell was not attached to but lying in front of the bell. The bell is rich in symbolic meaning and power. Mainly, the bell is the mandala of Prajnaparamita, the Great Mother, she from whom all reality comes forth. By its sound, the bell invites or attracts the deities to attend or participate and warns or drives away obstructing forces. The ringing of the bell can remind one of the emptiness of phenomena or bring the mind into greater awareness. As a musical instrument, its sound can be an offering to the Buddhas and Bodhisattvas. The hollow of the bell represents the void from which all phenomena arise, including the sound of the bell, and the clapper represents form. Together they symbolize wisdom (emptiness) and compassion (form or appearance). The sound, like all phenomena, arises, radiates forth and then dissolves back into emptiness.

Pelkor Chode (Auspicious Wheel Joy) is a landmark of Tibetan art history. It was built in 1418 by the Dharma King of Gyantse Rabtan Kunsang Phak and the first Panchen Lama Kedrop Gelug Pesang. It is unusual in that it is a nonsectarian Buddhist center where Gelugpa, Sakyapa, and Bontonpa coexist in harmony. When Olivia and her group arrived, monks were busy making huge swirl-type designs on the rock floor courtyard in front of the Lantang with a white and tan powdered chalk in anticipation of the arrival of a Rinpoche. Other monks were scurrying around, one carrying a large pot of flowers, another carrying a silver cooking pot. In the background sat a large cooking pot once used to prepare food for 180,000 monks that are now reduced to 80. The tallest prayer flag Olivia had ever seen stood in the courtyard, and beyond that a foreboding view of the 14th preserved dzongs in Tibet, perched high above the town of Gyantse on a huge spur of gray brown rock.

Late in 1427, the Great Stupa Kumbum (the largest in Tibet) was erected in the pattern of the Multi-door Stupa, one of the eight prototype stupas of Buddhism. The kumbum includes 9 floors, 108 altars where a hundred thousand Buddhist images are enshrined as statues and murals. The murals are famous, which center on Esoteric Buddhism and are presented in the Mandala style. They are mainly found inside the grand tower and the 2nd floor of the main Sutra Hall. The paintings have three types of themes: stories in Buddhist scriptures, stories about religious figures, and historical figures. The murals in the monastery have gained inspiration from traditional art genres in Tibet from its own natural and lively style. Named as the Gyangze Style, the murals have left deep influence on the Tibetan painting art. They are seen as representative works of the mature Buddhist art in the 14th–15th centuries and an important symbol of the peak that Tibetan Buddhist art reached in the 15th century.

There are 108 doors and 76 chapels in the Great Stupa Kumbum. Olivia stepped through every single low door and bumped her head so many times coming out that she started to laugh and call them "blessings." She took pictures in every chapel, some of them dark without any light (a flashlight is needed in order to see them). She was always looking for the old and original structure and lost count of how many ladders she climbed; however, she also wanted to capture images of Tibetan people arriving, eager to see an important teacher. For example, young mothers were helping each other in getting babies properly tied on their back. You would never see a carryall in this part of the world. Other women in traditional Tibetan dress, an apron signifying that they were married, were walking with a cane or prostrating. A few women were spinning a prayer wheel in one hand and holding a mala in the other. A khata was carried or tucked under an arm to give to their teacher. Olivia captured her best photographic shots of Tibetans on this occasion. In 1996, Kumbum was listed in the key state-level cultural relic preservation unit… a little too late, unfortunately, because thousands of statues were destroyed during the Chinese invasion and only hundreds remain. The murals survived the invasion much better than the statues.

Olivia looked forward to visiting Milarepa's Cave or Namkading Cave, six miles north of the town of Nyalam, below the roadside and above the Matsang River—a place of great beauty. Milarepa (c.1052–c.1135), the most beloved yogi of Tibet, is one of the Karma Kagyu Buddhist lineage Masters. He spent many years of his life meditating in this cave, which overlooks the entrance to the hidden valley of Lapchi Gang. From the roadside through the village, a stone path leads the way down a hillside, passing many mani stones and mani walls. Descending concrete steps lead to the Nyanang Phelgye Ling Monastery, or Phelgyeling. The Assembly Hall of the monastery has the statue of Buddha Shakyamuni in the center, which is seven feet in height. The cave is entered from the gompa's vestibule, a long narrow hall with practice benches on either side, displaying horns, trumpets and other sacred ritual items. A beautiful, large white statue of thousand-arm Avalokiteshvara is seen with turquoise, blue, and coral jewels laid in gold, and green, red, blue, gold, and white khatas (colors of the five Buddha families) are draped behind the hands, flowing down on either side of the statue.

The cave itself is kept as a shrine by two monks, guarding a gold statue of Milarepa, approximately two feet in height, enclosed in a glass case. Milarepa is sitting in the commonly seen depiction of right hand raised to his left ear, listening while singing his songs. Although 100,000 of his songs have been published, one example of Milarepa's songs arose when a disciple asked that Milarepa instruct them on the practice of the Six Paramitas, which is defined by Gampopa as generosity, moral ethics, patience, perseverance, meditative concentration, and discriminating wisdom (Gampopa, 1998):

Property and wealth are like dew on grass;
Knowing this, gladly should one give them away.

It is most precious to be born a worthy and
leisured human being.
Knowing this, one should with care observe
the precepts
As if protecting his own eyes.

Anger is the cause of falling to the Realms Below;
Knowing this, one should refrain from wrath,
Even at the risk of life.

Benefit to oneself and to others
Can never be achieved through sloth;
Strive, therefore, to do good deeds.

A perturbed, wandering mind never sees the
truth of Mahayana;
Practice, therefore, concentration.

Buddha cannot be found through searching;
So contemplate your own mind.

Until the autumn mists dissolve into the sky,
Strive on with faith and determination.
Milarepa, 1962, p. 100

Accomplishing the six paramitas leads to the ten perfections, the last four being:

1. Skillfull means—ability to act beneficially regardless external circumstances.
2. Resolute aspiration—strength of will towards progress and positive effort.
3. Effective spiritual power—unified application of being towards effort.
4. Knowledge—genuine understanding of "what is" that is unaffected by "what may or should be or not be."

On Milarepa's statue, a gold khata with auspicious signs is draped over his shoulder, a white khata lies behind it, and offerings of paper money from around the world lie inside and outside the case. In the dark cave is an impression in the rock attributed to Milarepa's sitting meditation posture and a hand print said to have been created when Milarepa helped Rechungpa (1083/4–1161CE), his student, use a boulder to prop up the ceiling. Olivia lit butter lamps as an offering and placed a khata at this site. She held her hand on the rock impressions, bending over, because the cave was not tall enough for standing. Khatas and paper money lay beneath, on a rock and on a couple of other large rocks in the cave. A glass case enshrined a gold statue of Padmasambhava (Guru Rinpoche) with a photograph of his face on the right outside corner of the case with a name plaque at the front, Holy Pema Loch, underneath a painted Buddha image. There were painted images on the wall of the cave of Milarepa, Tsongkhapa, and Shri Devi, a protectress whose mule is said to have left a footprint in the stone when she visited

Milarepa in a vision. Restoration work within the cave and the monastery was undertaken by artists and craftsmen from Nepal and was financed by the Chinese government in the 1970s (Dowman, 1988).

Olivia was often asked questions about Tibet. Some expressed that Tibet was gone forever; however, Olivia never felt that way. She had traveled in scenic, rural areas of Tibet that were untouched by the Chinese invasion. She laughed with Tibetan women in the fields, among their sifting baskets, fans, and metal bowls working with grains of barley that were spread out on blankets on the ground. She videotaped a Tibetan man, wearing a beige felt hat with a brass studded brown leather band around the brim. He was impeccably dressed in dark beige twill pants and a navy blue T-shirt, topped with a long-sleeved beige shirt and V-neck beige sweater. Holding onto a plow with both hands, he gave commands to a pair of yoked yak that were pulling a metal plow blade through straw-topped, brown soil. She watched a Tibetan woman, with a baby tied on her back, run in front of their bus, chasing a cow, and other Tibetan women herding their goats. She saw many Tibetan nomads called Drokpas who still have a presence in Tibet, identified by their large tents made of yak leather and wool. Olivia wished she would have had time to sit with them, in their tents. She learned to spot the many mani rocks and walls bearing the mantra Om Mani Padme Hung, painted in Tibetan.

Olivia also noticed rocks with white painted ladders on them, and asked their meaning. On Lhabab Ducehn Festival, which falls on the 22nd day of the ninth lunar month in the Tibetan calendar, one of the four events in the life of the Buddha is celebrated, and white ladders are painted afresh on rocks around many monasteries. It is said that the Buddha had left for heaven at the age of 41, having ascended to the Heaven of Thirty-Three (Trayastrimsa) in order to give teachings to benefit the gods in the desire realms and to repay kindness to his mother, Queen

Mayadevi, by liberating her from Samsara. This event is considered one of the Buddha's eight great deeds. After much debate, the Buddha returned to earth after three months as requested by his follower Maugalyayana, by a special triple ladder prepared by Vishwakarma, the god of machines.

Most notable in Tibet was that a white stupa was seen every few miles, and Olivia nearly jumped out of her seat on the bus taking pictures of them. Ten years ago a stupa was simply an architectural structure with symbolic meaning. Olivia learned to identify the five types of stupas, based on form and function and built for a variety of reasons: 1) A *relic* stupa contains the relics or remains of the Buddha, his disciples, and lay saints; 2) An *object* stupa contains objects that belonged to the Buddha or his disciples, such as a begging bowl or robe, or important Buddhist scriptures; 3) A *commemorative* stupa is built to commemorate events in the lives of Buddha or his disciples; 4) A *symbolic* stupa is built to symbolize aspects of Buddhist theology, for example, Borobudur is considered to be the symbol of the Three Worlds (*dhatu*) and the spiritual stages (*bhumi*) in a Mahayana *bodhisattva's* character; and 5) A *votive* stupa, constructed to commemorate visits or to gain spiritual benefits, usually at the site of prominent stupas which are regularly visited. However, all stupas are a treasury, filled with objects. Small clay votive offerings called *Tsa-tsas* (Tib.) fill a major part of the treasury and their creation of various types is a ceremony in itself. Mantras written on paper are rolled into thin rolls and put into the small clay stupas. Filling the treasury, one layer of Tsa-Tsas are placed, and the empty space between them is filled with dry sand. On the new surface appearing, another layer of Tsa-Tsas is made, until the entire space of a treasury is full, leaving no empty spaces. Jewelry and other "precious" objects are also placed in the treasury, and the more objects placed inside, the stronger the energy of the Stupa will be.

More Wishes! A very important element in every Stupa is the

Tree of Life, a wooden pole covered with gems and thousands of mantras, and placed in the central channel of the stupa. It is placed here during a ceremony or *initiation*, where the participants hold colorful ribbons connected to the Tree of Life. Together the participants make their most positive and powerful wishes, which are stored in the Tree of Life. In this way the stupa is charged up, and will start to function. There are also eight different kinds of stupas, each representing events in the Buddha's life: 1) Lotus Blossom Stupa; 2) Enlightenment Stupa; 3) Stupa of Many Doors; 4) Stupa of Descent from the God Realms; 5) Stupa of Great Miracles; 6) Stupa of Reconciliation; 7) Stupa of Complete Victory; and 8) Stupa of Nirvana. There was only one time that Olivia saw all eight of these identifiably different stupas lined up in a row—in Bhutan.

Despite this basic knowledge, Olivia was told by one of her teachers that it was impossible to learn about stupas intellectually, and Olivia found that it was true. The power and significance of stupas is beyond words, and building a stupa is considered extremely beneficial, leaving very positive karmic imprints in the mind. Usually surrounded by prayer flags, they now meant something to Olivia on a deep, spiritual level. Sadly, where a stupa had been destroyed by the Chinese, prayer flags were seen streaming out in a circle and from a central pole, commemorating and blessing the place. Destroying a stupa is considered an extremely negative deed, similar to killing. Such an action is explained to create massive negative karmic imprints, leading to massive future problems, leaving the mind in a state of paranoia after death has occurred and leading to unfortunate rebirths.

Regardless, colorful prayer flags were seen as part of the landscape, especially in auspicious areas where there was a river, wind, and mountains. Olivia could not stop taking pictures of them and videotaping them because they always looked different because of the way they had been blowing in the wind, sometimes tangled or falling to the ground. Every display of prayer flags appeared to be a new display of art. Thus, the history and spirit of Tibet will never be destroyed by the Chinese. As despicable as the Chinese invasion has been in regard to their forced genocide, murdering 1.2 million gentle and compassionate Tibetans and the attempted systematic destruction of all that is sacred to them—their culture, language, and religious freedom—all of which are egregious human rights violations with unspeakable suffering—the Chinese invasion did result in one positive outcome as Tibetans were forced to seek refuge in all corners of the world, as predicted by Guru Rinpoche (Padmasambhava):

When asked by his disciple when is the beginning of Dharma-ending age, Guru Rinpoche replied, "When the Iron Birds are flying in the sky and the Iron Horses [airplanes, cars and trains] are running on the roads, we know that the dharma-ending age has arrived. At this time, Tibetan Buddhism shall flourish globally. When the iron bird flies and the horses run on wheels, the Tibetan people will be scattered like ants across the world, and the Dharma will come to the land of the red men (Western Countries)."

Nepal: Last Resort—Manika Graveyard—Nuwakot

Just 7.5 miles from the border of Tibet, the group spent two nights at The Last Resort in Bungee, Nepal, set in a gorgeous, tropical spot on a ridge above the Bhote Kosi River. Undoubtedly, it is the most magical resort on earth. Reaching it meant walking across a long, four-foot narrow vertiginous suspension bridge that also serves as a launch pad for thrill seeking bungee jumpers, diving 525 feet and coming to a benching stop just short of the river below. Once arriving at the entrance, near the registration office, Olivia stepped up to a rock platform where a tall rock altar sits, a Buddha statue recessed on each side. Silver offering bowls, filled with water, sit on a ledge on the immediate side, and prayer flags are draped from the top and into the trees. There was such a feeling of tranquility that Olivia spent quite a bit of time there.

Accommodation at the resort is in comfortable and private two-or four-person safari tents with a covered porch and comfortable chairs, set privately in a jungle-type setting around a soaring stone-and-slate dining hall and bar. People not only eat buffet-style meals in the dining hall, but are seen lounging or working on their computers because of the Internet access. Most people register for all-inclusive adventure packages in order to enjoy swinging from a giant elastic band, rafting, trekking, mountain biking, and canyoning. For less endorphin-motivated travelers, there are gas-heated showers, and a sauna and spa is on site. After Olivia and the group were checked into their tents, several of them hiked down to the spa on a narrow path of stone steps, lined with trees, fern, flowers, and other green, lush foliage. They passed a square plunge pool, shallow steps leading down to its depth on three sides, the other side being a brick wall where a Buddha statue sat above a large spout pouring water into the pool. A couple of the women enjoyed a sauna while Olivia and the others had a massage in the spa, a Zen-like decorated brick building with high ceilings and intoxicating flowers floating in large, round metal bowls filled with water. Olivia loved listening to the birds, recording their songs, and taking pictures of exotic flowers, making it the most luxurious place to stay and a great place to escape the city or relax en route to or from Tibet. It would be a great honeymoon destination!

Upon leaving The Last Resort, the group was traveling in three Toyota Land Cruiser four-wheel drive vehicles, luggage tied and secured on the roof racks; however, with great concern they did not know if they would be able to travel on the Amiko Highway that connects Tibet to Nepal, which was necessary in order for them to reach Kathmandu. The highway had recently been destroyed in a landslide, along with the village of Manika, about 75 miles east of Kathmandu; thus, they proceeded with fingers crossed. Fortunately, once they arrived, they saw that a narrow road had been carved into the mountain that allowed them a safe but slow and bumpy passage. To complicate the landslide, a mountain river, causing the water to form a lake, was threatening to burst and sweep several villages; therefore, a lot of blasting and other maneuvering needed to be done in order to avoid further disaster. Controlled explosions by the army managed to knock down part of an earth wall that had blocked a river and created a temporary dam, allowing some water to flow out, but much of it still remained trapped, posing a threat to downstream villages as far away as India.

Olivia and her friends got out of their jeeps and stood on the very spot where Manika was buried in the middle of the night, killing over 150 people, and injuring even more, crushing over 60 homes that now lay beneath the earth. Olivia's jeep driver lost 21 relatives in the landslide and pointed out to Olivia where the homes of family members had stood, in which there was no trace whatsoever—just dirt. Hauntingly, they were standing on a graveyard and spent nearly half an hour walking over the area in reverent silence, feeling a great deal of sadness.

Devastating landslides such as this one are common in the mostly mountainous and remote areas of Nepal during the rainy season, which runs from June through September. They are mainly caused by the natural movement of land, erosion of land by rivers, earthquakes, melting glaciers, soil erosion, sitting riverbeds, and growing population. They claim a significant number of lives each year and cause untold damage to the environment. They have resulted in the loss of farming land, agricultural production, livestock, homes, villages, and road networks. Those who are able to keep their homes after a landslide may be affected by other consequences of the disaster, such as loss of power in the home or telecommunications. Tragically, due to treacherous terrain in Nepal, it is often arduous to send immediate help or equipment to landslide areas. Little did Olivia know that she would soon discover just how difficult it can be to get aid to people who desperately need it the most.

As they continued their drive to Kathmandu, one of the young women disclosed that her father had cheated on her mother for years before they got divorced. Olivia could tell that hearing the word "divorce" made the Nepalese driver very uncomfortable so she asked him about it. Yes, divorce was almost unheard of in Nepal and beyond his world experience. He married his wife at a young age for life, and he would never look at another woman. He even stopped at a roadside store to make a purchase for her while they waited in the jeep. They were impressed and jokingly concluded that they should start a buddhamatch.com for Western women who wanted to find a man with Eastern values. But somehow it was not a laughing matter. Every woman in the jeep had had experiences with cheating men.

Soon after returning to Kathmandu, a friend with a car drove Olivia to Nuwakot, a village 20 miles east of Kathmandu, which commands one of the broadest views of the Himalayas in the Kathmandu Valley—well-known for its hiking, scenic beauty and breathtaking sunrises. The name, Nuwakot, is made up of two words "nawa" and 'kort'. Nawa means nine in Nepali and "kort" means sacred religious site at the top of a hill. The district accordingly has nine hills over which various deities are said to dwell thus overseeing and protecting Nuwakot. Eight Himalayan ranges of Nepal can also be seen: Annapurna range, Manaslu range, Ganesh Himal range, Langtang range, Jugal range, Rolwaling range, Mahalangur range (Everest range), and Numbur range with views of the Kathmandu Valley and Shivapuri National Park. Situated in a strategic location, Nuwakot was an ancient fort of the Kathmandu Valley built to monitor the external activities of other kingdoms. Later, it became a summer retreat for the royal family before becoming popular as an international hill station.

After a scenic drive to Nuwakot, on narrow, winding roads, Olivia arrived at the quaint and charming, tucked-away Nuwakot resort, The Famous Farm. The main building consists of a renovated old Newar house with raised ceiling, tiled floor, central fireplace in a step-down room, and wraparound windows that offer panoramic views. The brick-walled guest rooms, situated in a long row, included a large window that faced a breathtaking view of the Himalayas, which appeared to be within one's reach. A burgundy colored Tibetan door curtain, trimmed in yellow with a matching pleated canopy, hung at the door to her room displaying the eight auspicious signs, embroidered in colors of turquoise, blue, pink, orange, yellow, and white. A young Nepali man built a fire for Olivia in a metal stove, planted in the corner of her room. He enthusiastically told her that the best view of the Himalayas would be early in the morning; thus, she set the alarm on her cell phone in eager anticipation of an unforgettable sunrise that would paint the sky, illuminating the mountains and uplifting the soul. She not only captured majestic pictures of the Himalayan ranges on film but shots that included flowers, trees, hills, prayer flags, and cloud formations. She heard a loud kha-kha-kha-kha bird call and zoomed in on a large eagle that soared above her, marveling at its dark brown, not less than 6 foot wingspan and white face—perhaps a migratory and rare Pallas's fish-eagle. She was sitting in the most tranquil spot on earth, experiencing another zone—and it was beyond words.

Retreat

Olivia began her familiar trip to the Tibetan Buddhist monastery on the outskirts of Kathmandu for retreat. Every cab ride was an opportunity to take pictures and watch the Nepalese people carry out their daily affairs. Occasionally, Olivia asked the driver to wait while she accessed an ATM machine, usually receiving a minimum of 10,000 Nepalese rupees and then purchasing fruit at one of the many colorful looking roadside vegetable and fruit stands: apples, lychee fruit, small bananas, tangerines, grapes, lemons (several varieties), pomegranate, guava, papaya, pears, mango, watermelon and Olivia's favorite Suntala oranges. After Olivia selected her apples, bananas, oranges, and tangerines, a young, male Nepali vendor placed them in a plastic bag and weighed it in kilos, the price amounting to a few rupees that converted to an inexpensive price when compared to the US dollar. When the cab driver reached a fork in the road, she knew they had nearly arrived at the tucked-away monastery, high on a hill, secured with a solid metal gate and the familiar guard at his post with two territorial watchdogs. The dogs had come to know Olivia, and there was always a warm greeting. The cab driver honked the horn, and the guard swung open the gate.

A panoramic view of the white, snow-tipped and majestic Himalayas awaited her. Olivia was in The Land of the Majestic Himalayas and always seemed to have them in her view—especially from the windows of her room that faced Ganesh Himal, a sub-range of the Himalayas located mostly in north-central Nepal with a direct view of the highest peak, Yangra (Ganesh I) at 24,350 feet, named after the Hindu deity, Ganesha, who is usually depicted in the form of an elephant. To demonstrate the expansiveness of the range, there are three other peaks over 22,966 feet, in addition to fourteen other peaks over 19,685 feet. A very clear day always meant that she should grab her camera, although pictures of the Himalayas do them no justice and cannot begin to capture their powerful beauty and energy. Chris wanted a picture of the Himalayas and Olivia now sent him one; however, when they exchanged e-mails she mentioned that she had processed so much in Tibet that she couldn't think. "For some reason I just cannot think about things. If I think about something for about 15 seconds, it's as if a lid is put on the thoughts because there are better things to do! However, while in Tibet I had a full recall of how much you humiliated me 30 years ago and how it was nothing to you to the extent that you didn't even apologize… but people who are humiliated have egos so the less humiliated I feel by you the less of an ego I have." This monastery was a place that Olivia needed, engulfed in peace, quiet, solitude, and no television—no Marilyn Monroe *Diamonds are a Girl's Best Friend*, no loud, more-often-than-not senseless noise running in every room. Noise pollution. Instead, there were yellow, white, red, green and blue prayer flags—representing the colors of the five Buddha families—attached to five vertical poles, blowing in the wind, sending prayers and mantras to the world. She could also see butter lamps flickering in the butter lamp house, especially at night when their golden glow seemed to shout their presence.

Olivia didn't realize what Nyungne (U-nae) practice was when she registered for four sets (two days for each set and a day of orientation for a total of nine days). Rinpoche (a title meaning "precious one" and nearly always a reincarnation) arrived from Singapore to give the group of registrants, including 12 Western women, an orientation to Nyungne. The familiar hike at the monastery began—up several flights of stairs in a world where elevators rarely exist—to see Rinpoche in the Green Tara room. The room, filled with statues of Green Tara, clearly identified by her posture of compassionate activity-sitting with one foot forward, ready to take quick, compassionate action. Rinpoche sat on a throne (Buddha seat) to talk with the group in broken

English, "I think you will have a little bit hard time." Laughing, Olivia had always loved his sense of humor! However, everyone stopped laughing as Rinpoche addressed the strict, arduous discipline of Nyungne and the importance of motivation, "The hardship you go through will have a great purpose and achievement. At the moment, you have come a long way to dedicate your merits and practice. Try to do it to the best of your abilities. Just doing one set, the merits are immeasurable… There are great merits within this practice. Observe it very, very carefully." He emphasized that hardship is a purification of negative karma.

Olivia quickly learned that Nyungne originated with the Buddha Shakyamuni himself, which is how transmissions are passed—from one master down to a disciple—and thus, the methods for Nyungne come from the sutras and tantras, the essence of Buddhas teachings. However, the practice was started by Gelongma Palmo, a beautiful, compassionate princess from Kashmir, an ancient Indian kingdom, in the 10th or 11th century. Because of her great beauty, she could have married one of the kings from a neighboring country but wasn't particularly happy with palace life and searched for greater meaning; thus, after finding masters who taught and inspired her, she chose to become a Buddhist nun. Her teacher appointed her as head of a monastic community because of her aptitude for study; however, her early life could not have predicted the horrors and hardships she endured when—at the age of 25—she noticed a small boil on her foot, which spread to painful boils that covered her body. Leprosy. Gelongma was a Leper. With the help of an attendant, she was able to hide her condition until her fingers fell off, which made it visible that she had a serious illness. She and her attendant were banished from the community. Living in isolation, Gelongma could only move by crawling. She realized that her leprosy was the result of a past karma so she didn't suffer emotionally but kept practicing. She was determined and very disciplined in her practice of Avalokiteshvara, the Buddha of Compassion.

Many people have known the feeling of isolation, perhaps not because of illness or physical appearance but because of beliefs or values that are not congruent with those around them. Olivia had suffered with that same feeling of isolation whenever she felt misunderstood. She had grown beyond the world in many respects, renouncing a lot of worldly concerns, but it simply did not resonate with many who were close to her. Olivia didn't fit the mold of wanting a 9–5 job with benefits and a house with a two-car garage, in which to park not one, but two cars. She had driven a convertible BMW Z3 for years but it was a pivotal moment for her when one day the manager of a restaurant walked over to the table where she sat. "I've always wanted to meet you," he said smiling. "You're the lady who drives the Z3."

Perplexed, Olivia asked, "You know me by the car that I drive?"

"Oh, yea," he replied. "Everyone knows that you're the lady with the Z3."

Olivia was actually uncomfortable as she thought, "Is this how I want to be remembered—by the CAR that I drive?"

Yes, Olivia loved to drive and had completed a Lou Holtz NASCAR driving course. She was notably the only woman in the course and the men hated her for it, revving up their engines on the track as they waited for her to pick out which jumpsuit she was going to wear. She knew how to take curves and accelerate on the straightaway. She knew how to put "pedal to the metal," and it saved her life once when she threw the stick shift of her Z3 into gear and peeled out, missing being run over by a huge semi-truck that didn't see her on the road because of how low she was sitting. But Olivia didn't want to be defined by material possessions in her life nor did she want it to become her legacy. She didn't want to be remembered by the car that she drove. It is as though her wish manifested, because within days a gentleman knocked on her door, asking to purchase her Z3. She sold it to him, without hesitation. She hasn't felt the desire to purchase a car since then although not owning a car in America can be unacceptable and somewhat strange, even if living in a walking community where a car is not needed. Olivia identified with Gelongma's situation, although on a much smaller scale. Was there a place where she could be different from others and fit in—accepted for who and what she was? She often reflected upon the words of Tulku Trinlay Rinpoche's American mother, who truly was "different" from the norm when she turned her three-year-old child over to Kalu Rinpoche: "I grew up in a very privileged milieu," Anne says, "among millionaires, debutantes, rock stars, politicians. None of them were particularly happy. It was the Lamas who had the key to real happiness. Through them, my child could learn what most people need a lifetime to catch a glimpse of. I wish someone had given me to Rinpoche when I was three!" (White, 2005.)

One of the key themes of Buddhist life stories is that our experiences are not only made up of circumstances, but more importantly, our reaction to those circumstances. Whatever happens externally may not be in our control, but we have a choice as to how we react and choose to let those experiences shape our lives. Gelongma Palmo did not let herself fall into anger, bitterness, or self-pity. Instead, she generated *bodhicitta*, the wish to free all beings from their suffering and wanting to attain enlightenment in order to achieve that wish. Subsequently, she had a vision of Avalokiteshvara, the Buddha of Compassion, in the form of Thousand-Armed Avalokiteshvara. Understanding the powerful symbolism of a Buddha always helped Olivia understand its emanation, and for generating compassion, no image is more powerful than that of Avalokiteshvara. His mantra is OM MANI PADME HUNG, probably the most commonly seen mantra and one that is so powerful that it can transform disturbing emotions into wisdom (Nydahl, 1999):

Om – transforms pride and egotism
Ma – transforms jealousy and envy
Ni – transforms attachment and egotistical wishes
Pad – transforms ignorance and confusion
Me – transforms greed and avarice
Hung – transforms hate and anger

Gelongma vowed to Avalokiteshvara that she would remain in one place meditating until she attained the highest realization; thus, she became devoted to the practice of 1000-Armed Avalokiteshvara whose image is so powerfully symbolic that identifying with him is an efficacious way to develop compassion. In summary, the 1000 arms of Avalokiteshvara are reaching out to all of the suffering in the world, his 1000 wisdom eyes in every palm see the suffering of the world, and his 11 faces see the suffering of the world in all directions.

And so Gelongma remained. She fasted without food or drink. She remained completely silent. Whatever inner demons hounded or tempted her, she sent them compassion and, therefore, they were subdued. One year later, like a snake shedding a skin, Gelongma's leprosy was cured and she became *even more beautiful than before*. She discovered the true source of beauty: a compassionate, altruistic heart, an enlightened intention, with the wish for the benefit of all beings. She transformed, was liberated, and attained enlightenment. It is said that many people saw that she was a dakini, a highly realized woman. The practice, which she began in Nepal, soon spread to India and became very popular in Tibet.

Gelongma's life and practice of Nyungne became her legacy. She passed the methods and blessings of Nyungne down through a lineage of great practitioners that continues to this day. The fasting and meditation practice was carried on by both male and female practitioners alike, monastics and lay practitioners, making Gelongma Palmo one of the few Tibetan Buddhist women who was the founder of a major Tibetan Buddhist practice. This intensive practice involves maintaining the eight Mahayana precepts, not to kill, steal, commit sexual misconduct, lie, take intoxicants, take high or luxurious seats, sing, dance or wear ornaments or eat after midday on the first day. On the second day, additional vows are taken of not eating, drinking or talking for twenty-four hours. The meditation and practice sessions include praises, prostrations, and mantra recitation.

After the Nyungne orientation with Rinpoche, a few of the nuns (Anis) were smiling at Olivia. Olivia asked one of them, "Are you betting that I won't show up in the morning for Nyungne?" They had been instructed by Rinpoche to be standing outside the Gompa at 4am wearing no makeup, jewelry, or perfume. Being in the raw like that and giving up attachments really does make a difference in mindset. The Anis didn't answer but continued to smile. "They don't think I can do this," Olivia thought. She often wondered what it would be like to be a nun. The most difficult part wouldn't be shaving her head of nearly waist-long hair but awakening early enough every day to attend Green Tara practice at 5am. Green Tara, the female aspects of Avalokiteshvara, is the Buddha of enlightened activity and one of the 21 forms of Tara, who vows to always be reborn as a woman. Green Tara, as succorer, hears the suffering cries of beings, associated with protection from fear and the following eight obscurations: lions (= pride), wild elephants (= delusion/ ignorance), fires (= hatred and anger), snakes (= jealousy), bandits and thieves (= wrong views, including fanatical views), bondage (= avarice and miserliness), floods (= desire and attachment), and evil spirits and demons (= deluded doubts). Her mantra is OM TARE TU TARE SOHA. Olivia recognized her not only by her green appearance but by her sitting posture of compassionate activity with her right foot forward.

Olivia reminded herself that Nyungne is an excellent practice for the purification of one's negative karma, the accumulation of merit, and developing and increasing one's compassion for all sentient (thinking) beings. It involves taking vows every 24 hours (the highest vows that can be taken by a layperson), recitation of Tibetan text, often at speed reader pace, and recitation of the mantra of Avalokiteshvara, OM MANI PADME HUNG; fasting, periods of silence, and prostrations—all of which requires very strict self-discipline on all levels.

At 4:45am it was still dark outside—one of the monks was standing outside the Gompa, holding a cord that suspended a 14″ flat disk metal gong, the surface etched with a gold double dorje. With his other hand he sounded the gong with a mallet, its deep, penetrating sound meaning that it was time to roll out of bed—you've got 15 minutes to get to the Gompa. Olivia found that this routine didn't work well for her because it didn't allow her enough time to awaken, and she would feel drowsy all day; rather, it was best for her to set the alarm and awaken at 4:00am, always listening for three loud, booming blasts from the conch shell—those similar to the sound of one loud and sustained note on a trumpet. The sounding of the conch shell meant serious business: get to the Gompa RIGHT NOW or you are late! Olivia was only steps away so as long as her belongings were tucked away in her tote bag (coral mala beads that she found in Lhasa, sacred texts, meditation shawl), she could get there on time.

After climbing a few steps to the Gompa from her room, she removed her sandals, and after a purification ritual outside the door of the Gompa of rinsing out her mouth with alcohol, and then spitting it out over the railing, she headed straight to her practice bench and sat down on a cushion with her back to the east wall. Her bench was one of several benches placed in a horizontal row in front of a magnificent mural wall painting of the Karmapas. A matching row of benches were lined up in front of the west wall facing her. The altar at the north end of the Gompa was to the left of Olivia, displaying a large gold 15-foot Buddha statue, draped in a gold cloth. The altar in front of it was adorned with fresh flowers, smaller statues, and artistically made tormas. Olivia could not believe the time and effort that the Anis placed into the making of lovely tormas, decorating them with greater effort than making holiday cookies. In front of this altar with the Buddha Shakyamuni was another altar set up on the floor with a magnificent gold statue of Thousand-Armed Avalokiteshvara. There was a chant master who chanted throughout the day. "Talent, pure talent," she thought. Everyone recited for hours from Tibetan text, and sometimes they had to skip pages so it was easy to get lost; however, sitting next to Olivia was a young woman from Singapore, and she would literally poke Olivia. Then she would show her what page they were on!

A Rinpoche sat on one of the thrones in the Gompa and presided over the session. Across from Olivia, facing her, were a row of practice benches. Taking vows in the morning was difficult for Olivia because it was painful for her to kneel and put weight on her right knee due to an old knee injury that had required surgery; however, prostrations were the bigger concern. On the first day they were painfully impossible. Olivia brought her bed pillow on the second day to place on the floor so that she would at least hit the pillow with her knees instead of the floor. The pillow helped but was not the entire solution. The second day also involved taking a vow of silence. Within two hours, Olivia accidentally bumped into the woman sitting to the right of her. "Sorry," Olivia said. The surprised reaction on the woman's face said it all. Olivia's hand flew up and covered her mouth! Oh, no, she had broken her vow of silence. She had to see Rinpoche for a type of confession and purification. But that didn't seem to work as a deterrent because later in the day, she accidentally bumped into one of the Anis, "Excuse me," Olivia said. OMG… she had broken her vow of silence again! How can being in silence be such an impossible task? Off to see Rinpoche again!

On day two of the first set of Nyungne, Olivia's knees were

killing her from trying to do prostrations even when dropping on a bed pillow on the floor in front of her. She felt sleep-deprived from awakening at 4:00am, she had broken her vow of silence twice, she had a migraine headache from fasting, and her stomach was producing more acid instead of less. She had been prescribed a proton inhibitor medication for stomach acid production but she rarely had to rely on it. She thought that fasting would decrease stomach acid, but in this case it was significantly increased to the point of causing stomach pain and discomfort. The only fix for the pain was to sneak into the monastery souvenir shop during a short break to purchase a small lime green bag of Lay's Sour Cream & Onion potato chips. Olivia preferred Lay's Classic potato chips in the yellow bag, which usually wasn't available. But that also meant breaking her vow of fasting. Olivia wondered if the Anis would see her entering the shop, and then as she handed the attendant Ani 20 rupees to pay for the potato chips, Olivia thought, "Is she going to tell the other Anis that I am breaking my vow of fasting? Probably not… Anis don't thrive on gossip, useless chatter, or idle talk. They'll never find out… but what if they do—or what if they suspect?" Olivia discretely dropped her potato chips in her tote bag and found her way across the courtyard, past the butter lamp house, and past the tall prayer flags—to her room.

At the end of the first set of Nyungne, sitting at her seat in the Gompa, Olivia gathered her belongings and sacred text, put them in her tote bag and looked at her iPhone to check the time. It was 5:15pm. "I'm done," she thought. "No more… I'm throwing in the towel. I've had enough. I'll go shopping tomorrow morning in Thamel and then stop at Roadhouse Cafe for Caesar salad and a medium pizza that I'll eat all by myself."

The next morning, at 4:45am, Olivia heard the deep, penetrating sound of the 14" round gong, which triggered a long-forgotten memory. She was 12 years old. Sinking with each step, she struggled to walk across an area of deep sand that led to a field where she and her friends played softball. She wore a large topaz birthstone ring that her father had purchased for her in Africa; however, when she attempted to put her softball glove on her hand it wouldn't slide over the ring. She twisted it off her finger and placed it in the front pocket of her jeans.

After a couple of hours of playing softball, she discovered, to her sorrow, that her cherished ring was gone. Her careful search of the softball field was futile. She retraced her footsteps to the area of deep sand. She started to sift through the sand but believed that the ring had probably sunk so deep that she would never find it. She decided not to dig, gave up the search, and her prized possession remained lost; however, she never could reconcile the fact that she hadn't searched harder and dug deeper. She quit. She hoped that her aborted effort and lack of perseverance would not become a metaphor for her life.

And now, somehow, she could not find it within her to quit. She knew she had to keep going. After all, Olivia had grown to be hard driving, persistent, and tenacious, not only completely a PhD but a postdoctoral fellowship. She had registered for and made a commitment to complete four sets of Nyungne. She remembered Rinpoche's final words in the Nyungne orientation, "Inspiration is like lightning… it doesn't come often and for only a few seconds… grab it." Yes, this was one of those "carpe diem" seize-the-day moments in life that she had to grab. She knew that the Anis would soon bring breakfast to them in the Gompa, ending their first fast. She scurried to put her belongings into her tote bag, and was back in the Gompa five minutes later, sitting on her cushion. The Anis gave them each a cup and carried in big thermos bottles. Some of the bottles contained hot water or hot lemon water, which was Olivia's favorite. Most of the thermos bottles contained yak butter tea, a Tibetan mainstay that Olivia delicately avoided. Porridge was served with a piece of Tibetan round, white bread. Then she saw every kind of jar of peanut butter—creamy, chunky, with chocolate; Nutella, and mixed fruit jam was passed around. They had ended their second day of fasting, which would begin again the next day.

Olivia couldn't do prostrations that put pressure on her knees so she had to find a way because she didn't want to sit on her cushion and visualize them. Again, dropping out was no longer an option. After two days of practicing, she finally found a way in which she could execute a prostration. She put a bed pillow on the floor where her knees would hit before sliding supine on the floor, hands out in front of her; however, when she stood up, she would shift all of her weight forward and onto her hands so that no weight was put onto her knees. She also wore a Lululemon shirt with sleeves that covered the hands via an opening for the thumb. This allowed her to easily slide forward on the marble floor with open hands. It was arduous, physical work. Then, there was fasting every other day. After the first fast, Olivia ate what she thought was a red pickled dish that she spread on her bread only to run out the door of the Gompa seconds later… it was red chili pepper! The Anis giggled and told her not to drink water but to fill her mouth with sugar.

Olivia couldn't understand why she had not grown to tolerate hot spices when she loved Mexican food and hot—not mild—salsa. The food, the food… her biggest challenge in this part of the world. The staple food is dal bhat, which consists of rice and lentil soup, generally served with vegetable curries, achar, and sometimes chutney. Rice is served twice a day, at lunch and dinner, with dal, and Olivia reached the point where she could not eat it probably because in the West, she might eat rice twice a month, not twice a day. Mushrooms! Mushrooms were served every day, and Olivia didn't like mushrooms. Mushroom soup, mushroom salads, and mushrooms cooked in food. You can imagine Olivia's delight when she was once sick with a throat infection and missed nine meals only to have an Ani show up at her door with mushroom soup. Sometimes noodles and potatoes are served. Her favorite dish was actually a spicy potato dish but she couldn't eat much of it or she would get sick from the spices. Her next favorite dish was a shredded cabbage salad with carrots. But lettuce and her much-loved salads were not often seen. A "green salad" meant tomatoes, cucumbers, and radishes. Don't try telling anyone that tomatoes aren't a green salad. Olivia didn't like tomatoes but grew to like cucumbers that were almost as plentiful as rice.

Actually, Olivia was told that the last American who attempted to complete Nyungne cracked up because of the stress, and the Anis took her to the hospital. Olivia does not know what was more difficult: the lack of sleep, the prostrations, or the fasting, but regardless, it was challenging. Yes, it was a task in purification. But soon Nyungne was completed. The group took a field trip to see where Gelongma Palmo practiced Nyungne, which is now a temple erected in her honor. There is a statue representing her in the temple that is normally kept locked. The kitchen where she cooked is in back. Plates are seen nailed to the walls throughout the courtyard, a Nepali tradition, believed to remove obstacles. They also drove to Pharping to Guru Rinpoche's cave and the Vajrayogini Temple. They had such a wonderful, celebratory afternoon although many of the women felt as though they had run a marathon. Rinpoche had arrived before they departed to tell them that Nyungne is the most meritorious dharma activity that one can perform so they were all very thrilled that they completed all four sets of practice. Any exercise in self-discipline is a good one! "You did the impossible," one of the women said to Olivia, smiling. Yes, the perseverance kicked in, and Olivia was beyond happy. Now it was time to complete three more retreats over the next three weeks: Mahakala, Chod, and Shinay meditation. As challenging as they were, they were quite a breeze when compared to Nyungne and certainly not as physically demanding.

It was Olivia's birthday. She looked down at her iPhone and saw that a Nepali by the name of Deval had messaged her, wishing her a happy birthday. Touched, Olivia thanked him. She scrolled back through archived messages and was surprised that he had first messaged her over four years earlier, prior to her 2010 trip to Nepal. Of course, she had not responded. "How did he get through to me then and now?" she thought. Hundreds of messages from adoring men were stacked, sitting in a spam folder that she didn't look at—but Deval's message came through. He seemed to desperately want to meet her although she told him that she had no free time because she was in retreat at the monastery; however, when he learned that she was going to light 108 brass butter lamps (an auspicious number) in the red brick butter lamp house, he asked if he could be there. She didn't agree because she viewed the event as sacred—nothing to gawk at and certainly not for curious viewing. Besides, she was lighting many of those butter lamps at the request of students and friends; Olivia would say their names and express their written wishes while lighting their lamp(s), which required focused concentration. Deval did ask her to light a lamp for him, which she was more than happy to do. He expressed that he needed more peace in his life, and she wholeheartedly wished that for him. She lit a long, tightly rolled up piece of paper, which created a tall flame in which to light the white, cotton wick, stuck in yak butter. An offering of that many burning butter lamps, with wishes made, created a profound energy. She took pictures of the blazing butter lamps from her iPhone and again during the night as the flames from the lamps continued to dance, lighting up the entire butter lamp house in a massive golden glow.

Deval then wanted to meet Olivia when he visited a nearby friend, offered to take her on a hike to a stupa, and wanted to assist her with public transportation. Olivia replied that she had a cab driver who would wait for her, which was necessary because whenever she had to briefly leave the monastery she was always in a time crunch to return for a teaching. On one of those days she was at the Indian Visa Service Center applying for a visa to India. Afterwards, Deval told her that he lived near the center and wanted to surprise her by meeting her there, but decided against it in fear that she would think he was stalking her. Finally, he messaged her and asked, "Am I ever going to meet you?" She replied, "We'll see," to which he replied with a puzzled looking sticky-face. He was nothing short of relentless. And with that relentlessness, he made a bold statement that grabbed Olivia's attention: "You're sexy. That is what I see." Then he sent her his e-mail address and asked her to e-mail him in the future because he was deactivating his messaging service.

Olivia was still in retreat and had no time to meet anyone; however, one day she had to travel to Thamel for a couple of hours and reached for her iPhone to message Deval, hoping he could meet her for lunch. She saw that his messaging service really had been deactivated, and how unfortunate, because she didn't know his e-mail address offhand; however, within a couple of weeks the day came when Olivia's two-month retreat was completed, and she departed from the monastery.

Caste and Culture

Olivia checked into the same hotel in Thamel where she had met her Tibet group of friends—now one of her homes in Nepal—and after a few days, invited Deval to come to the hotel for tea. She didn't want to be rude to someone who had so persistently wanted to meet her, but at the same time, she intuitively felt that there was something very special about this man. "10am," she said. As irrational at it seemed, now that she was preparing to leave Nepal, she knew that she would get involved with him in some way although it was also her strong belief that one should know someone for six months before getting involved because it takes at least six months to get to know someone! When the day finally arrived for their meeting she flat-ironed her long, highlighted, past-the-shoulder brunette hair and spent extra time on her makeup. She didn't wear the black Donald Pliner high heels that were among her packed eight pairs of shoes but pulled on her classic tall black suede UGGS and topped her black Lululemon pants and shirt with a long, front angled, black Eileen Fisher sweater. After all, it was beginning to get chilly in Kathmandu.

At 10am, Olivia was in the comfortable and charming hotel lobby, which displayed a huge 4x6 painting of the historical Buddha Shakyamuni in earth-touching mudra. She sat on one of the three overstuffed fabric couches that were arranged against the walls, each back draped with a colorful Tibetan yak wool carpet. A beautifully carved Newari wood coffee table, covered with a sheet of glass, was centered in front of the couches. She waited 15 minutes, returning to her room up two flights of stairs on the second floor. Then she received a message from Deval saying that he would be late. She returned to the lobby a few minutes later, and saw him standing there in a beige jacket, gray slacks, and dress shoes. He was less than six feet in height but looked tall because he was thin and had the thickest black hair she had ever seen. His eyes were dark brown, lips pouty, skin light for a Nepali, and he was better looking than his pictures although he had noticeable periorbital dark circles under his eyes, which added years to his actual age. She suspected that it might be due to a nutritional deficiency rather than a hereditary factor or lack of sleep. Olivia never could believe how un-photogenic he was, later concluding that only about one out of twenty pictures of him was flattering and looked like him. She smiled and said, "Let's have some tea," as he followed her steps down the hallway and through an ornately carved entryway to the small restaurant with five 3x4 rectangular tables, covered with a white tablecloth, each table seating four people. She especially liked the eating area because it included an altar against the east wall and above it, a large, six foot tall carved statue of 1000-arm Avalokiteshvara that would forever trigger virtuous impressions, including Gelongma Palmo and the practice of Nyungne. One of the Tibetan Buddhist men who worked at the hotel kept fresh flowers on the altar and filled the silver offering bowls with clean water on a daily basis. He also lit incense and a butter lamp at night as additional offerings.

Olivia selected a table by a window that overlooked a meticulously landscaped courtyard, the lawn in the middle lined with terra-cotta planters that overflowed with plants and colorful flowers. As she sat down on the right side of the table, he selected a seat on the left, directly facing her. Deval seemed a little nervous and never removed his zipped-up jacket. Taking a long look at him, Olivia felt an instant recognition and connection to him although she had never met him in this lifetime. There was also an unexplained attraction that Olivia could have never justified to herself or to anyone else, especially family and friends, who would immediately suspect that he was a foreigner trying to get a green card via an American. She knew they had a story—karma. He seemed to feel an intensity, also, later telling her, "Your lips almost drove me mad." Perhaps it was really the auburn Mac lipliner and the CB96 lipstick she was wearing that day, she thought—her favorite. Regardless, she was always amused when people thought she was magically ageless or growing younger by the year, and no one could ever put a finger on why because it was beyond having young looking skin with no wrinkles on her face. It was "everything—the way you dress, the way you act—everything that you're doing." However, she never hid the fact that she had grown children and joy-of-her-life grandchildren, which put an approximate chronological age on her life. Deval and Olivia appeared to be the same age—or he could have even looked older—although it shouldn't have been relevant. When someone is discriminated against because of their age, it is called ageism. When someone is discriminated against based on their gender, it is called sexism. When someone is discriminated against because of their race, it is called racism. There are far too many *isms* in the world to buy into it.

There are characteristics of a karmic relationship that Olivia had heard about years before when Richard Gere stated, "When someone has a strong intuitive connection, Buddhism suggests that it's because of karma, some past connection." And now—what was going to be a 20-minute tea drinking session with Deval resulted in two hours. Olivia loved his laughter, his big Nepali smile. He smiled at least 20 times during their conversation, which was especially meaningful to Olivia. Chris never laughed and rarely smiled, not even for a picture, which is why she deleted so many pictures of him. Much to Olivia's chagrin, Chris actually seemed depressed half the time, even when Olivia broke out in her full smile and laughed—a laughter that many people loved, claiming it was "authentic" and real.

Deval was an intellectual, from the Brahmin caste of scholars, intellectuals, and educators—the highest of the four-category caste system that is further divided into a total of 124 castes in Nepal. The caste system intrigued Olivia because it was still very much alive in Nepal, despite equality before the law. For example, if she mentioned the last name of a Nepali to another Nepali, the usual response was to tell Olivia the caste of that person; thus, from Deval's last name, she was told on *several* occasions that he was from the Brahmin caste. Another time when she met a Nepali woman and asked her what her name was, she said, Laxmi, from the Chettri caste (which falls under the category of Brahmin). In addition, when Deval talked about some of his friends, he would mention their caste affiliation. She learned that scholars often used a body metaphor from the oldest Hindu texts, the Vedas. Brahmin priests and teachers orchestrate from the head, Kshatriyas rulers and warriors govern with powerful arms, Vaishya merchants and financiers circulate goods and wealth from the belly, and Sudra farmers, builders, and artisans undergird the body on firm legs. The metaphor is used to represent ideal hierarchy, showing how priests, rulers, and financiers cooperate to control the system, and its relation of caste to ritual purity. Brahmins may rise above the unsavory aspects of ruling, trading, and banking because their head transcends bodily impurities. Yet, the political power and wealth was among the Kshatriyas and Vaishya castes. In renouncing this for spiritual purity, many Brahmins became farmers.

The caste system, originating as an ideal way to divide labor, got quite muddled as sub-castes proliferated. They became rigid about their interaction with other castes, often segregating themselves. The powerful relegated "impure" jobs to those increasing number of people who became known as Dalitis, the untouchables, who fall outside of the caste system all together and still face discrimination to this day. In December 2015 it was reported that milk, although in demand in Nepal, was being unsold because Kumal sellers belong to the Dalit caste. One Kumal man had to sell his buffalo, valued at RS. 50,000, because the milk was going to waste. Dalits are also not supposed to stay in hotels in Piluchour and Kabad bazaar. Even though there is a single water source, there are separate taps for Dalits and non-Dalits in almost all areas of the Bajura district, where so-called upper castes still practice untouchability. What is dismal is that people are afraid to speak out about discrimination in fear that they themselves will be discriminated against. Thus, even though a law was passed in 1962 making castes equal before the law and it illegal to discriminate against other castes, the caste system still exists, particularly in the villages. Some progress has been made, however, in that education is free and open to all castes.

The caste system didn't discriminate among village children, however, like Deval, who rode on a raft up and down a river in order to attend school. Olivia had seen pictures of children on round, rubber, black inner tubes, traveling on a river en route to school, knowing that some of them would drown. In the USA mothers put their children on yellow school buses, knowing that they'll return at the end of the day whereas in many of the remote villages of Nepal, mothers watch their children climb onto rafts or tubes in order to be pushed into the river, realizing the risk. Deval claimed it was why he is such a good swimmer. He had to learn how to swim with currents rather than against them in order to survive.

Olivia always noticed the cables spanned across rivers in Nepal, which were used to transport children. She saw one cable with a suspended large metal basket full of schoolchildren, creeping along, moving from one side of the river to the other. Other cable lines would simply suspend children from individual chairs on a pulley while they used their hands to pull themselves forward along the cable. It looked absolutely terrifying. Olivia had to appreciate the overt value placed on education while at the same time believing that the Nepalese government should immediately install bridges in order to allow children safe passage to and from school. Deval later moved to Kathmandu to receive his university education. Olivia related to his intellectualism as a safe, comfortable, and even enjoyable place for her because being more intelligent than the men in her life—and loving academics—always became her Achilles' heel. Nothing is more fragile than male ego.

DE JA VU. Deval and Olivia left the restaurant and parted in the lobby but within minutes her cell phone rang. "I thought we were going to have lunch," he said. "Oh, I had a very late breakfast so perhaps some other time." And then the next day he telephoned her. He was leaving town for a few days. He could hear the disappointment in her tone of voice but, regardless, he departed. They messaged each other, and by the next day he was regretting his decision. She reminded him that she was going to a party that weekend at a Thamel restaurant where an extraordinary group of musicians were performing. "I don't take hints!" he said. "You needed to say, 'Deval, I want you to take me to the party.'" But soon he was on a train back to Kathmandu, creeping along at a snail's pace in the smog, sending her repeated messages. He couldn't be more frustrated at the weather-induced delay because, in just a few days, Olivia would be leaving for a meditation retreat in New Delhi, which she had planned and registered for months prior.

When Deval finally arrived later that night, they were able to see each other for a couple of days before she departed for New Delhi. He wanted to go to New Delhi with her, "Please don't leave me alone." However, she couldn't see the prudence of that given that she would be in retreat. "What would you do all day?" she asked. She believed that he would be a distraction—how could she possibly focus on meditation if he was sitting around a hotel waiting for her? He wanted her to return to Kathmandu earlier than she had planned. Clearly, she wanted to keep somewhat of a distance to slow down the progression of their relationship although there was already an intensity to it, another characteristic of a karmic relationship. She felt a deep bond with him and sensed they had been together in other lifetimes although they never talked about it. But now they lived half a world apart from each other. It was difficult for her but she repeatedly told him that she had just ended a relationship, she didn't want to be in another one yet, and at the present moment, she really didn't want a boyfriend.

Olivia saw Deval before she departed to the airport for a flight to New Delhi. Once settled in at her hotel in New Delhi she was thrilled to see old friends. Most of the time she walked with them to and from the retreat but one day while walking alone the song *Jar of Hearts* (Lawrence, Perri, and Yeretsian, 2010) popped in her head. She downloaded the album *Lovestrong*, sung by Christina Perri, onto her computer and her iPhone. For the next few days, she sang it whenever walking alone, almost as though a message was being driven into her psyche. Olivia smiled while listening to it because it wasn't a touchy-feely song that made you want to cry, but more like a wrathful deity "don't mess with me" type of song. The lyrics were creating a distance necessary for non-attachment, expressing a goodbye, what Westerners would call "closure"—this was Olivia's final letting go of her minutest amount of attachment to Chris. The Buddha stated it quite bluntly, "If you cannot find a companion equal to or better than yourself, journey alone—do not travel with a fool" (Buddha, 1985, p. 32).

No, I can't take one more step towards you
'Cause all that's waiting is regret
And don't you know I'm not your ghost anymore
You lost the love
I loved the most.
I learned to live, half alive
And now you want me one more time

And who do you think you are?
Runnin' round leaving scars
Collecting your jar of hearts

And tearing love apart
You're gonna catch a cold
From the ice inside your soul
So don't come back for me
Who do you think you are?
I hear you're asking all around
If I am anywhere to be found
But I have grown too strong
To ever fall back in your arms...

Don't come back for me
Don't come back at all

Once back in Kathmandu, Deval and Olivia spent a few days together. He continued to want Olivia to make a commitment to him, not wanting to introduce her to his family until she did. He wanted her to be his girlfriend and mentioned to her that he took the longest route walking home one night in order to really think about their relationship. He was wishing that she was his wife rather than a hoped-for girlfriend, looking into her eyes and telling her, "I want to make you the happiest woman on earth." If she suggested to Deval that she was too old for him, he would adamantly reply, "There is not a holy book in the world that says a man has to be older than a woman." When she expressed that he needed to meet a younger woman whom he could have children with, he responded, "If I want children I can walk out the door and find children on the street." It was true. UNICEF once reported that there are 650,000 orphaned children in Nepal for an array of reasons, including ten years of civil war—children who needed parents and a home. Olivia loved the fact that Deval loved children and knew he would want to provide a home for any child who was in need of one. Once when she told him about a baby boy in the Mt. Everest region whom she had grown to adore, Deval asked for a picture of the baby and then asked

Olivia if they should go there and try to adopt him. All she could tell Deval was that they needed to spent a great deal of time together before they developed a serious relationship, and although she was returning to the US soon, there were reasons for her to return to Kathmandu in April. She promised him that she would return, although she usually traveled to Nepal every other year and certainly not twice within a year.

Deval was annoyed that a good friend of Olivia's had arranged to drive her to the airport although this friend was helping her with a possible luggage weight problem. It was always difficult to leave Nepal, and even more so this time, because Olivia felt that she had met someone who loved her and wanted her in his life. But, Olivia's father had recently been seriously ill, undergoing surgery for cancer, so she felt it would be inappropriate to delay her trip; thus, she just kept reassuring Deval that she would return to Nepal. She messaged him during her layover in Hong Kong, and he begged her to return to Kathmandu. Immediately she was receiving messages: "I'm missing u… I'll always miss u ok… missing u so much… it's so hard to be without u…" In the morning it was typical to see a message of: "Good morning, honey! I hope u did rest well! It's so hard to be without u" and at night: "Take rest. I'll visit u in my dreams. XOXO." The intensity of his feelings didn't subside. He wrote, "I seriously think, if we'd met 2 days more, you couldn't have left me." A month later, he said, "I just wanted to let u know I'm thinking of u constantly."

The day that Olivia and Deval parted, and as he walked out the door, he put on an earloop cloth facemask that is commonly seen worn in Kathmandu. After all, Kathmandu is the largest city in Nepal, with a population of at least a million people and with traffic congestion that causes pollution, especially since Kathmandu lies in a valley where the pollution tends to get stuck. Later, Deval told Olivia that when he took off the mask he saw her red lipstick, a trace from kissing her goodbye. He lamented that he didn't have other tangible items to remind him of her. This nostalgic comment reminded her of when he had seen a strand of her long, highlighted brunette hair resting on her shoulder while they were eating dinner in a restaurant. He reached for it and carefully wrapped it in a white paper napkin as a keepsake. Those kinds of unexpected gestures meant more to Olivia than wealthy men buying her expensive gifts while they sat on big bank accounts and collected homes and cars.

Olivia viewed monetary "things" as a distraction from what was really important in life—love—the kind of love that seemed to always elude her. Yet, her painful experiences with materialism and wealth, that caused her to feel devalued, discounted, and isolated, perhaps caused her to swing too far in the other direction. She appreciated Deval's words, "All I have to give you is the love in my heart," but she couldn't appreciate that he was ambitious. She couldn't appreciate how hard he had worked to become educated and his ambitiousness to escape a poverty-stricken life in Nepal because she feared he would lose sight of what had become so important to her. Human values. She had seen many of her students come from a life of poverty and rise to fame, particularly some of her students who became professional athletes, and in every case it went to their head. They were star struck with new cars, Hollywood, a big house, Ray-Ban sunglasses—all of it. Olivia would have preferred that Deval remain a village boy than be lost in a world of materialism. She needed to trust that he would remain grounded. One of the last words he said to her was, "We'll love each other until our last breath." Had she waited her entire life to hear those words?

After departing from Kathmandu, it was only a matter of days before Olivia wrote, "I have always believed that good pedagogy is to get where someone is—regardless of how lost they are—and simply take them by the hand and take them where you want them to go. This is what you did. You went where I was, took me by the hand and led me through what I perceived as an impossible maze. I didn't know where we were going but you knew that I was slowly growing to love you... In reality, growing to love you is probably your greatest accomplishment." Deval loved this. He said that he read it three times. He interpreted it as meaning that they were in a relationship, which became the most dominant relationship in their lives. Their deep connection became almost addictive, which is also characteristic of a karmic relationship. He stated, "I want to tell the world that you are my wife. I want to show you my world, I doubt you've seen most of the Nepal. The rest—95% of Nepal is so beautiful, honey. I'm sure you'd fall in love with it." Surprise! Olivia received an e-mail from Chris. He had just bought the home in Florida that they had talked about so many months ago. He was still trying to hide his relationship with Barb, not realizing that Olivia knew about her. Olivia could have telephoned him and sang the *Jar of Hearts* song... "No, I can't take one more step towards you... Who do you think you are? Don't come back for me." She simply replied to his e-mail with six words, "I'm sure Barb will love it." Olivia was no longer in the game, a prudent decision she first made at the young age of 21. To think that for over 30 years she wondered if she had made the right call in not marrying him.

In the meantime, Olivia's relationship with Deval was a long distance one under difficult and frustrating conditions. Deval had accepted a two-month contract to relocate and teach in a remote village in a mountainous region with no road access. He was only able to access electricity and an Internet connection on the weekend when he stayed in a nearby city, which he had to walk two and a half hours to reach; thus, they were limited in their communication with each other. There were also frequent electricity outages and load shedding, typical for Nepal, and his computer use was limited. Whereas they had started to Skype when he was in Kathmandu, it was now discontinued for the most part. However, because of their 12-hour time difference, even Skyping was difficult. Either he was falling asleep or she was falling asleep! Imagine setting your alarm in the middle of the night in order to communicate—half asleep—with someone, and then speculate how long the enthusiasm for doing so would last. Olivia was simply not thrilled about him being in a remote area without any modern conveniences—not even running water—but he felt that he had no other alternative as this would generate income for him. Olivia was fast learning that, beyond the tourist industry, Nepal was not a land of opportunity. Deval firmly believed, "I think our relationship is strong enough to survive all of these [sic]… why do u think it won't?"

One of the biggest hurdles for Deval and Olivia was the fact that English was not his primary language, and there were often misunderstandings when they messaged and communicated in writing. He commented once that he misunderstood "everything" she said but it did improve somewhat over time, in addition to an improvement in his command of the English language. But his words, "I love you so much baby, I'm so head over heels in love with u, i just want to be with u for always until eternity, i love you sooo much Olivia!" were consistent. One time when they were Skype-typing, he said, "U r so beautiful." She told him that he had caught her in the raw—she had on no makeup. He replied, "pls never ever put makeup then… u look more beautiful now than at any other time." He often told her that she was beautiful. Olivia once told him about one of her favorite poets, Elizabeth Barrett Browning (1806–1861), and shared her words:

> How do I love thee? Let me count the ways.
> I love thee to the depth and breadth and height
> My soul can reach, when feeling out of sight

After a month of rarely being able to communicate with each other, Olivia was discouraged enough to write, "I can't do this anymore. I need to be able to communicate with someone and we've been having a communication challenge as it is. I think we've given it a good try but there are just too many things getting in the way so it would be best if you would find the perfect Nepali girl for you. It has to be someone you can communicate with. Talk to her, Deval, and if she asks you a question always, always answer the question." He quickly responded, "I need your help and support at this point of my life. Please make me cool and help me to overcome this distress. I'm so messed up at this point. u said its [sic] called up in the air. so I'm that… so messed up now. if u also add worries, do u think that's going to help me… I love u unconditionally and pls be patient with me… I'm trying to figure out how to communicate well with u… I can't handle everything at the same time. Please love me and be patient with me, ok honey." That was all she needed to hear. She couldn't walk away. He asked her to be patient, and she could do that, especially since it was apparent that he was having a difficult time.

Olivia initially did not have a deep insight into the cultural differences or power dynamics between she and Deval, especially in regard to the nuclear family. She perceived herself to be in a subsidiary position and would never be on the inside circle with his family. For example, one of his in-laws was in the hospital for a week, and because he never left the hospital, he never contacted her during that week. His excuse—there was no accessible electricity in the hospital in which to charge his phone; however, he understood Olivia's frustration and wrote, "u r so very very perfect for me, and I feel so stupid not to appreciate u as well, as I feel so fortunate to have u in my life." As far as marriage, despite some Westernization in Nepal, arranged marriages were still normative in Nepal. The mother or parents choose a spouse with qualities such as: similar caste, similar family reputation, qualifications (education, employment), qualities (appearance, hobbies, background), and cultural/religious understanding. There is no dating. Olivia could not begin to understand why

Deval had no concept of what dating was until she realized that it was nonexistent in his culture.

Believe it or not, the Nepalese bride and groom often do not set eyes on each other until the wedding; thus, there is no premarital sex but there is also no divorce, except in the rarest of situations. If it is discovered that the bride is not a virgin, even after the wedding ceremony, she will be returned to her family, will not get a chance for a second marriage, and will be abandoned from society. Once married, the bride belongs to the groom and his family, which demonstrates how patriarchal this family unit is, and yes, if the bride gets past the feeling of being "owned," it is wonderful that a bride could become so "part" of a family unit; however, she cannot return to her parents' home but does keep close ties with them, which is why she often prefers to marry someone from her village. The bride's family must also prepare a dowry, and if the dowry is not transferred, the bride will be returned to her home and can even be mistreated by the groom's family. Olivia observed that some couples from arranged marriages do eventually fall in love or grow to love each other over time, but sometimes these marriages are loveless "business arrangements." Once children arrive, it is the paternal mother (Big Mom) who is more responsible for the raising of the children than the children's mother. This ensured the continuance and strength of the patriarchal line; thus, once the bride gave birth to a baby, especially if it was a son, her status was slightly elevated in the family—but not much.

Olivia talked with a young 15-year-old Nepali Brahmin village boy about marriage and asked him if he would marry outside of his caste.

"No."

"Why not?"

"Culture."

"Would you marry an American?"

"No."

"Why not?"

"Culture."

"Who is responsible for choosing who you will marry?"

"My mom."

"Why?"

"Culture."

What was interesting during this dialogue was the body language of this young boy. His arms were folded in defensive posture, he never smiled throughout the conversation, and he had a determined air about him, as if warning Olivia that he was entrenched in his beliefs and wasn't about to budge—not at all.

Olivia's friend, Raj, a Buddhist Nepali, had a unique experience in regard to his marriage. While Raj was trekking on an expedition to Annapurna, his parents met with the parents of the girl they wished Raj to marry. Together, the parents set a wedding date. When Raj returned from his trek, he was informed; thus, he contacted the girl and asked her to marry him. When she asked "Why?" he replied that his brothers and parents liked her. They married; however, his younger sister was against an arranged marriage and chose to marry someone from a different caste, which still has Raj's parents upset, ten years later. Raj, from the Tamang caste, the largest Tibeto-Burman ethnic group within Nepal, told Olivia that he has friends from villages who will not drink tea or eat food that is prepared from his house if they are of a higher caste. Even if Raj says, "I can feed my dog but not you. What kind of teacher do you have?"

Olivia also talked with two Nepalese Hindu men who had two different experiences after they became involved with Western women. The first man, Ramsel, who received a university degree in Europe, could never persuade a European girlfriend to move to Nepal. Visiting Nepal was one thing but living there was another. Eventually, he agreed to an arranged marriage to a Nepali woman. His mother selected this woman and arranged for them to meet. When they met, they found that they had a couple of things in common and were subsequently married. But, was he happy? Not really. The marriage "worked" similar to a business partnership.

The other man that Olivia talked with, Himal, was frequently pressured by his family to marry a Nepali girl but when his marriage to one was actually scheduled, he told his family that he was traveling to Europe to purchase a suit for the wedding, only to return to Nepal with a European wife! The European wife, however, although she had loved traveling to Nepal for a short vacation—which is how they originally met—could not live in Nepal, especially as a Nepali wife with four generations living under one roof. After being banished by the family, they left Nepal, and moved to her native country in Europe before she had a "mental breakdown." The fact is, she couldn't think for herself—everyone in the family wanted to think for her and constantly told her what to do. That there would be conflict between a Nepalese mother and a European daughter-in-law didn't surprise Olivia because she had heard of conflict between a Nepalese mother and Nepalese daughter-in-law when a daughter-in-law would refer to her mother-in-law as *Sasu*, often in a derisive tone, and the mother would refer to her daughter-in-law as *Buhari*, meaning that lazy, good-for-nothing daughter-in-law with whom I've been cursed. Himal, however, remained devoted to his family, often traveling alone to Nepal to see them despite his marriage that did not at all fit the stereotypical Nepalese marriage.

Olivia couldn't see Deval prioritizing a wife in this manner, defying Nepalese culture, which might have caused his observable confusion about how he would marry. At times he wanted to marry Olivia instantly, while at other times he wanted her to get close to his mother, referred to as Aama, in order that his mother would choose her to be his wife. He respected and adored his mother, telling Olivia, "She is so sweet. If you meet her you will love her more than you love me." They would have "secret" telephone conversations and code names for when someone was in the room and they couldn't talk freely. This "secretiveness" seemed characteristic of Nepali culture. Why? Fear of retaliation was real. It was also common for Nepalis to call someone a "best friend," and fellow Nepalis were "brothers" and "sisters"; however, even if they slept in the same bed and bathed together they still only knew their best friend, brother, or sister on a very superficial level because of secretiveness and lack of disclosure.

The consequence of lack of forthrightness is always suspicion, and the enigma of expressing "empty words" was always baffling to Olivia. Deval's unmistakable bond with his mother was characteristic of Nepali men, although a Westerner might view this bond as extreme. For example, Olivia once tried to console a Nepali male friend whose mother was dying. "I am nothing without my mother… I miss eating dinner with her." Another friend was still grieving endlessly over his mother's death a year later, saying, "She was my religion." Undoubtedly this son-mother bond created conflict for Deval. One time when he told Olivia that they needed to be "legal" as soon as possible she smiled and said, "And how do you intend to do that?" With a puzzled look on his face he replied, "I don't know." The topic of love and marriage was certainly a very complex and bewildering one for him. The Nepalese also believe that arranged marriages last, particularly since divorce is virtually nonexistent in their culture, and love marriages as a result of "falling in love" will fade. These beliefs and attitudes are radically different from beliefs in the Western world.

Seeing a picture of Deval posing with his family for a family group picture is what spoke a million words; yes, it may have only been a small oddity but perhaps demonstrated another difference between them. The men were standing in a line on the right side of the picture facing the camera, and the women were standing on the left side as if they were preparing to pass through security at the Tribhuvan Airport in Kathmandu. The men and women are segregated, and proceed through security in separate lines. There was no way that Olivia would stand with the women in a family portrait. She would want to be standing next to her man, and he, next to her, together—where they belonged.

Grown Nepalese men are also highly committed to and responsible for their parents, partially because of their belief that it is now their turn to return the support and care their parents gave to them, and partially because the poverty rate in Nepal is very high. This is different from a growing Western trend where children often do not feel responsible for their parents, which is why America has seen a rise in Senior Citizen Homes and Assisted Living facilities. It is a tragedy and cries for a compromise between East-West values. Nowhere in the world are backs turned on the aging as in America. Ageism exists, and honoring parents is disregarded. Deval began to provide monetary support to his parents at the age of 18. When he asked Olivia if her own son would take care of her, she replied, "Absolutely not. He has a wife and family that he is responsible for." Deval couldn't begin to understand this. He also seemed to bear more responsibility to his parents as a single man when compared to his brothers (*dais*) who were married. Furthermore, everything that a Nepali child possesses is owned by the parents as long as they are alive, and when they did die, until recently, it was the son(s) who inherited their estate.

These cultural differences were the source of much discussion between Deval and Olivia, and as much as she tried to explain her position, Deval never budged an inch, entrenched in his beliefs; however, Olivia later came to believe that this devaluing of her opinion was cultural—women do not have much of a voice in Nepal. Olivia discovered that women can even be invisible. One day she wanted to wire money to herself from Western Union via her credit card, which she later discovered cannot be done in Nepal. Deval wanted to go to the Western Union office with her; however, once inside the main branch office, Deval and the gentleman behind the counter had a discussion in Nepali and then Deval walked out of the office without telling Olivia what had transpired in the conversation. This was an entirely new experience for Olivia. She had been invisible to both of them! Her presence was not acknowledged in any way. She wished that she would have gone alone and forced the Western Union representative to speak to her in English, since she was the one who was requesting the service and trying to figure out how to obtain cash without withdrawing small sums of money from ATM machines with bank charges. Deval had reached a conclusion alone, without discussing it with Olivia. According to him, she simply needed to have someone in America access her bank account and then wire money, which Olivia would not do. She was slowly discovering that her feelings—even about the handling of her own checking account—were dismissed. They weren't important. They didn't matter.

Olivia's assessment was accurate about women in Nepal. Although Nepal has made some progress in this regard, the treatment of women is far below Western standards. Some would go so far as to say that Nepali women were second-class citizens. Olivia's assessment was validated when the National Human Rights Commission released their report, "Progress of Women in Nepal, 1995–2015; Equality: non-negotiable," in December 2015. The report hailed the progress on gender equality in Nepal, especially with girls and women gaining greater access to education, but at the same time concluded that much more remained to be done in order for women to realize their rights. Barriers to progress included traditional cultural norms and values, which legitimize violence and discrimination at home, in the community, and in the market against them; inadequacy of laws, institutional and financial, and the human resources to address them. Bottom line—there are discriminatory social norms and attitudes towards women in Nepal and interventions are needed in order to transform these attitudes while empowering women. However, whenever Olivia and Deval did communicate, his expressions of "I'm missing you terribly… Love you so much… I loveyousomuch" never subsided. They looked forward to seeing each other again, which he anticipated would be a couple of days after her arrival in Kathmandu, when he completed his work in the village. Olivia missed Nepal. She told him, "I can go to the mall here in the USA and pass people and it's like passing cars… there's no human connection, but yet in Nepal anyone can go out onto the streets and connect with everyone." Olivia looked forward to walking the chaotic, narrow streets of Thamel, past brightly colored graffiti-painted walls, the town as alive during the day as at night; clusters of telephone wires piled, wrapped, and hanging; crowded with adventurous tourists from all over the world and jammed with taxis, bicycles carrying huge baskets of oranges, motorcycles in non-delineated traffic lanes and bicycle rickshaws. Olivia never knew what a shock absorber was until she bounced around for 15 minutes on a bicycle rickshaw through the bumpy streets of Thamel, the driver often stepping down to the ground to walk the rickshaw through puddles of muddy water. She loved to see and hear musicians walking the streets, playing their four-stringed sarangi, a wooden folk instrument similar to a violin. She would sit for hours in one of many CD shops and discover music from around the world, browse through books she had never seen before in bookshops, and hang out in her favorite singing bowl shop, playing singing bowls and always finding at least one that she added to her collection.

Invariably, Olivia would always run into friends. *Everyone* in Nepal seemed to be a friend—whether a tourist or a Nepali. But more than anything, she loved to see and feel the beauty, power, and presence of the majestic and diverse Himalayas. The flora and fauna of the Himalayas vary with climate, rainfall, altitude, and soils. The climate ranges from tropical at the base of the mountains to permanent ice and snow at the highest elevations. This diversity of altitude, rainfall, and soil conditions, combined with the very high snow line, supports a variety of distinct plant and animal communities. For example, seeing a mountain range covered with a forest of red rhododendron flowers (the national flower of Nepal) in March and April is a sight never to be forgotten.

Pokhara is a major tourist hub in Nepal, and Olivia and Deval planned to spend some focused time there together before her friends arrived for some scheduled events, which included the consecration of a nearby monastery. She had invited Deval to attend the consecration and wondered why he insisted that she answer the question, "Will you let the monks see me holding your hand?" Stymied, she didn't answer the question only because she had never seen anyone holding hands at such an event, not even married couples. Paradoxically, one evening when he saw a young Nepali woman showing affection towards her boyfriend in a restaurant in Thamel, Deval was greatly disturbed by this, putting his hand over his eyes and stating that such displays in public are not appropriate among Nepalis. When Olivia didn't respond to one of his questions, which occurred more than once, Deval began his next sentence with, "I demand that you answer me..." Initially, this didn't disturb Olivia but, rather, amused her and made her grin to think that he would try to be controlling. After all, she wasn't what anyone would call obedient or submissive enough to be controlled by anyone.

The day came, however, when Olivia no longer felt humor about his "I demand" assertion, but rather oppression, as if being squeezed into a corner. She asked him, "Where did you learn this from?" She suspected that he had learned this one-up, superior behavior from his father, and she was correct, although Deval was very sensitive about talking about his father's controlling, mentally abusive behavior towards his mother. As children, he and his brothers and sisters would beg his father to stop the abuse, which made their mother cry every night. He simply refused to talk about it, and threatened Olivia, "If you mention this again, we're done." Sadly, as much as one can be traumatized by the behavior of one's parent, who is a role model, it can become a learned behavior that cannot be learned anywhere else. And in order to change that behavior, one must be willing to recognize it and want to change it, which Deval was not willing to do. Not that he was selfish—because in so many ways he wasn't. He simply had a very different belief about the role and function of a woman in an intimate relationship with a man. There was an intimacy chip missing—and it seemed to be cultural. Later, Olivia learned that women with Brahmin husbands suffered the most ideological abuse of all of the castes and some physical abuse, also.

Olivia accepted Deval as Deval, knowing there was no one like him on earth, not wanting to change anything about him except his notion of "Buddha time." She had to explain to him what "being flakey" meant because he didn't know the meaning of "flake." If he said he was arriving at 6:30am she didn't want him to arrive at 9:30am... after her stomach had churned for three hours. On the other hand, she didn't mind his often funny haircuts, beige socks that didn't match his gray polyester-blend pants, and his general non-attention to the clothes he was wearing. Small, round Tulsi neck beads (kunti mala), made from genuine Tulsi wood that is found in Vrindavana, India, were always seen wrapped three times around his neck, signifying that he was an initiated devotee of Krishna. (If not initiated, the beads are wrapped one time around the neck.) Srimati Tulsi-devi is a pure devotee of Krishna; thus, by wearing Tulsi neck beads the devotee benefits from constantly associating with a pure devotee of Krishna. The Tulsi neck beads, worn all of the time by devotees of Krishna, have a purifying and protecting effect and also signify that one is a vegetarian.

No, Olivia didn't mind that Deval was a vegetarian, perhaps because Olivia had already been on the fence about becoming one herself. Deval's entire family became vegetarians not because of their Hindu religion but because of an experience Deval had as a child. When he saw exposed muscle on a man who had been stabbed and murdered, he ran home to tell his parents that it looked exactly like the animal meat they ate. They immediately became vegetarians and then vegans. What was interesting to Olivia was developing an awareness of food that contains egg. Whenever she would offer Deval food, such as a muffin, he would ask her if it had egg in it, and in most cases it did; however, when he asked her to immediately brush her teeth if she had eaten a dead animal, the wry look on her face expressed her revolt. What a blunt way to refer to meat. Ugh.

Beyond being a vegan, Deval ate food with his right hand, which is customary in Nepal, India and many parts of Asia, Africa, and the Middle East; however, the first time Olivia saw him shoveling rice and dahl into his mouth, she grimaced. Somehow they seemed to be transported to a cave in Bedrock, Deval was suddenly Fred Flintstone, and Olivia wondered if he would yell "Yabba-Dabba-Do" at any moment. He responded to her jaw-dropping reaction with "I won't embarrass you" and subsequently, always used a utensil to eat; however, because he never defended or explained why he ate with his hand, Olivia decided to research the topic, always concerned that her feelings might be based on in-the-box judgement. Yes, she had been taught Western eating and drinking etiquette, and it was taboo to eat with the hands. It was interesting, then, to discover that: 1) The ancient tradition of eating with the hand is derived from mudra (hand postures) practices and are widespread within Hinduism. 2) According to Vedic knowledge, the hands and feet consist of the five elements: Space, Air, Fire, Water, and Earth. According to Ayurvedic texts, each finger is an extension of one of the five elements: thumb (Fire), index finger (Air), middle finger (Heaven/Ether), ring finger (Earth), and little finger (Water). 3) Each finger contains millions of nerve endings and becomes an extension of the digestive system as it causes digestive juices and enzymes to be released as food is handled before it passes to the digestive system. Improved digestion enhances the pleasure of eating as taste, texture, and smell is felt better while eating food with the hand. For example, the skin sends messages to the brain about the appropriate temperature and texture of food, which acts like a catalyst in the action of generating necessary salivary juices. 4) Some believe that the hands act as an energetic cleanser when the food passes from hand to mouth because food contains various external energies. This could explain why people who normally eat with the hand—and experience a divine feeling—feel suffocated with negative feelings when they eat with utensils, almost as though they were holding a weapon in their hands. It is believed that eating with utensils can change the arrangement of normal flora, especially in the gut, which results in reduced immunity to environmental bacterial germs.

The bottom line was that eating food with the hand in Nepal was considered a polite thing to do but involved some rules that included washing the hands before and after eating, trimming the nails short, never eating with the left hand, and never eating from or taking food from someone's plate. Also, if drinking from a communal jug, the jug never touched the lips; rather, the head was tilted back, and liquid was poured into the mouth. Germaphobic Olivia cringed at the thought of sharing and drinking from a jug or water bottle in this manner but learned and practiced the technique out of necessity. However, as far as eating with the hand, she preferred not to trim her nails short. She had only lost them once years ago when she attempted to scuba dive from La Jolla Shores in California, struggling to pull fins on her feet while being tossed to and fro by waves in shallow water. Thus, she reserved for another day the technique that involved scooping food with four fingers, bringing it up to the mouth and pushing it into the mouth with the thumb. Her fingernails were long enough that she would have to tediously remove trapped food from underneath them.

Part III

Gorkha 7.8 Earthquake

After being separated from Deval for three and a half months, Olivia landed at the Tribhuvan International Airport in Kathmandu, Nepal, on April 25, 2015, five minutes before the 11:56 NST earthquake, known as the Gorkha earthquake, measured at a 7.8 magnitude. Its epicenter was east of the district of Lamjung, and its hypocenter was at a depth of approximately 5.1 miles. The following day, Sunday, there was no electricity, which Olivia heard had been cut because live electrical wires were hanging everywhere. Thus, with no Internet in order to contact family and friends, Olivia hailed a cab to the US Embassy Monday morning in order to send out an e-mail, which detailed her experiences upon arriving in Nepal. The last she had heard from Deval was a couple of days earlier when he wrote, "I'm not feeling good so won't go to the village again. I might just go and grab my belongings though… then I'll go to Kathmandu since now u r going to be there as well. I better be with u. love u." She didn't believe it would be possible to reach Deval under such circumstances but knew that he would be en route to Kathmandu.

Olivia wrote: "It is 6:19am on Sunday, April 26, and we do not have electricity yet so I am simply going to start this document after purchasing three large bottles of water at a nearby local market and taking pictures of more destruction and damage, including people sleeping outside in the hotel courtyard and on the ground level floor in the restaurant. I am so grateful that I was able to purchase bottled water because there is no running water.

The videos I shot seconds and minutes after the earthquake did not post with the information I was conveying so I will e-mail these videos to my son who is a guru at photography/filming to see if he can get them posted. Most of you thought I had arrived in Kathmandu a day earlier but I was detained in Los Angeles for a day; thus, my plane landed at the Kathmandu airport only 5 minutes before the earthquake hit on Saturday. We are fortunate because our plane could not have successfully landed during the earthquake. I was standing in the visa line inside the airport when the power suddenly went off, and about ten seconds later the ground was shaking so badly that people were thrown. It was impossible to stand. Most people were so terrified that they ran outside. I remained on the tile floor, leaning against my Brighton brown and black wheeled suitcase. I immediately fumbled for my iPhone in the wallet-purse that was hanging around my neck and started videotaping the shaking table in front of me that held immigration and arrival forms.

Once I was able to stand, I was now the only person in the visa line to obtain my visa. I snapped a picture of the ceiling immediately above me, showing that a white ceiling tile was cracked and giving way, ready to collapse. When I walked downstairs to luggage claim, I couldn't believe that it was practically vacant because normally the Kathmandu airport is wall-to-wall people. I walked past the baggage claim area and saw luggage on luggage carts that had been abandoned by the men driving them. Presumably, in fear, they had run to safety, which meant to an open area. As I started looking for my luggage, a Nepalese policeman, in blue uniform, waved and directed me outside where people from my flight were standing. The airport personnel and policemen were terrified, and given the earthquake history of Nepal, I cannot blame them. Of course, people wanted their luggage. In addition, we thought it was going to start to rain, and it was getting chilly. I remained almost exclusively with a police officer during this time who said "no" to my every request; i.e., I offered to go inside the brick enclosure baggage claim area and bring out *everyone's* luggage.

I worried about my driver who was picking me up from the airport and soon discovered that he waited two hours for me. He is now hours away from Kathmandu at his home, believing that his home is gone and worried about his family because he was unable to contact them. You learn some invaluable lessons during a time like this. I am beyond grateful to him because I do not know what would have happened to me if he would have left me. For one thing, there was sheer pandemonium at the airport. It was only because of my determination that I found my luggage and then, when I was told that I could not leave the airport with it, I kept repeating that I would NOT leave without it. I showed many police officers the visa that I did obtain and the claim checks for my luggage. Finally, a police officer allowed me to depart and go outside where sure enough, my loyal driver was standing, holding up an 8x11 white piece of paper with my name written in large, black letters.

I saw this earthquake coming like a freight train. I had researched the 1934 earthquake and shared that information with a lot of people. Many of my family and friends have heard me talk about the earthquake that would inevitably hit Nepal again. I was here four months ago during a late-in-the-evening 5.9 magnitude earthquake, which caused my bed to sway and awaken me. Immediately, a friend in Kathmandu texted me, and another Nepali friend telephoned me, updating and assuring me. But that 5.9 was nothing compared to this. So, why am I here, and what have I learned? At the outset, the most frustrating experience is not being able to console the inconsolable. Last night, a Nepalese young man was sitting in the dining area of my hotel, sobbing uncontrollably on the telephone, obviously listening to bad news, and no matter what I did, I could not begin to console him. My arms around him did nothing. My breaking heart did nothing. [NOTE: It was too dark for Olivia to recognize who this young man was but a month later when she couldn't find her sunglasses at the hotel, a young man gave her his sunglasses. She couldn't understand why he would do that until he said, "You don't remember me, do you? I'm the one you had your arms around in the dining room the night of the earthquake." He then told Olivia that he was on the phone receiving news that his endeared grandmother, who had recently lost both her husband and one of her sons, had jumped into a nearby river at the onset of the earthquake. Her body was never recovered.]

Interestingly, I did learn that I have no fear in situations like this. I chose to sleep on the top 5th floor of the hotel last night rather than outside on the ground because I needed a good night's sleep after such a long, arduous trip and being detained in Los Angeles for a day to obtain a new passport Thursday at the US Embassy. (My passport was valid for five months, and Nepal requires six months' validity upon arrival so I was not allowed to board my Cathay Pacific flight Wednesday night at midnight.) However, last night, in support of each other, everyone was wishing everyone a safe night's sleep. We experienced three terrifying aftershocks last night, the worst at 5:00am after a dog awakened me at 4:30am with frantic barking. I pay attention to animals because they have an awareness of impending danger that we do not. At 1pm we had another earthquake—a 6.7. Events do not necessarily happen in this order: earthquake, aftershock, tremors. SO many tremors! As an aside comment, I actually don't like to use the word aftershocks because these aftershocks are really like additional earthquakes. I discovered what I do in situations like this. I don't run or scream. I just keep repeating OM MANI PADME HUNG, and I am grateful that I feel a sense of peace with those words.

I have 149 e-mails in my inbox, and I cannot begin to respond to everyone, but thank you so much for your concern, and continue to pray for Nepal as events continue to unfold. You are probably receiving more updated information than I am here in Kathmandu but from what I hear, there is destruction throughout Nepal. When I arrived at the hotel there were a reported 900 deaths and over 1,000 injuries but it was anticipated that those numbers will grow." [NOTE: The total death toll was 9,061 and more than 23,447 were injured. If the earthquake hadn't occurred on a Saturday, 75,000 children could have died when their schools collapsed.]

Olivia e-mailed the above message from a computer at the US Embassy in Kathmandu on Monday, April 27, and although grateful for the Internet availability, it was her experience at the Embassy that seemed to put her into a state of post-earthquake shock. She had believed that the US Embassy was her home away from home. It wasn't. Nepal was her home away from home. She was greeted at the US Embassy door with a great deal of politeness but she did have a hotel cab waiting for her. When Olivia asked the young man at the Embassy door if she would be able to get a cab back to her hotel he said, "Yes," which was incorrect information, unfortunately, because she told her cab driver to leave. Taxis were not up and running, and she did have difficulty finding another one to transport her back to the hotel. But disseminating wrong information at the front door of the US Embassy isn't what was so shocking. Rather, it was the level of stress she felt inside the Embassy.

The Embassy Resource Room was busy but quiet, a person at each one of the ten computers; however, the open areas, which included a large cafeteria, were extremely stressful. An adult woman who worked at the Embassy yelled at a woman for taking some cereal that was on a table: "Don't eat any cereal. That is for the children, and that is all we have!" There were families staying at the US Embassy. They clearly didn't have enough food. A few US Military flameless ration packets of food were on a table. The ration heater contains finely powdered magnesium metal, alloyed with a small amount of iron, and table salt. To activate the reaction, a small amount of water is added, and the boiling point of water is quickly reached as the reaction proceeds to warm the food. They served meals buffet style, and Olivia was there for breakfast. They gave her a spoonful of fried potatoes and told her there wasn't enough food for more than that. How could she possibly eat any food at the US Embassy when the people staying there were in a situation like that? This is the US Embassy, and it does not take a rocket scientist to know that Nepal was due for a huge earthquake. If anyone should have been prepared, it truly should have been the US Embassy! Olivia had been talking about the earthquake coming for months. Olivia sighed at her lack of faith in bureaucracy, big organizations, and government. When she later read that Obama called the Prime Minister of Nepal and offered assistance, she thought, "Are you kidding me? The Prime Minister is the LAST person I would telephone. The biggest problem Nepal has right now is government."

It is difficult to walk away from a karmic relationship because its roots go beyond this life. Whenever Olivia thought that she should walk away from Deval, she found—over and over again—that she couldn't. After she returned to her hotel from the US Embassy she found that Deval had been there looking for her and, subsequently, left a note at the front desk with his phone number, telling her to telephone him. One of her daughters had actually messaged him, terrified that Olivia was MIA (missing in action) because they didn't hear from Olivia the day after the earthquake when there was no electricity. Olivia read Deval's note, written on a small piece of white paper in noticeably small cursive, and proceeded to her hotel room that had been moved from the 5th floor main building to a new, safer building with her room close to the ground. She was in shock and wondered if she should telephone him under the circumstances. She simply wanted to collapse on the bed, feeling numb and exhausted.

Within a couple of hours, there was a knock at the door. Olivia wouldn't have suspected that hotel personnel at the front desk would give Deval her room number. Olivia opened the door. He stood there facing her, leaning against the balcony railing, looking frustrated and frazzled, as if he hadn't slept in days. She stepped back, and he rushed in, throwing his arms around her in tight embrace, whispering, "I love you." As he held her, it was a raw, penetrating moment that will never escape her memory. There was no way that she could walk away and leave him… not now… although she also wasn't in the mental frame of mind to act as though there hadn't been a disastrous earthquake two days previous. Deval told Olivia that he had gone to look for her at the US Embassy; however, he could not enter the building because he was not a US citizen; thus, they missed each other.

Olivia and Deval spent a couple of days together but he soon discovered that his parents' home had been seriously damaged in the earthquake, and he needed to travel to their village, hours away, to assess the damage, which would probably involve demolition. He anticipated that he might not return to Kathmandu for two weeks but returned within the week. It's a good thing because Olivia could never open the door to her hotel room but Deval could. It was a little tricky having to pull the door forward before dropping the handle down while turning the key several times in whatever direction worked. Perhaps it was the turning the key part that was challenging but there were clearly three different actions going on. Deval reached the point where he didn't even want her *try* to unlock the door, sometimes taking her key and walking ahead of her in order to have the door unlocked when she arrived. It always made her smile because she was a child who never let her mother tie her shoes, even if it took her hours to tie them herself, and here she was as a grown woman, surrendering to someone else unlocking the door for her.

Walking ahead. Hmmmmm. Olivia had heard that Brahmin men walk ahead of women, acting superior, impure, intelligent, and carrying nothing whereas the women walked behind them, carrying children and heavy loads. Perhaps this would explain why Olivia would often find Deval yards ahead of her, sometimes nearly losing sight of him. She could see where behavior like this could truly be cultural, deep in the caste DNA; thus, Deval would not see it as being strange or rude behavior. The other explanation to his behavior is simply that Olivia was a

Western woman, not of his caste, and he needed to be careful about who saw him with her in public.

Karmic relationships can be so intense that they can seem addictive, either on an emotional or physical level. This is because the forces of karma are stronger than what most people realize. There is truth to the statement that one is "driven by the winds of karma." Once karmic imprints (seeds) are left in the mind-stream consciousness, it only takes the coming together of causes and conditions for those imprints to activate and come to fruition, the same way that a planted seed comes to life when the causes and conditions of light, temperature, and rainfall come together. And because the emotions are so deep in karmic relationships, it is understandable that buttons can be easily pushed. Olivia was always perplexed at how Deval could be instantly consumed with jealousy if another man gave her attention, or how they could argue over the most trivial things. Emotions were deep. Buttons were being pushed. Deval didn't speak to Olivia for two hours because he saw her give a big hug to a friend who, as a surprise, came to see her at the hotel. Deval expressed something to the effect that a Nepali wife wouldn't behave in such a manner.

One day after a high-ranking military official wanted to meet her for coffee, Deval suspected that the man had been in her hotel room and, thus, Deval wouldn't come near the room. That was the final straw. Olivia reasoned logically with him, "I have never done anything to you to cause you to suspect that I would be with someone else behind your back. If I had ever done that, you would have a reason to be suspicious or jealous but you don't have a reason to feel this way." It was curious that he would feel distrust and suspicion when he expected and demanded blind allegiance from Olivia. He shared with her that when he was very young he had beaten a boy at school one day, and when the boy's father confronted Deval's father that night at their home, Deval's father (Buba) sent him away, telling him that Deval would never do such a thing. His father believed it to the extent that he wouldn't even question Deval. That kind of head in the sand devotion is what Deval expected from Olivia—never to question him even if he should question her. There was a double standard—they were not on an even playing field—and what was good for the goose wasn't good for the gander. Nepal had never experienced Betty Friedan or the bra burning second wave feminists of the 1960s. Olivia couldn't help but wonder how Betty Friedan would take on a Nepali Brahmin.

A couple of days after the earthquake, Olivia was observing the cleanup at her hotel. For the most part, the hotel received little damage although there was a large horizontal crack, about ten feet in length, on one of the interior restaurant walls. Many potted plants, on five levels of the hotel, had been thrown and smashed during the quake, and several outside terra-cotta structures had been damaged. It would take weeks before the buildings in Kathmandu would undergo inspection to determine if they were inhabitable or uninhabitable. The outcome of the assessment certified no structural damage on the exterior, or the exterior and interior, via a green notice with the date and time attached to the outside of the building, signed with an inspector ID, his Agency with further identification as Government of Nepal, Ministry of Culture, Tourism, and Civil Aviation, Department of Tourism. On the other hand, if the building was condemned, which was often the case, another notice would indicate that it was uninhabitable.

"Come with me," Ganesh said, as he approached Olivia. She followed him, turning right at the entrance to the hotel and walking down the street, turning right again through another narrow street, noticing the destruction of buildings and debris in the streets, usually consisting of piles of dirt, brick, and boards. Telephone poles were leaning and wires were hanging. Often chunks of a wall or an entire wall or walls from a building were missing. Huge vertical cracks were seen in buildings as large as

12 inches in diameter. At the corner of the street a house had collapsed on top of a white Suzuki car that was still buried beneath the rubble. Olivia saw a black sandal lying in the road and 20 feet ahead saw its match. A mother was walking down the street with a naked child, approximately four years of age, carrying his clothes. They came across a dead little black and white dog in the street, now partially decomposed. Olivia saw a group of women sitting on a blue plastic tarp in an open space, one woman holding a large gray umbrella over their heads to protect them from the sun. Nearby sat another group of women, holding a turquoise plastic tarp over their heads. Everyone feared close proximity to buildings because of the danger of them collapsing, especially with the continuing aftershocks. There were always screams heard when there was an aftershock, and people ran to open areas, away from buildings.

That day there were mass cremations underway among grief-stricken Nepalese, especially at Pashupatinath Temple, a UNESCO World Heritage Site, and one of the largest and holiest Hindu Temples of Lord Shiva in the world. Pashupatinath was first erected on the banks of the Bagmati River more than 1,000 years ago because the Bagmati River is considered sacred, eventually flowing into the Ganges River in India, ultimately reaching the holy city of Varanasi. As Olivia arrived at Pashupatinath, she could not help but remember that it was there where she had witnessed a cremation for the first time, years ago, and a Nepalese woman gestured to Olivia that she should not be wearing red lipstick for such an occasion (red lipstick was worn at weddings). What was unsettling at the time was knowing that Hindus believe in cremating the body minutes after death; therefore, people are sometimes brought to Pashupatinath before death actually occurs; thus, Olivia did see people who were there waiting to be cremated, some housed in a hospice-type facility at the entrance. Olivia observed the body of a deceased man being prepared on a concrete ghat by the river, covered in saffron silk cloths and garlands of orange marigold flowers placed around the neck. The male members of the family, heads shaved in respect, carried the body to a pyre, and the body was laid on top of wooden logs with straw. The eldest son lit the pyre, flames soon engulfing it, the smell distinctive but, surprisingly, not like the smell of burning flesh. After about four hours the cremains were dispersed on the river. Olivia recognized that the river was used for a number of things; i.e., she saw a man dump a couple of large garbage cans into the river and below him a few yards was a woman washing food utensils for eating. You can see why Westerners must be careful about drinking only bottled water. However, the scene at Pashupatinath years ago was nothing like the scene now.

Pashupatinath had not suffered too much damage in the earthquake, but in the back, spilling out of the cremation area onto a main path, was a row of corpses covered in saffron sheets. Extra cremation pyres had been set up, but it was not enough. Whereas there are normally 20–30 cremations a day at Pashupatinath, in the three days following the earthquake there were over 1,000 cremations with thousands more to come. And sadly, there was no pomp and ceremony for those whose bodies were not identified or claimed by family members. There simply was not enough room at the morgue at Tribhuvan University to store bodies; thus, large flatbed trucks lined with the dead, swarmed by flies, arrived. After entering the temple compound, the trucks drove down a crude, mud-worn slope and into the Bagmati River, through the shallows, and onto the grassy shoal at the river's center. There, volunteers, many of them monks dressed in plain clothes or maroon robes, latex gloves, and medical masks, climbed into the flatbed, lifting, dragging, or pushing the bodies, wooden with rigor mortis, onto waiting stretchers for deposit atop hastily arranged funeral pyres. The unclothed and uncovered bodies were simply tipped off the stretcher, two bodies to each pile, and set alight by the young volunteers as a small crowd looked on.

The entire cremation process—outdoors, under the sky—and open to the public, seemed so sacred to Olivia, as it did to the Nepalese, because there is a belief that those who are cremated on the Pashupatinath Ghat will enter heaven. What Olivia witnessed was nothing like funeral rituals in the West that drag on for days with big business funeral homes trying to sell consumers one thing after another, including metal clad coffins that are guaranteed for 100 years. What is even more ludicrous is when the deceased body is fastidiously groomed by professionals with makeup, hairdo, and manicure so that the body doesn't look dead but asleep, which is one reason why cremation is usually so unacceptable.

Olivia and Ganesh walked past another group of people sitting silently, as if confused and in shock, and then down a narrow street to the location of a rescue and recovery mission. This is what Ganesh wanted her to witness. There were approximately 20 Nepalese policemen standing in their beige uniforms with black, brown, and green camouflage; matching helmets on their heads, and black leather laced-up boots on their feet. Equipped with rope and shovels, they were prepared to take action when needed. Chinese rescue workers were on the scene, attempting to recover a little boy and an older woman who were buried beneath a collapsed house. Olivia stood on the nearby step of a house, videotaping. She could not believe the danger that the rescue workers had placed themselves in, attempting to climb in open areas underneath debris that could easily collapse on them. One Chinese rescue worker walked away from the scene, approximately 20 yards in front of Olivia, and then past her, looking for a bottle of water. It was hot, and the look on his face was intense. Ganesh led Olivia closer to the collapsed houses, and as she walked past policemen she repeatedly said, "I'm so sorry." Once she arrived at the area where the rescue workers were working, they motioned for her to move away, recognizing the danger she was in and also clearing the way for the bodies that were about to be dragged from the rubble. Olivia learned that the group of people she had passed prior to walking down the alleyway were waiting family members.

These kinds of horrific scenes were typical during the days following the earthquake; hospitals were operating in the streets, turning away people with cuts, scrapes, and abrasions in order to treat those with serious injuries. Dead bodies were lined up in front of the main hospital in Kathmandu, family members grieving. In Thamel, Olivia saw a cab stop, and two men got out of the cab to remove an elderly man from the back seat of the cab. He wore gray shorts, a gray shirt, and was barefoot but had a white bandage wrapped around his left foot. They sat the elderly man down on the street against the concrete step to a building and laid his aluminum crutch on the step. He immediately fell to his left side, and streams of urine ran from underneath his shorts, into the street. The men in the cab had already driven away, but a man passing by, wearing a helmet, ran over to the man and attempted to sit him upright—to no avail. Another bystander attempted to help but the elderly man had rolled to the edge of the street and was lying unconscious, on his side, almost in fetal position. Olivia rushed over to him—but he was gone. He was someone's husband, someone's father, someone's son, someone's brother, she thought—and here he was alone, dead on a Kathmandu street. It was beyond heartbreaking—beyond comprehension. And the poor animals. The birds, especially the crows, were going crazy, constantly squawking and flying around. People commented that the city of Kathmandu should be renamed Crowmandu.

Olivia soon learned that her reasons for being in Nepal, except to see Deval, had been cancelled. Her friends and teachers from around the world were not coming. People were streaming out of Nepal in droves, especially because of the unpredictable series of aftershocks. Aftershocks are earthquakes that occur following a large earthquake, in the same general area as the earthquake, during the following days-to-years, and have the potential to create damage, just like other earthquakes. Usually, the number of aftershocks following an earthquake decrease in number; however, the unusual fact about the Gorkha earthquake was that aftershocks occurred on nearly a daily basis for months; thus, people needed to be aware of the possibility of aftershocks, especially when working in or around vulnerable structures or in landslide-prone areas that were weakened by the initial earthquake. Many people at Olivia's hotel booked flights to continue their vacations in Vietnam or some other country. However, the Tribhuvan airport, sustaining some damage in the earthquake, was a chaotic mess. Their normal activity of 40 flights a day was now doubled, with crowds of people trying to leave Nepal and planes with relief aid from other countries attempting to land, some of which were turned away.

The ground continued to shake. One night at dinner, Deval got a startled but terrified look on his face as he said, "Earthquake!" Olivia was bouncing her leg, and it shook the table. "It's just my leg," Olivia exclaimed. "Look," as she pointed to her leg. He breathed a deep sigh of relief. She never did that again. Everyone was hypersensitive to an aftershock, not knowing if it would result in a full-blown earthquake. Hearing people scream and seeing people run to open spaces was a typical scenario. Olivia wondered how she could return to the USA just to watch events in Nepal unfold on CNN, knowing that media spin is not an accurate depiction, especially since they would focus on Kathmandu and not the remote villages of Nepal.

A longtime friend and Buddhist nun (Ani), devoted to the Disability Rehabilitation Center (DRC) near Boudha in Kathmandu, immediately told Olivia about the desperate needs of the 55 children there. As a result of the earthquake, they were sleeping outside because of damage to their school where they also lived, and they needed food; thus, the Ani and Olivia traveled to the DRC. Olivia personally donated food, providing juice and ramen noodle soup for the day and food that would last a couple of days: rice, dal, sugar, and flour. Once at the DRC, Olivia immediately fell in love with the children who, in anticipation of her arrival, were sitting at their tables in an open area. They clapped and expressed such genuine appreciation. Olivia will always remember the DRC as the Land of the Grateful Children.

Olivia noticed a boy named Tufan who was about eight years of age, and asked about him. Tufan had arrived at the DRC yesterday. He was one of 50 people rescued, via helicopter, from the Langtang area, 35 miles north of Kathmandu. The snow, ice, and boulders sitting on the steep hillsides above the valley ripped off, free-falling for about 1,640 feet, an avalanche that triggered a mudslide at Langtang village and completely buried it—wiped off the map, killing about 350 people. It was reported that the energy involved was roughly half that of the Hiroshima nuclear explosion, or more, a detonation of 7.6 kilotons of TNT. The horrifying air blast, exceeding 200 miles per hour, blew away large swaths of the village, including sturdy stone hotels. In an area of hillsides stretching about 0.6 miles around the landslide, the air blast snapped trees like matchsticks. A small forest was flattened by the blast of air as far as 1,300 feet up the opposite slope of the valley. The limbs, leaves, and branches of trees were removed, and in many cases, the bark was removed. Olivia was already messaging with Yasmine Habash whom she would meet the following week when Yasmine arrived to conduct a dangerous helicopter search for her mother, Dawn Habash. Roads leading to Langtang were so badly damaged that search teams could not reach it by land for four months after the earthquake. Dawn, a 57-year-old yoga instructor from Augusta, Maine, loved Nepal and had traveled there for many years, often with Yasmine. What was most difficult for Yasmine was that her mother had a trekking partner who was about 200 yards ahead of Dawn at Langtang, and she lived through the avalanche; however, Dawn's body was never recovered. All told, the earthquake triggered a total of 4,312 landslides.

Tufan was brought to the DRC because he has a disability. His mom, dad, and two brothers were safely outside their home when the earthquake hit but they thought Tufan was still inside. They all hurried inside to find him. The house collapsed, and they were all killed, buried beneath the rubble. Tufan was outside all along. Olivia believed that Tufan's story could well be the most heartbreaking story she would ever hear. She tried to comfort him, knowing that he was facing a long healing process. He was having dreams about his family at night, which would cause him to cry for hours. The words of Shantideva (1979, pp. 20–22), the 8th century Buddhist Master, echoed now more than ever:

Thus by the virtue collected
Through all that I have done,
May the pain of every living creature
Be completely cleared away.

May I be a doctor, medicine
And may I be the nurse
For all sick beings in the world,
Until everyone is healed.

On April 30, five days after the earthquake, Olivia decided that it was time to do what she could to help the people of Nepal. It shouldn't have surprised her family because her father always said that even as a child Olivia always advocated for the underdog. She joined a team of dedicated, young Nepali men who were distributing food to remote villages although her family would have preferred that she return to the USA. Her brother expressed that he would "get out of there even if it was on a camel," which made Olivia laugh, because there were obviously no camels in Nepal. Olivia reached out to her family, friends, and students with an e-mail: "It has been so heart-warming for me to witness the efficacy of this proactive group that I have decided to join their efforts, participating in a purchase and distribution via the funds that I raise, while documenting it with pictures and video footage. I will post it on my Facebook page along with my other Kathmandu coverage. Thus, if you would like to donate, whether it is $1, $2, $5, $10, $20, $50, $100, $500 or more, it can provide much-needed food, water, and other necessities. Please use Western Union because they are currently not charging a fee for money sent to Nepal, and it is instant, whereas it takes 3–5 days for donations to process through a bank. [NOTE: Later Olivia found it easier to receive donations via her PayPal account and prior to her establishing a GoFundMe campaign account.] From the bottom of my heart, I thank you with the deepest of gratitude. May we dedicate these efforts for the benefit of all beings, particularly those affected by this disastrous earthquake."

On Ground Earthquake Relief

Olivia's first relief run with a team of six volunteers on May 5 was to Dhading, a picturesque, mountainous district west of Kathmandu. It took six hours to purchase and another 13 hours to distribute about 3,000 pounds of food to approximately 2,000 people. There was so much involved in the preliminary work of getting ready for a run: coordinating with the villagers who were to receive goods, shopping at many stores in order to accumulate the amount of food needed, then loading, transporting, and unloading it at a storage room in a nearby school, then loading it onto a truck the next day. The team had blisters on their hands from loading and unloading sacks of rice. No one seemed to know the meaning of work gloves. Olivia had one pair of gloves and offered them to one of the volunteers but he wouldn't take them unless all of the volunteers were given a pair. She was often addressed as Ma'am, a respectful form of address.

It was well-known among Nepalis that Dhading was in need, and Olivia and her team made about a dozen stops in that area to distribute to groups of people. She could not believe the devastation—heaps of scattered boards and debris where homes had once stood. Originally, Olivia felt relief when she saw standing homes with cracks in them, but later discovered that most of these homes were uninhabitable and needed to be demolished before they could be rebuilt. Being a mountainous region, it was HOT in Dhading, which made it even more difficult for people to be without shelter. The sun was scorching and penetrating. Olivia understood why she saw a few people with umbrellas, and she relied on her own animal print umbrella to save her from the discomfort of that sun.

Whenever Olivia and her team arrived at an area and stopped the truck, people immediately gathered and formed a line to receive their food distribution in a fair and efficacious manner.

Some had been patiently waiting for the team's arrival, sitting under the shade of a tree. Olivia and her team didn't have enough rice to give each family a full bag of rice on this run but every individual, whether a man, woman, or child, received a pink or turquoise plastic bag that was filled full of rice with a metal scooper or a makeshift scooper, made by cutting off the bottom of a large, plastic water bottle. The people were astonishingly resilient—grateful, patient, polite, and always seemed to have a radiant smile on their face despite having lost their homes and, for many, everything they owned.

The Nepalese went on with life the best they could under such circumstances. Olivia saw a young couple plowing a field with a white and a black water buffalo, a wood beam (yoke) extending over their shoulders, enabling them to pull together through the reddish soil. One of Olivia's favorite scenes was passing a family—two teenage children, their mother dressed in an ankle-length cotton red skirt under a knee-length peach top, and the father wearing a pointed traditional Nepali hat, representing Mt. Everest, a reminder that he should have self-esteem that is as high as Mt. Everest. Nepal was The Land of Men's Pointed Hats because they could always be seen. They were all together at a waterfall that was cascading over a rock, happily giving their two black water buffalos a bath. The buffalo closest to Olivia turned his head as if to smile for her camera, and he was impressive—obviously very stocky and strong, unlike many skinny water buffalos she had seen in the past throughout Nepal.

Olivia often saw groups of people, mostly women, standing in open areas because their homes were gone. She saw women at the open bathing areas, water pouring out from a pipe enclosed in concrete, either taking a bath or washing clothes by hand. Olivia saw so many beautiful women wearing their jewelry—always a necklace and bangle bracelets. One older woman, without makeup, was more than Hollywood gorgeous; Olivia had to stop to take photographs of her as she remained sitting in a typical squat, gazing at Olivia as if she was now a subject, posing for an oil painting. Her feet were flat on the ground, one foot forward, exposing her left bare foot with left hand resting at the ankle, bare fingers spread, pointing downward. She was wearing a long light orange skirt with white swirl-like patterns throughout the material. A matching fabric, without the white swirls, was wrapped around her hair, exposing only a few wisps of white hair around her oval face. She wore a checked, gray and burgundy, long-sleeved blouse. Sure enough, there was a pearl necklace wrapped twice around her neck and a gold, metal bangle bracelet on each wrist. Olivia learned that when a woman marries, her husband gives her a necklace and a bracelet that are never removed. She can only remove them if the husband dies, and the bracelet must be broken off rather than simply removed.

There were hundreds of scenes with women that Olivia will never forget but she was particularly touched by an elderly couple. The woman, clad in a red cotton blouse, a short pink skirt and a longer pink and yellow striped skirt that fell to her ankles, was walking with a tall stick held in her right hand, giving her support. Her left hand was behind her back, tightly holding her husband's left hand close to her as he provided shade by holding a plain, gray umbrella over them. He was carrying a stuffed full-looking black backpack on his back and was sporting a knit cap, a long red and blue plaid shirt and long pants, evidently to protect himself from the penetrating sun. When Olivia would see a woman sitting in an odd location, such as under a wooden table or under a sheet of galvanized corrugated roofing material, she knew that the woman was seeking shade and relief from the sun. Olivia couldn't help but remember this area as the Land of Gorgeous Wives.

At one of their food and supply distribution stops on the road, a vehicle passed and stopped. A man with white hair soon joined Olivia and her team—Nepali Congressman Arjun Narasingha KD, Member of the Consulate Assembly in Nepal, Former

Minister of Education, Health, Housing and Physical Planning, Member of the Central Working Committee. He was assessing damage caused by the earthquake and the needs of the people. He talked with Olivia, giving her all of his contact information, including his cell phone number. He also told her to call him at any time; thus, she had made a very important contact out in the field. However, many Nepalis did not have positive feelings towards him or any political figure for that matter, which raised Olivia's curiosity about Nepal's political history. There were reasons why Nepal was plagued with years of civil war and immobilized political groups, and understanding it helped Olivia to understand the current plight of the Nepalese.

Unfortunately, Nepal, with a population of approximately 31 million people and the size of the state of Arkansas, became a Land of Ineffective Government due largely to three major events: the creation of a multi-party parliamentary system of multi-party politics in 1980, a decade-long (1995–2006) Maoist bloody war against the monarchy where thousands were killed (the monarchy was abolished in 2008), and political instability demonstrated by frequent changes in Prime Minister; i.e. in 2000, GP Koirala returned as Prime Minister to head the ninth government in ten years. To paint a brief historical overview: In 1768, Gurkha ruler Prithvi Narayan Shah conquered Kathmandu and laid the foundations for a Unified Kingdom. During 1814–1816 there was an Anglo-Nepalese War, which resulted in a treaty that established Nepal's current boundaries. In 1846, Nepal fell under the sway of hereditary chief ministers, known as Ranas, who dominated the monarchy and cut off Nepal from the outside world. In 1950, anti-Rana forces in India formed an alliance with the monarch. In 1951, the Nepali monarch under King Tribhuwan ended the century-old system of rule by hereditary premiers, and anti-Rana rebels in the Nepalese Congress Party formed a government.

King Mahendra, a true patriot, ascended the throne in 1955,

and a multi-party constitution was adopted and conflict ensued. He died in 1972 and was succeeded by King Birendra, whose reign saw years of conflict, civil disobedience and boycotts until a multi-party democracy within the framework of a constitutional monarchy was established in 1990. This event resulted in a landmark in political party history: the first free and fair Nepal elections were held in 1991, and all Nepalese citizens of 18 years and older became eligible to vote in the elections.

Olivia often wondered if Nepal would ever recover from their unfortunate history, one blow after another, which included the Nepalese royal massacre on June 1, 2001, at a house on the grounds of the Narayanhity Royal Palace, the then residence of the Nepalese monarchy. It was reported that the heir to the throne, Prince Dipendra, in a drunken and drug-induced state, killed nine members of his family and himself, armed with a H&K MP5 9mm submachine gun, a Franchi SPAS-12 shotgun, a Colt M16A2 rifle, and a Glock 19 9mm pistol, during a monthly party of the royal family in the house. Five were injured, and ten were killed, including his parents, King Birendra and Queen Aishwarya. Olivia visited the site, now a museum, where placed markers denote where each member of the royal family was shot. The structure, to the side of the Palace, has been torn down to its foundation; however, some markers are outside prior to entering a beautiful garden and grounds. Several tourist guides have told Olivia that the number of Americans visiting Nepal decreased radically following the massacre.

Five years prior to the royal massacre, in 1996, an insurgency led by Maoists broke out. The ensuing 10-year civil war between Maoist and government forces witnessed the dissolution of the cabinet and parliament and assumption of absolute power by King Gyanendra in 2002, which led to a state of emergency being declared for two years. From 1991 to 2002 the Parliament (*Sansad*) had two chambers: The House of Representatives (*Pratinidhi Sabha*) had 205 members elected for a five-year term in single-seat constituencies. The National Council (*Rashtriya Sabha*) had 60 members, 35 members elected by the Pratinidhi Sabha, 15 representatives of Regional Development Areas and 10 members appointed by the King. Parliament was subsequently dissolved by the King in 2002 on the pretext that it was incapable of handling the Maoist rebels. On February 1, 2005, King Gyanendra suspended the Parliament, appointed a government led by himself for direct royal rule, declared a three-month state of emergency, and enforced martial law. The King continued to argue that civil politicians were unfit to handle the Maoist insurgency. Telephone lines were cut, and several high-profile political leaders were detained. Other opposition leaders fled to India and regrouped.

A broad coalition, the Seven Party Alliance (SPA), was formed in opposition to the royal takeover, encompassing the seven parliamentary parties who held about 90% of the seats in the old, dissolved parliament. Nepal had joined the United Nations in 1955. The United Nations set up a monitoring program in 2005 to observe and assess the human rights situation in Nepal. On November 22, 2005, the Seven Party Alliance (SPA) of parliamentary parties and the Communist Party of Nepal (Maoist) agreed on a historic and unprecedented 12-point memorandum of understanding (MOU) for peace and democracy. Olivia was in Nepal during this time and remembers hearing discussion about the 12-point memorandum and also complied with an enforced curfew. Nepalese from various walks of life and the international community regarded the MOU as an appropriate political response to the crisis that was developing in Nepal. Against the backdrop of the historical suffering of the Nepalese people and the enormous human cost of the last ten years of violent conflict, the MOU, which proposed a peaceful transition through an elected constituent assembly, created an acceptable formula for a united movement for democracy. As per the 12-point MOU, the SPA called for a protest movement, and the Communist Party of

Nepal (Maoist) supported it. This led to a countrywide uprising called the *Loktantra Andolan* that started in April 2006 and led to victory. All political forces including civil society and professional organizations actively galvanized the people. This resulted in massive and spontaneous demonstrations and rallies held across Nepal against King Gyanendra's autocratic rule, which were so pervasive that he feared being overthrown. On April 21, 2006, King Gyanendra declared that "power would be returned to the people." However, the people continued to protest and occupy the streets until at midnight he conceded to one of the demands of the SPA and announced the reinstatement of the House of Representatives. Twenty-one people died and thousands were injured during the 19 days of protests.

On that date, the constitution was altered by the Constituent Assembly to make the country a republic Assembly; a unicameral interim legislature replaced the previous parliament. The new body consists both of members of the old parliament as well as nominated members. On May 19, 2006, the parliament assumed total legislative power and gave executive power to the Government of Nepal (previously known as His Majesty's Government). Names of many institutions (including the army) were stripped of the "royal" adjective and the Raj Parishad (a council of the King's advisers) was abolished, with his duties assigned to the Parliament itself. The activities of the King became subject to parliamentary scrutiny and the King's properties were subjected to taxation. Moreover, Nepal was declared a secular state abrogating the previous status of a Hindu Kingdom. An agreement was made for the monarchy to be abolished and the country to become a federal republic with the Prime Minister becoming head of government, and the President, head of state. Defying political pundits, who had predicted it to be trounced in the April 2008 elections, the Communist Party of Nepal (Maoist) became the largest party amidst a general atmosphere of fear and intimidation from all sides.

On July 19, 2006, the Prime Minister, GP Koirala, sent a letter to the United Nations announcing the intention of the Nepalese government to hold elections to a constituent assembly by April 2007. As of December 2007, there were 11 parties; however, three of the parties dominated: Nepali Congress with 133 sets, Unified Communist Party of Nepal (Maoists) with 84 seats, and Communist Party of Nepal (Marxist) with 83 seats. A remaining 30 seats were spread among 8 other parties. In May 2008 the elections for the Constituent Assembly saw the Communist Party of Nepal (Maoist) as the largest party (among 25 parties) in the Constituent Assembly, with a term of two years. Thus, a federal republic was established in May 2008, with only four members of the 601-seat Constituent Assembly voting against the change, which ended 240 years of royal rule in Nepal. The government announced a public holiday for three days, May 28–May 30, to celebrate the country becoming a federal republic.

Major parties such as the Unified Communist Party of Nepal (Maoist), Communist Party of Nepal (Unified Marxist-Leninist) (CPN UML), and the Nepali Congress agreed to write a constitution to replace the interim one within two years. However, uncooperative and self-centered behavior of the political parties has been cited as the major cause behind the derailing of the peace process. Between this chaos and a monarchy, the building of desperately needed infrastructure and roads in Nepal was thwarted—infrastructure that was rapidly being developed in other parts of the world. (However, the Mahendra Highway, also called East-West Highway, that runs along the entire Terai belt in southern Nepal was constructed during King Mahendra's reign.) The Maoists, as the largest party in Nepal, took power after the elections and named Pushpa Prachanda as Prime Minister but the Nepali Congress took the part of the main opposition party. Prachanda fell into a dispute with the army chief Rookmangud Katawal and decided to fire him but President Yadav, as the supreme head of military power, revoked the decision, which angered Prachanda to the extent that he and his party quit the government and decided to operate as the main opposition to the government. Madhav Kumar Nepal was named the Prime Minister. The Maoists demanded civilian supremacy over the army and forced closures—commonly known as *bandhs*—in the country, and declared autonomous states for almost all the ethnic groups in Nepal as a part of revenge against the action that foiled their decision to sack the army chief. Elections were held in November 2013, in which the Nepali Congress won the largest share of the seats in the CA and in February 2014 formed a coalition government with the second place UML (Unified Marxist-Leninist), with Nepali Congress President Sushil Koirala as prime minister.

Political leaders have consistently demonstrated that they have not been able to end the turmoil, and a number of conflicts between police and the public have taken place since 1991. Despite advancements in the political oversight of the country, there has been little improvement in the lives of the people. There are a myriad of special interest groups fighting for specific demands or conditions, which cannot coexist at the same time, creating problems for a government that has repeatedly proven itself to be ineffective, indecisive, and immobilized. That it would take Nepal seven long years to complete the writing of their Constitution, deadlocked over a dispute over Federalism, was outlandish enough; but then to see Nepal's border checkpoints with India blocked was even more preposterous—most of them blocked by Indian border police and customs officials. One of the borders was blocked by activists from Nepal's plains-dwelling Madhesi community, who were unhappy with the country's new constitution.

The political party members who suddenly wanted to rush through the release of the Constitution, because of criticism about the way in which they handled the earthquake aftermath, seemed to ignore the red flags. Many people in the neglected far west of

Nepal and along the southern plains bordering India were not happy with the boundaries of new federal provinces in the draft constitution, arguing that it did not give them representation in proportion to their populations. Seven policemen were lynched by angry protesters on August 24, 2015, and the violence soon spread and escalated. Fifty people were killed in August and September in protests. And yet, the Constitution was passed on September 20, 2015. New Delhi officially denied that it was blocking the border, and a limited number of cargo trucks entered Nepal, but imports of petroleum, medicine, and earthquake relief materials were choked. The country came to a halt, schools were closed, hospitals turned away patients, public transportation was severely limited, industries shut their doors, and tourist arrivals plummeted because 70% of international flights in and out of Kathmandu were cancelled, unable to refuel in Kathmandu. Thus, the swearing in of new Prime Minister, KP Oli, and the passing of the Constitution was celebratory, followed by civil unrest and political turmoil. So typical. It brought the people of Nepal to their knees and posed an even more serious problem than the earthquake. On November 28, 2015, BBC reported that tens of thousands of schoolchildren protested, shouting, "Stop the blockade. Education is our right. We will not bow down to India." They formed a human chain around the Ring Road in Kathmandu. The schools were still closed—a shutdown of longer duration than post-earthquake.

However, despite its tragic and turbulent history, with a fuel blockade waiting to unfold in the near future—as Olivia and her team departed Dhading and headed towards Kathmandu, Olivia gazed out at The Land of Exquisite Beauty, its mountainous landscape covering 75% of Nepal, speckled with gorgeous lavender flowers growing among the trees. She took a moment to make a wish: "May Nepal rebuild better and stronger so the world can still love and enjoy this country and its people—as I have done for the past ten years."

Olivia's team enjoyed a stop along the road where fresh, clean mountain water was streaming down in pipes and bamboo shoots. There was actually an excitement in the air as they unloaded from the truck and saw that a couple of Nepali women had set up to sell bottled water and sliced watermelon and cucumber. One of the women was busy slicing, trying to keep up with the demand, while the other woman collected rupees. The cucumber was not sliced horizontally in small slices but, rather, a long, vertical slice that cut the cucumber in half. Olivia was learning to like cucumbers because of their abundance, and when sprinkled with salt they tasted even better!

A couple of hours later, towards dusk, Olivia and her team decided to make an unplanned stop in a village called Kushal Basi. Olivia often didn't know what was transpiring on runs to the villages because her team spoke in Nepali, the primary language of Nepal. If Olivia didn't ask for a translation from one of them, it wasn't offered to her. She recognized that there was not available manpower to provide her with a constant translation service, and it would have been impossible in the rural areas because at least 93 different languages are spoken in the wide regional variations of Nepal with all the dialects not mutually intelligible; however, Olivia sometimes felt frustrated when she was "out of the loop" and could not understand what was being said, particularly when her team spoke in Nepali but could have spoken in English in her presence. She learned a great deal from this experience because when she was at the monastery or in Thamel, English was the language of choice; thus, she assumed that English was widely spoken; however, in the rural villages, it was rare that anyone spoke English. She wanted to videotape a few interviews with villagers and was surprised to find only one—a passionate, young Nepali boy in his teens—who could speak English fluently enough to communicate with her.

Because Kushal Basi is a village near Kathmandu, it was assumed that they would receive relief assistance; however, in reality, they had been completely overlooked. No assistance had gone to them despite having lost their homes and now living in makeshift tents. It was dark when Olivia and her team arrived, and as soon as the truck stopped, four young boys, about the ages of 9–10, were next to Olivia's partially rolled-down window with their big Nepali smiles, asking her, "What's your name?" Approximately 500 people were forming the longest line of the day, and there was a feeling of desperation in the air. They were hungry. Someone turned on a flashlight and the headlights of a car in order to provide some visibility. This first run was the result of $1,000 in donations that Olivia collected within the first couple of days that she asked for them.

Olivia was soon receiving messages from Nepalis and foreigners who wanted to talk to her about the earthquake or the rebuilding of Nepal. She surmised that Nepalis love to talk, which can impede quick action, forcing Olivia to develop what she called her manta: "My mantra is—I don't talk. I GO." Truthfully, that is all she wanted to do—go where help was needed, without talking about it. Fortunately, she could depend on her team to know where they should go because most of them had been raised in villages and knew the territory firsthand.

Olivia and her team were ready for their second run to Sindhupalchowk, focusing on Syaule of Sindhupalchowk (in the mountains). Food was purchased with another $1,800 in donations. Syaule had also been completely neglected, which is why they went there. En route to Syaule, they made several stops to distribute food, people always lining up in a very organized manner. Colorful clothes hanging out to dry became part of the landscape. Often the clothes hung on a wire or a line of rope strung randomly in the oddest locations; however, clothes were also seen draped on top of fences and other objects. People were frequently seen standing in the rubble of what was once their home. Sometimes they were looking for something. Sometimes they were still trying to perform their daily duties from what once was. One older couple sat on a board in front of their crumbled house—in silence—as if still in shock. Olivia noticed a large piece of plywood in the rubble of their house with the word HELP printed in two-foot tall, black, capital letters. She saw one woman walking at a distance towards them on a dirt road leading to her village—a long walk—a metaphor for what laid ahead. But the children were what stole Olivia's heart.

Olivia never saw one child who was not clean. She did not see one little girl who did not have her hair fixed, often pulled on top of her head in a ponytail or pulled back in pigtails with a rubber band, secured with a colorful ribbon. Many of the girls wore dresses with ruffles. One darling little girl was about two years of age, with short, brown curly hair and huge brown eyes. She wore a silver, metal bangle bracelet on her left wrist, a coral beaded necklace around her neck, and was wearing a pink sleeveless dress with four horizontal rows of ruffles on top. Noticeably, the shoes on her feet that did not match. On her right foot sat a turquoise scrappy sandal that was meant to be worn on the left foot, and on her left foot was an open-toed pink shoe. Olivia was in the Land of Precious Little Girls. Olivia sat with her for a while, simply wanting to hold her, until another young girl, about ten years of age, approached her. This girl had shoulder-length black hair, and wore a long-sleeved, pink cotton blouse with an apple appliqué on the front with the word apple printed underneath. She was pointing while saying, "My home, my home." Olivia saw that she was pointing at the white stucco-like, three-story house sitting behind them—full of cracks and, thus, uninhabitable. Olivia took her hand and they walked back to the house as Olivia took pictures. The little girl seemed proud that it was her home even though she could no longer live there, apparently not realizing what would lie in the days ahead. The home would certainly need to be demolished.

The paved road to Syaule now had a one-foot-wide, deep, rugged crack running down the middle of it as if it was about to split in half—the road they were driving on but the road that these people needed to walk on. Olivia stopped to take pictures of another little girl, beaming with a radiant smile, hands folded in gassho in front of her heart, saying, "Namaste." She wore at least half a dozen plastic, red beaded bangles that hung on each wrist, and red polish was painted on her fingernails. The little girl's mother, purple scarf tied on her head, was standing next to her, beaming with the same kind of adoration and pride that Olivia has seen on the faces of mothers all over the world. "Beautiful," Olivia thought. This area in Sindhupalchowk is what she would always remember as the Land of the Doting Mothers.

Olivia again wrote to her friends and donors: "Yesterday we were in Syaule, which is in the mountains of the Sindhupalchowk district, about four hours northwest of Kathmandu. We did make some food distribution stops in Sindhupalchowk. Syaule village has been completely ignored because of the risk and difficulty in getting there. Yes, several of the guys on our team did have to push the truck part of the way up rugged, dirt roads, but we got there. We had to take an additional cab for five of us because some of our volunteers got sick from riding in the back of an open truck. (There were seven guys that rode in the back of the truck, on bumpy roads, sitting on top of sacks of rice for hours, and one of them was dressed up to the nines in a three-piece suit that ended up being covered in an inch of dirt.) The people were so happy to see us, and the psychological benefit is beyond measure because they are feeling abandoned and forgotten.

However, as we were finishing our food distribution we felt a few drops of rain. Our cab driver had terror in his eyes as he pulled me out of the truck and insisted that I come with him. He was so afraid that he was shaking, and as he drove he kept repeating, 'We shouldn't be here. We shouldn't be here.' He wanted to get past a mountainous area where there was risk of a landslide. The weather turned volatile—thundering and lightning as Nepal has never heard or seen. Hailstone, the size of golf balls, started pounding down, hitting objects with a bounce, which was also unheard of in Nepal. In the downpour I videotaped some footage of us speeding through a muddy road next to a steep, mountainous ridge of dirt that was ready to collapse in a landslide. Later, the rest of my team was upset that the driver grabbed only me and abruptly left but he was terrified; however, THE POINT IS—We left about 2,000 people in the rain with no shelter when we could have taken them tents. We can get 2,000 tents to these people so please, whoever has them—whoever can get them to me—message me. I have received another $1,000 from all of you. We are going to continue to collect donations for the next week, and hopefully we will have a BIG truck when we go out again. Our transportation costs are taking 20% of our donations because we are going to areas that are hours away from Kathmandu. If someone has a jeep or SUV we could use, please message me because it will reduce our costs. But the main thing I want right now is TENTS, and yes, we need food until other relief can get there. I want to mention, also, that there have been 140 aftershocks and other earthquakes since the initial earthquake 14 days ago. It is unbelievable. Arriving into Kathmandu last night we saw candles lit everywhere for the important 13 days of grieving since the passing of so many people. My camera battery was dead, and my cell phone was full but I hope to find and post a picture."

Just days ago, on their return from Dhading, Olivia had seen three men sitting by the side of a road, each dressed in white pants and a white shirt, with a white scarf tied on their heads. They were mourning their mother who had died in the earthquake. Olivia got out of the truck, approached, and talked with them. She was relieved that she did not touch any of them because even if she would have done so accidentally, they would have had to begin their 13 days of mourning over again. As Olivia visited with them, they fought back tears, and once again she felt helpless in wanting to console the inconsolable. So much grief—

so much loss—so much suffering.

Mother's Day found Olivia herself compiling pictures that she had taken of Nepali mothers and their children. "HAPPY MOTHER'S DAY TO THE MOTHERS OF THE WORLD," she wrote. Her own children had created a YouTube video of scenes from the earthquake with Olivia's daughter, Lindsey E. Myer, LEL (2014), singing a song (music) she had written and playing it on guitar. *OM to Nepal*:

OM to Nepal
The earth has shaken
Homes are breaking
People fallin' to their knees
With a plea and a prayer
For grace to shine upon them there
When the light begins to dim
That's when hope lights our flame within.
Let's rebuild, revive, keep your spirit high
[chorus]
om mani padme hum
om mani padme hum
om, om, om
Let love unite us
Joy ignite us
Invite compassion in our hearts
This is where the healing starts
So please share your love and spark
May God be with you till we meet again
May grace shine upon your head
May your joy inside never subside
[chorus]

Olivia couldn't help but think of mothers, not only because it was Mother's Day but because she saw mothers hovering over their children, and whenever she heard a telephone ring, it was usually a Nepalese mother or a mother somewhere in the world calling for assurance that her child was safe. Olivia's mother didn't begin to grasp the situation in Nepal because when boots-on-the-ground Olivia was fundraising, her mother told Olivia that her Methodist Church was raising money for Nepal; thus, she would make a donation to her Methodist Church and even sent Olivia the church bank account information so Olivia could make a donation. Olivia could only shake her head.

The word on the streets in Nepal was that the Nepalese didn't want aid from religious organizations because bags of rice had been received with "Jesus Saves" cards inside, which was another reason for the now increased delay in items being inspected and processed through customs. These deeply spiritual people would not tolerate this kind of invasion or opportunistic Bible-toting proselytizing of vulnerable people in crisis, although Christians comprise nearly 2% of the population now that proselytizing is no longer illegal. There were also at least two reports that during the earthquake, while people were running to safety, two different Christian Pastors who were in two different buildings, one of them a church, told people to remain still and "pray." One of the pastors actually locked the door to the church. Those who did not run—but remained praying—met their demise as the buildings collapsed and killed them—7 people in the first building and 41 people in the church. Nepal was the Land of Spiritual Strength.

AID Organizations. Another problem was that aid organizations, especially in the USA, weren't able to reach the Nepalese people in rural areas who needed assistance *now*. In fact, Olivia sighed when she heard about the millions of dollars that had been given to the American Red Cross when she had only seen two tents on the ground representing the Red Cross, and they were both from China. The Kathmandu airport was receiving an outpouring of goods from around the world that were being stockpiled. Customs couldn't begin to deal with it. The situation was nothing short of a mess, especially once the government got involved.

Dolakha 7.3 Earthquake—Hijacked

Two days later, on May 12 at 12:50pm Nepal was hit with another earthquake—a 7.3 magnitude. Olivia was sitting on the back porch of the hotel—her favorite spot overlooking the garden, where birds are always heard singing and a monkey occasionally drops in. She was working on her computer when the shaking began. Terra-cotta lanterns were swinging above her with a glancing noise when a female waitress, Binu, ran past her for an open, safe area. She glanced over, and when she saw Olivia, she stopped, ran onto the porch, grabbed Olivia's hand and pulled her, saying, "Come... come..." Together, they ran to an open area at the back of the hotel and sat for hours with at least a dozen other people, some of whom were guests at the hotel. Dolakha, one of the districts worst affected by the April 25 earthquake, was affected again, with the epicenter located in the border of Sindhupalchowk and Dolakha districts, which resulted in massive damage, 218 deaths, and over 2,500 injuries. The earthquake was followed by several aftershocks, the largest one being a magnitude of 6.3. [NOTE: In the first month alone, following the April 25 earthquake, there were 270 aftershocks that measured 4.0 or greater on the Richter scale.]

Olivia was still sitting outside with a group of people from her hotel in an open, safe area on May 12, trying to wind down from yet another earthquake, when they heard that six Marines, two Nepalese soldiers, and five injured civilians who were aboard a US Marine helicopter UH-1 "Huey" crashed during a relief mission northeast of Kathmandu. Olivia's heart sank. She understood the urgency of relief aid and the danger because she and her team were also delivering rice and tarps to villagers in remote, rural areas. It took three days to recover their bodies because of treacherous terrain. The helicopter crew had been delivering rice and tarps in Charikot, the area worst hit by

Tuesday's quake. They dropped off supplies and picked up injured civilians, deciding to take the most direct route to Kathmandu in order for them to receive medical care. The terrain was unfamiliar, an investigation later concluding that it was most likely that the aircraft was enveloped by rapidly developing clouds or lifted into a cloud by rising air currents, which probably caused them to lose sight of the ground.

Five days later, on May 17, with over $2,000 in donations used to purchase tarps and with rice, dal, sugar, and oil donated by the Tzu Chi Buddhist Foundation, Taiwan, Olivia and her team traveled six hours to Gaikhor in Gorkha. It was a long and very hot day. They departed Kathmandu at 7:30am and didn't return until 9:30pm. Driving through Kurintar en route to Gaikhor in Gorkha, Olivia noticed banana trees and saw a man with his huge Nepali smile, carrying a large bowl of bananas on his shoulder. Another man carried a big silver bowl of halved cucumbers. Olivia met a medical doctor from San Francisco who was working in the area, providing medical treatment to earthquake victims for ten days. He could not believe how people could lose everything and still have a smile on their faces. He remarked that they are deeply spiritual people. Olivia told him, "They are spiritual practitioners. It is their practice. It is their way of life." It was true; life was going on among the Nepalese, and Olivia remembered all of Nepal, particularly Gorkha, as the Land of the Nepali Smiles.

They passed a suspension bridge and saw a man crossing it with a large, gray umbrella. They came to a bumpy dirt road, and once again, everyone had to help push the truck. They saw more umbrellas. Gaikhor became the area that Olivia remembers as the Land of Colorful Umbrellas because the first people she saw were women holding open red, blue plaid, pink, and green plaid umbrellas above them, as protection from the intense rays of the sun. They were smiling and happy, relieved that they had safely arrived. There weren't roads to some of the villages so many villagers, mostly women, had walked 20–30 minutes from their village to meet them, waiting for an hour under shade trees. Olivia and her team distributed tarps because 90% of the homes in these villages had been destroyed or were uninhabitable. Although many relief agencies were purchasing tarps from out of the country, which would not only take time to arrive in Nepal, but would also get tied up in customs, Olivia found tarps in Nepal and purchased over 200 of them. Her team had a written list of heads of households in each village where they distributed, which is organization to the nth degree. As one of the team members called each family name, a family member would come forward one by one, and Olivia handed them a tarp and other food supplies. This was the most efficient manner of distribution she had ever seen. If supplies are just dropped off to a villager, the supplies get hijacked and are not distributed to all of the people in a fair and equitable manner.

Olivia and her team were then invited to one of the villagers' homes, parking the truck on the main dirt road and hiking up to the house. Olivia immediately saw a sophisticated outdoor bed setup; however, the fabric covering over the bed wasn't waterproof for the approaching monsoon season. It was vitally important that they get tarps to these villagers. Noticeably, Olivia wasn't used to the heat she was experiencing, especially without access to air conditioning. As she sat outside on the ground, a teenage girl carried out a white, 14-inch fan, and with an extension cord ran it into the house so she could turn it on and direct it towards Olivia. "How sweet," Olivia thought, "for her to care like that."

The next day, on May 18, Olivia and her team delivered approximately 700 pounds of food to the Disabled Rehabilitation Center (DRC) for the 55 children, which fed them for three weeks. Olivia had grown to love these children and was so happy to see them again and grateful for the opportunity to inquire about Tufan. He was doing better but still cried when he dreamed about his parents and brothers who died in Langtang. Driving to and from the DRC was an opportunity for Olivia to notice the tents that lined the streets of Kathmandu, mostly comprised of blue, sometimes orange, white, or yellow plastic tarps. In areas where the tents were placed several feet from the road, motorcycles lined the street in front of them. Inside the tents were straw mats and blankets for sleeping. Olivia asked her driver to drive into the grounds of the Hyatt Regency Hotel where as many pitched tents as tarps were seen, set up a little more spaciously. Families with children were sitting outside in groups. Olivia got out of the cab and wandered in the space between some tents and saw an open tent with a man sleeping on blankets, a woman looking at her phone, and a teenage girl sleeping on a mat on the ground in front of the tent. She was using a white terry cloth towel for a pillow. An elderly gray-haired older woman with deeply wrinkled skin sat barefooted on a brick ledge in the yard, saying mantras with her coral mala held in her left hand.

That night, in her hotel room, Olivia had an unusual but foreboding experience. She felt that her maternal grandfather was with her. She had never been particularly close to him but, rather, very close to her maternal grandmother. However, she felt his presence. At first she couldn't begin to understand the why of it but later, after living through the next two days, she understood completely. Her grandfather had a big, humanitarian heart. He was the one member of her family who would identify with what Olivia was doing in her attempts to help earthquake victims in the rural villages of Nepal, and he would have understood why. He was supporting her, protecting her, and more than that, zealously joining her. He had been a volunteer firefighter for 40 years and captain of his fire department in the days when firefighters were all volunteers and not paid a salary. Helping other people and risking his life in crisis situations, even in the middle of the night, was never about money to him. At a young age, he lived through the terror of the disastrous Great Baltimore

Fire in Baltimore, Maryland, on February 7–8, 1904, a fire that burned for over 30 hours in high winds and freezing temperatures, destroying 1,545 buildings and spanning 70 city blocks—over 140 acres; 35,000 people were left unemployed and $150,000,000 in USD 1904 worth of damage was done, which equates to approximately $3.84 billion in 2014 dollars.

We do not realize that in this day of strict fire codes, fires regularly swept through cities, and every city had their own unstandardized system for fighting fires. One reason for the Baltimore fire's 30-hour duration was the lack of national standards in firefighting equipment. Although firefighting crews from outlying cities and states brought their own equipment on horse-drawn pumpers, most could only watch helplessly after discovering that their hoses could not connect to Baltimore's gauge size of water hydrants although there were over 600 sizes and variations of fire hose couplings in the United States. [NOTE: As a result of the Great Baltimore Fire, there was a nationwide standardization of fire hydrants.] This is probably why Olivia's grandfather was always so intent about inspecting fire hoses, fire trucks, and other firefighting equipment when he would take her to firemen's conventions during summer vacation. She had never understood any of his passion for firefighting but she understood now and he was the one family member who wouldn't tell her to get the hell out of Nepal. Instead, he would join her. For the first time in her life, Olivia felt bonded to her grandfather and deeply appreciated what he had lived for—other people.

The following day, May 19, Olivia and some of her team departed for the villages of Chilaumektanka, Pokhare, and Paiti in Dolakha because Dolakha was affected more than any district by the third 7.3 earthquake on May 12 where 240 people died and thousands were injured. They departed from Kathmandu in a jeep and a huge truck carrying over 230 tarps (purchased with $2,300 in donations), and rice, dal, sugar, and oil donated by the Tzu Chi Buddhist Foundation in Taiwan; however, after hours of driving they were faced with deplorable road conditions. In retrospect, this was a helicopter drop area that was inaccessible via the roads. Their contact person in the village had not been honest with them about the road condition, probably because the people were desperate and needed food and supplies; thus, the villagers wanted them to take the risk or at least get as close to their village as possible.

Deval and nine young men volunteered to help with this large relief run. They had hired two drivers, one driving a jeep, and the other, a very large sky blue Eicher truck. Everyone was upbeat and enthused about this much-needed run. They stopped and enjoyed a typical Nepali late morning lunch but soon came upon unspeakable devastation… collapsed buildings on either side of the road with piles of rubble, dirt, rock, boards, bricks, and sheets of galvanized corrugated metal that once were part of a roof. When the debris extended onto the road it made passage through it all quite difficult. Olivia spoke with one woman sitting in the midst of some of that rubble; her newborn baby asleep in a basket, lined with a small blanket. She learned that the earthquake had caused much psychological trauma to pregnant women because there was a belief that an earthquake could cause damage to an unborn child and, thus, birth defects. Unfortunately, counseling for those pregnant women was nearly impossible. What was even more tragic was that counseling was unavailable for the many children who were not in school every day because most of their schools had been destroyed or were uninhabitable. Instead, children sat among the ruins, confused and traumatized. And for the thousands of orphaned children in Nepal, their suffering was intensified without parents. Olivia once asked why there were so many orphaned children in Nepal, knowing that the country had not been hit by a wave of HIV/AIDS. Of course—there had been ten years of civil war with thousands of deaths, and some children had been abandoned by impoverished parents. Olivia liked to wander among the people, talking with them and photographing them, but it did cause Deval to worry about her safety. One time when she wandered off to photograph a mother with her baby, Deval yelled when he found her, "Olivia, you cannot do this!"

After about six hours of driving on bumpy dirt roads, replete with holes and mud puddles, the jeep driver stopped the jeep, stating that he would no longer continue. Several of the volunteers got out of the jeep and truck, and started walking ahead on the road to inspect it. Yes, it looked impossible. They were wondering if they had made a wrong turn, although they were being directed on the phone by a man in their destination village. The jeep driver had been standing on the road—hands on hips—frowning with a disgusted look on his face. He then got into the jeep and turned it around on the road to return to Kathmandu. Five of the volunteers decided to return with him. The remaining five piled into the truck to continue but every few minutes the truck driver would stop the truck and tell them that he would not continue. Olivia pleaded with him. With tears in her eyes, she begged, "We have to get there. This food needs to get to these people. You cannot quit. These are YOUR people." At least 30 minutes transpired. The driver got back into the truck and continued driving but he was trembling, terrified that he would get stuck and/or his truck would get damaged. Finally, he said that he would no longer continue. He was returning to Kathmandu. He told the volunteers to unload the food and supplies onto the ground by the side off the road, which they proceeded to do with the heaviest of hearts.

Olivia's heart sank to an unknown depth. The driver, acting erratically, asked who wanted to return to Kathmandu with him. A couple of the volunteers said that they would return, and one of them tried to persuade Olivia to return, also. No, she would proceed with Deval and Ram. She felt responsible for all of the food and supplies, and Deval didn't want her in the truck. He didn't trust that the driver would drive safely because he was now late for a scheduled medical supply run that he had to make at midnight from Kathmandu.

Once the white sacks of rice, identifiable by a navy blue insignia on front, orange and yellow sacks of dal, yellow plastic tarps, and other supplies were unloaded into a huge pile by the side of the road, Ram covered the heap with one of the yellow tarps. Olivia literally sat on top of the pile as if to guard it, wondering if she would be sitting there for days. She reached into her black Lululemon bag that housed her computer and pulled out a bag of Peanut M&Ms. The only thing better at that moment would have been a box of thin mint Girl Scout Cookies—the perfect deterrent to not thinking about the dire situation in which they found themselves. Deval and Ram were talking on their phones. Soon, their contact person from the village was on the scene with a few other villagers.

Among four villages in the area, there was one man who owned a tractor with a hitch and a trailer, which Olivia called the "tractor cab." The "tractor cab" was on its way. They sat and waited. After about 30 minutes they heard its loud, generator-type noise—a green, 5310 John Deere tractor, pulling an open green trailer, with an orange plastic cover above the driver's seat providing shade. Deval, Ram, and Olivia were elated. There were four older men riding in the trailer, wearing the traditional pointed Nepali hat, and three teenage boys. Once the tractor stopped, they immediately hopped out and began to load the stockpiled supplies into the trailer.

Olivia and Deval sat on the tractor, directly behind the driver, who might as well have been Captain America, Superman, or both but, definitely, the village shining knight who had rescued an American damsel in distress. He appeared to be in his late 30s, wearing a noticeably expensive gold watch on his wrist and a couple of gold rings on his fingers. Ram joined the men and boys who were sitting in the trailer behind them. Deval and Olivia were extremely uncomfortable because the ride was bumpy on a treacherous road, and they were tossed around onto metal supports. All they could do was hold on as tightly as they could to the metal bar nearest them. By now it was beginning to get dark as they crept along. The lights on the tractor dashboard gauges blinked and the headlights shined a few feet onto the dirt road. Otherwise, they were traveling in pitch darkness on terrain that one could never call a road. When they passed a wall of dirt, Olivia knew there was the possibility of a landslide. She had learned as much about landslides as she had learned about earthquakes because they were equally as dangerous. The sound of the tractor was so deafening that Olivia had to yell in order to be heard. "How much longer?" Initially, the tractor driver told Deval one hour and then it was three hours, which Deval communicated to Olivia, translating the information from Nepali to English.

They crept ahead in darkness at a snail's pace. After about 45 minutes the tractor stopped. Large logs lay in the road ahead of them as if they had been placed there. The men and boys riding in the trailer quickly jumped out and moved the logs to the side of the road. They hopped back into the trailer, and the tractor continued to creep forward. But lying ahead were more logs on the road, obstructing their passage. The tractor stopped again, and again, the logs were moved to the side of the road; however, it was now apparent that the logs had been placed there on purpose… "But why?" Olivia thought. Soon she noticed three men on the right side of the road who climbed into the trailer, sitting on top of the supplies. No one seemed to react to this; thus, Olivia believed that the men were joining them in order to help. But very soon she realized that they were not joining them, but rather, were part of a hijacking.

They were being hijacked! Within minutes at least 20 men, nearly half of them in their 20s, were standing in front of the tractor. The driver had no choice but to stop. The men in front of the tractor were soon joined by a few other men and two women, and their crazed behavior began: arguing, screaming, and shouting. Olivia wondered if this was a "Bandh" that she had heard so much about but had never actually witnessed—a term used most often to describe a strike that can be suddenly called at any time, which happens on a frequent basis in Nepal. Some bandhs are quite small and isolated while others grind the entire country to a halt; thus, Nepalis were experienced in staging these kinds of demonstrations. The men were from different villages and fighting about the food and supplies being delivered, believing that one particular village was getting preferential treatment. Ram was running around troubleshooting, trying to communicate with them, telling them that he, Deval, and Olivia did not represent any one village but planned to distribute the supplies at one village for four villages, in a fair manner. Olivia could not understand what they were saying, which only added to the suspense.

It was obvious that the hijackers had been drinking, and many of them were drunk. Olivia had heard about the home brewed alcohol, raksi, usually made from kodo millet (kodo) or rice—a strong drink, clear like vodka or gin, tasting somewhat like Japanese sake, and one didn't have to drink much of it in order to be full-blown over-the-top intoxicated. One young man, approximately 25 years of age, started to climb up onto the tractor where Olivia sat. She feared that he was going to pull her off of the tractor because there was no room for him to sit, stand, or talk to her. For once she hoped that she really did have a protective energy field around her from the gau that she wore around her neck, the melong in her purse, a 7th century piece of protective armor from Tibet that was on her key chain, and a few other items. Regardless, she braced herself, realizing that she could be robbed, raped, murdered, or taken as a hostage. The young man said something to her in Nepali that she didn't understand but then he climbed back down to the ground. Olivia heaved a sigh of relief. The volatile arguing amongst the men continued for at least another 15 minutes until Olivia screamed, "Stop it! Stop it! This is NOT appropriate!" They got quiet and looked at her. Then she said, "If you steal this food, it will be on CNN all over the world." Deval immediately translated what Olivia had said from English to Nepali. Suddenly, the men were coming towards Deval, not realizing that he was simply translating for Olivia. One very muscle-bound young man, consumed with explosive anger, lunged for Deval. Three men grabbed him to restrain him, inches away from Deval. Deval calmly turned to Olivia, as if to prepare her: "They're going to beat me." Olivia looked at Deval, and for the first time she thought that they might actually die together. It was very possible that they were not going to get out of this situation alive.

Instead of feeling the tension and rage around her, Olivia simply felt connected to Deval in an indescribable bond. She quickly learned that Nepalis are extremely sensitive to perceived threat. They thought that Deval had threatened them about CNN but all Deval had done was translate what *Olivia* had said about CNN, and she didn't intend it as a threat but simple fact. Ram was talking nonstop in Nepali and was brilliant in how he got incited men settled down. The men who were restraining the enraged young man from beating Deval were finally able to release him. Then three of them jumped into the trailer, screaming a primitive-sounding victory yell, grabbing bags of rice and lowering them down to villagers who were standing on the ground. Their celebratory war whoops and rebel cries echoed with no language barriers. Olivia clearly understood what was going down, and she was helpless. Deval was relieved that one of their team members, Mriti, from the Kshatriyas rulers and warriors' caste, the caste of the Gurkha warriors, had returned to Kathmandu. "He would have instinctively fought them all, believing he could take them all down but there were too many, and he would have gotten hurt." For Olivia, this suggested that generations of breeding within a specific caste produced characteristics that were in the DNA. No wonder the Gurkha fighters were unstoppable. She appreciated Mriti. He was so solid, buff, and strong that she felt as though he was her bodyguard, and he had protectively wanted her to return to Kathmandu with him—as if he sensed the danger that lay ahead.

Olivia started to cry. She believed at that moment that all of their food and supplies were being stolen by a group of drunken villagers, and who knows what would become of those supplies. The young man who had previously climbed onto the tractor to speak to Olivia now climbed all the way up to where Olivia was sitting. Leaning, a foot in front of her face, he looked at her and said, "Sorry," in English. Then, the hijackers who were standing in front of the tractor and blocking passage moved away and allowed them to continue on the road, leaving most of the food and supplies in the trailer. Olivia once again felt relief. She didn't mind if hungry people stole some of the food, although the manner in which it was done could not have been more outrageous. Notably, the tractor driver was suspiciously calm throughout the entire incident. Perhaps he wasn't Captain America. What if he was Red Skull, instead? What if they had been set up and he was part of its contriving orchestration? Nevertheless, they continued to the village where they had intended to distribute food, arriving at about 1:00am.

They stopped to unload the food and supplies into a storage-type wooden shed with a metal roof. It was too late to distribute; thus, they scheduled distribution for 6am in the morning. Then Deval told Olivia that they would be spending the night at the home of one of the villagers but assured her that it would be okay. Villagers always opened their home to anyone in need. That was not a concern. A young man soon appeared with a flashlight, and Deval, Ram, and Olivia began a trek to what was considered to be the nicest home in the village. The terrain was rugged. Deval had to hold Olivia's hand the entire time, leading her. At times the young man leading Deval would shine his flashlight on slopes that they had to climb. Olivia let out a small scream more than once and wished that she had on her hiking boots instead of sandals. She did not believe they would ever arrive at any home, especially in one piece. Once they did arrive, however, an older couple was cooking food over an open fire. There was a mat on the ground, and Olivia believed it was where they were going to sleep so she laid down, asking Deval if he could find something to cover her feet because they were cold. She was so exhausted that she fell asleep on the mat only to be awakened a short time later after Deval and Ram had eaten dinner—rice and dal that the villagers had prepared. Deval told Olivia that they would be moving to a sleeping area but first one of the young women in the family wanted to show Olivia the outdoor bathroom. As they left the eating area and walked past the family's home, Olivia noticed the massive damage that had been done to the home. The cracks were enormous—she knew the home would have to be demolished.

Once Olivia returned to the cooking area, and with the help of another villager, Deval guided her down a steep dirt area to the family's temporary shelter where she would sleep. She crawled onto a very comfortable double mattress, covered with a Nepalese-made quilt, and immediately fell asleep. She did have to get up in the middle of the night and find her way up the hill to the outdoor bathroom using the flashlight on her iPhone. Middle of the night outdoor bathroom treks were Olivia's dreaded nemesis and always a bit frightening, especially when she needed to do it more than once. She thought she was alone in her sleeping area but when she awakened in the morning, the first thing she saw was a cow outside the open door. Then she realized that everyone in the family was sleeping in the same, but very large room.

The father and grandfather were to the left of her with one of the grandsons (Krishna), about ten years of age, who was visiting from Kathmandu. Olivia had heard stories that five generations of a family were known to live in one home in Nepal, and she was experiencing an overnight stay with three generations in one room. What struck her was that everyone was smiling and happy to be together, even though their home had been destroyed, and they were forced to live in a one-room temporary shed. She experienced an unforgettable feeling of love among family members that she had never experienced before. They were more important to each other than their home, or anything else, for that matter. She had to wonder how an American family would handle such a situation—Americans who cannot tolerate visiting family for two weeks, much less live with them indefinitely in one room. And would any American give up their beds and invite strangers to sleep with them in that room? Perhaps, but not any American that Olivia knew. These villagers acted as though it was a sacred duty not to turn away anyone from their door, and it had become so engrained in their emotional makeup over the generations that they didn't consider discomfort. Rather, it seemed to bolster in them a sense of human dignity.

Deval and Ram were in the corner of the room to her immediate left, and they laughed about trying to talk to Olivia the previous night but she was completely out. She had never experienced exhaustion to the extent that she could literally lie down on the ground and fall asleep. They had also slept in the same clothes they wore the previous day because they had not planned for an overnight stay. Considering the circumstances, they looked presentable for a group picture after they scrambled from the makeshift sleeping room. They hiked up to the storage shed where they had stored their supplies, now visible in the daylight. Olivia could see the narrow path on uneven terrain where they had hiked the night before in the dark, passing a cornfield with stalks about a foot high. Krishna, wearing black pants and a short-sleeved white shirt, walked ahead of Olivia, carrying her black bag on his shoulders. Every once in a while he would stop and turn around to wait for her, smiling. He was a happy child, she thought, and happy that he could be helpful. They soon arrived at the shed in order to distribute food and take more pictures with some of the nearly 100 villagers who were patiently waiting for them. They were concerned about how they would get back to Kathmandu and were told that the "tractor cab" would pick them up and give them a ride to a transportation center a couple of hours away where they could take a bus back to Kathmandu.

Ram, Deval, and Olivia quickly started a brisk walk down the main village road to where the "tractor cab" was supposed to meet them. It was now that Olivia could see a view of the village. It was truly mountainous; the reddish-looking dirt road ahead of them carved into a one-lane passage, winding uphill in front of them. What appeared to be pine trees were everywhere, and there was a cleanliness to the air and a stillness that she had never experienced before. She could understand why villagers loved their villages. Even when it was more practical for them to move from their destroyed village to relocate and rebuild elsewhere, they did not want to leave their beloved village. A young man walked with them, escorting them while talking on his phone. Olivia looked back and saw a man and a woman standing in the ruins of their house. They passed the village school, built with cinder block, sitting on a hill to the left, demolished. The open public water area lay ahead, two concrete walls about three feet tall on either side of a wall with a large pipe from which water was flowing. A young boy, about eight years of age, was bathing and washing his hair while his father, wearing a purple ball cap, looked on, brushing his teeth. A young teenage boy in a red T-shirt, hand on hip, leaned against an outer wall, where clothes were draped. Olivia noticed a woman in the distance through cornstalks, bent over, working a 10x10 dirt area with a pick; a large straw work basket laid on the ground. In villages you meet families living with no money. They simply live off the land. Nepal was the Land of Poverty and Work Baskets because they were part of the Nepalese scene, always. Olivia never saw a wheelbarrow—only work baskets, often filled with brick and rocks, carried on the back, supported by a strap across the forehead, usually by women. Olivia never dreamed that women could work so hard and endure such hard, physical labor. When wages are earned in Nepal, the GN (gross national) per capita PPP is US $1,500, and nearly half of the population lives below the poverty line.

After about half an hour of walking, the young man on the phone informed Deval that the man with the tractor had another obligation and was not going to give them a ride to the bus station. He had bailed out! Olivia could not believe it. The tractor guy was definitely not a knight in shining armor but possibly a villain, as she had suspected. It was a six-hour bus ride to Kathmandu, and here they were stranded in the middle of nowhere in a remote, mountainous area of Nepal that had just experienced a second earthquake with aftershocks to come. As they walked, they stopped at every home that had a motorcycle. They inquired about possible transportation. Soon, they stopped at a small village where food was being cooked, and a wonderful meal was prepared for them. Chickens were running everywhere. Olivia actually enjoyed sitting there taking pictures, particularly of a little girl sitting on a woven, 3x3 mat that had been placed on the dirt ground. She was happily playing with a couple of aluminum round pots as chickens ran around her.

Time. They were running out of time. The bus would soon be leaving for Kathmandu. They found one young man with a motorcycle who would take Olivia to the bus station but it was not guaranteed that Ram and Deval would get there. Olivia refused to leave them or depart by herself on a motorcycle with a complete stranger. Minutes of agonizing indecision transpired, and then, as if a miracle dropped out of the sky, they heard that a group of relief workers was in the area from Kathmandu to deliver a few tarps to villagers, and they had three empty seats in the back of their SUV for Ram, Deval and Olivia to return to Kathmandu with them in a couple of hours. It was a thrill to see the SUV arrive, which had a Human Appeal sticker on the doors and a sticker of the Nepal flag on the side view mirror. They breathed a sigh of relief. They were going back to Kathmandu; however, they were only driving a matter of minutes before they saw that the road ahead of them had been destroyed by a landslide, and at least a dozen men were placing rocks on the road in order to rebuild it for safe passage.

To the left of the impassable road were two distinct pools of water in a mountainous area; a very narrow passageway stood where the road had once been, and to the right was a steep drop-off to a ravine with a river below. It was a real possibility that they would be unsuccessful in driving on the passageway. Olivia had to close her eyes after she looked down at the steep ravine where they would plummet; however, after a few minutes they were told that they could attempt to creep over the makeshift road, which they did at about 1mph. But that wasn't the end of it. Now they had to drive up and through a river in order to reach the main road. Olivia did not know how they could possibly get through the river in a vehicle but they moved forward until the road back to Kathmandu was in sight. She started to laugh and said, "People go to Disneyland for a ride like this!" The driver then said that he wanted to get the vehicle washed so everyone jumped out. Olivia remained, thinking she would go to the carwash with the driver. However, within moments the driver backed into the river they had crossed, and everyone stood in the river around the SUV throwing water on it. This is what they meant by a carwash! The river was gorgeous, full of large grayish rocks that could be easily seen in the clear water, winding through the mountains.

The remaining drive back to Kathmandu was actually enjoyable although destruction from the earthquake was seen everywhere. They stopped at least half a dozen times on the road to purchase organic cauliflower and greens that were being sold by groups of 2–3 women. They returned to Kathmandu on May 20, nearly 34 hours later. Ram told Olivia that Dolakha meant "double slap," and they had indeed suffered at least a couple of those. True, they had been betrayed, hijacked, and abandoned by some but there was also a wonderful family who had shared a meal and makeshift sleeping quarters with them. Thus, with mixed emotions, Olivia viewed the Dolakha area as The Land of Betrayal and Kindness. As far as Deval's reaction to the betrayal and the fact that he was almost beaten, he said, "No more runs."

Olivia didn't recognize it at the time but it was all beginning to take a toll on her. She was beyond exhausted. She wished she had a secretary to handle the flood of e-mails and messages that she couldn't begin to respond to. She spent hours each day taking pictures, uploading and editing them, and then posting them with descriptive information, often in the middle of the night. She had taken on the role and responsibility of a fundraiser when she wasn't a fundraiser. It simply was not her forte although she wanted to execute the job with perfection. She was also working closely with Janet Bass, Lightning Tree Films, who was producing incredible film footage to promote Olivia's fundraising efforts; however, because of their 12-hour difference in time, it often meant that Olivia had to look at footage in the middle of the night. She was caught in a torrent of social media trying to come up for breath. One day she couldn't stop crying, which was uncharacteristic of her because she's wasn't a crier. The needs of the Nepalese were overwhelming, and Olivia couldn't begin to meet them. She wanted to do more but couldn't. She needed more sleep. She needed her Vitamix blender to blend protein powder, ice, and berries; she needed more of the fuel and nutrition that her body was accustomed to. Deval couldn't have been sensitive to any of this but at the same time she was growing to believe that he had never been taught to recognize the unspoken needs of a woman, especially one who was not Nepali. Or perhaps it was

Nepalese culture or Brahmin caste culture to dismiss the needs of any woman even when they *were* recognized. There was an intimacy language he didn't understand. But then, Deval was dealing with his own kind of stress and grief. After all, this was *his* country and *his* people in the midst of a humanitarian crisis.

On the main road leading to Olivia's hotel, two very tall, four-story brick buildings were on the verge of collapse with only wooden and bamboo stilts propped against them, at an angle from the ground, for support. For three weeks, people had been quickly running past these buildings while holding their breath, observing that the cracks in the walls grew larger, and being very careful not to run into one of the stilts. It was finally due to public pressure that demolition workers began to arrive on the scene, as owners of the buildings threw clothes and other household items from the windows to family members standing on the ground below, waiting to catch them before they hit the ground. The labor crews that arrived, which included women, were usually the poorest of Nepalis who came from villages in order to work for unthinkable wages. Olivia could not believe the risks that these workers would take, one day noticing a woman standing on the second floor of a building near a brick cracked wall that was ready to crumble. Workers began demolishing these homes, brick-by-brick, with shovels and picks in tow. Before the road was blocked off, one young worker called out to Olivia, asking her if he could have some water from the large water bottle she was carrying. She handed it to him, and it is true—you will never see a Nepali touch their mouth to a container they drink from. Whenever he saw Olivia in the following days, he called her "sister." It is common for Nepalis to refer to other Nepalis as brother and sister but foreigners—never. Olivia will always remember that moment because it suggested that she was no longer a foreigner but truly one with the Nepalese people.

Being with Deval was always comfortable for Olivia, but there again, it was as though she had known him for eons of time. He was often always willing to go along with whatever she wanted to do and enjoyed himself. At any moment she could say, "Let's dance," and he'd be on his feet. He didn't know how to dance so she taught him the box step, and they were working on the waltz. When she told him that her fantasy was to do the Argentine tango with him, he didn't respond. Obviously, he didn't know anything about ballroom dancing and didn't know what he was getting himself into! They had also purchased the Nepalese two-player board game Bagh-Chal, meaning "Tiger game." However, Olivia called the game "goats and tigers." It is a strategic offensive-defensive game, asymmetric in that one player controls four tigers and the other player controls up to twenty goats. The tigers "hunt" the goats while the goats attempt to block the tigers' movements. Every time they played, Olivia became more adept. It seemed that because Deval was raised in a third world country village, the simplest things left him contented, and he knew how to roll with everyday life, as if there was never a set expectation; however, Olivia was always amused at his limited world experience. One night at dinner when she asked him if he was going to order a glass of wine, he said, "I've never had a hard drink... only a soft drink." She couldn't stop laughing, probably because of what she had gone through with Chris's alcoholism; thus, soft drinks it was, and that was more than okay with her. It was difficult for Olivia to admit that Chris was an alcoholic, despite the genetic component. His brother had died from an alcohol-related death.

Olivia and Deval spent time at Olivia's favorite neoclassical Garden of Dreams, an oasis of tranquility in the central hub of busy Kathmandu, also known as the Garden of Six Seasons. The six seasons of Nepal are represented by six exquisite pavilions in the garden, meticulously landscaped with flowers, shrubs, and trees. The garden was created for the late Field Marshal Kaiser Sumsher Rana (1892–1964) in early 1920, and although massive at 6,895 sq. meters, only half of the original garden remains. After the completion of this garden, it was considered one of the most sophisticated private gardens of that time. Olivia was eager to see how much damage the garden sustained in the earthquake and was relieved that she and Deval could still sit on benches and enjoy the sounds of running fountains, especially in the centrally located breathtaking lotus pond. The long pond has a large, black fountain near each rounded end and is filled with beautiful pink lotus flowers. She and Deval watched in interest as the gardener meticulously groomed and thinned out the lotuses, and Deval waited patiently while Olivia took pictures of every single flower in the garden; however, sadly, there was structural damage to some of the pavilions, fountains, decorative garden furniture, and European inspired features such as verandas, pergolas, balustrades, urns (Olivia noticed one that was completely missing off of its wall, presumably because it was destroyed), and birdhouses; thus, there were areas roped off, restricted to the public.

The Garden was beautifully designed and inspired in the famous Edwardian style by Kishore Narshingh, a prominent architect. After the death of Kaiser Sumsher, the garden was given to the Government of Nepal but was not properly managed for decades. The Austrian Government financed seven years of extensive renovation in order to revive the garden as per the original concept with added modern facilities. One of those facilities is a wonderful outdoor restaurant where she and Deval ate lunch and then wandered to a bench near the amphitheater. They sat there for so long that they called it "their" bench.

Magical Pokhara

There were rumors circulating that Nepal was bracing for another earthquake, and since Thamel and Kathmandu were the most dangerous places to be during an earthquake—because of its population and densely situated buildings—Deval suggested that this was the ideal time to travel to Pokhara (124 miles west of Kathmandu) for a few days in order to ensure greater safety. There was no doubt about it. Olivia was exhausted and drained on all levels. Her days and nights had been long with little sleep. That they had wanted to spend a few days together, away from the devastation of the earthquake and its aftermath, sounded wise. No one could believe that Olivia had visited Nepal for ten years but had never been to Pokhara, known as Nepal's tourist center of adventure. Fortunately, although an enigmatic quandary to scientists, Pokhara did not feel the effects of the April 25 earthquake nor the additional earthquakes and aftershocks. There was no damage and destruction in Pokhara. Olivia had to see it to believe it.

Deval flagged a cab while Olivia waited around the corner, as per Deval's instructions. They found that a cab driver would charge 1/3 less if Deval bartered with him without flashy American Olivia on the scene, which would result in the cost being significantly escalated. They found this was true regardless of what the bartering situation was; i.e., Deval could purchase two T-shirts for $6.00, and one of those T-shirts would cost Olivia $10.00. The price differential increasingly disturbed Deval; however, once in a cab, they traveled to a transportation hub where bus tickets and tickets for other modes of transportation were purchased. Although there is no air conditioning in a minivan, Deval said that the trip would be more economical, faster, and safer than a tour bus. Over the years, Olivia had seen many large trucks and buses turned on their side on the narrow, winding roads in Nepal, and saw one bus plummet over a guardrail into a river; thus, she did feel safer in a minivan. Since a minivan to Pokhara pulled up at the hub about every 20 minutes, they were able to secure two front seat spots for a six-hour trip to Pokhara. Olivia noticed vehicle windows that were decorated with stickers, promoting the tourism industry in Nepal that officially started in 1950—the tourism industry that keeps the country alive. It was common to see a large sticker on a van with hands folded in gassho with the word WELCOME written underneath or two crossed Gurkha knives, symbolic of the famous Nepalese Gurkha Army. It was also common to see the flag of Nepal, not only in tourism shops but displayed by the Nepalese, who are fiercely proud of their country. Most notably, it is the only flag in the world that is not rectangular. The crimson red is Nepal's national color, which indicates the brave spirit of the Nepalese people and the blood that has been shed defending Nepal. Nepal is the only country that has never been under the control of another country, due in part because of their renowned Gurkha Army, which could not be defeated even by Britain.

Historically, before the creation of the Nepal State, the kingdom of Gorkha had a powerful military called Gurkhall. The Britsh were so impressed by Gorkhas in the Anglo-Nepal War of 1814–16, and after suffering heavy casualties and defeat, the British East India Company signed a hasty peace deal in 1815, which allowed it to recruit Gorkhas into the British Indian Army. Alongside the British Army, Gorkhas, now referred to as Gurkhas, fought in wars all over the world. More than 200,000 Gurkhas fought in World War I and II, and 43,000 of them lost their lives. Following India's Independence from Britain, six out of 10 Gurkha regiments joined the Indian Army and the remaining regiments joined the British Army. Out of the 30,000 Gurkhas in seven Gurkha regiments of the Indian Army, 70% are from Nepal. The Gurkha Regiment has won 28 Victoria Crosses so far, UK's highest military award, and have also won three

Param Vir Chakras, India's highest military award. It has been said that if a man is not afraid of dying, he is either lying or he's a Gurkha. They still carry their traditional weapon, an 18″ kukri knife, and they adhere to their Nepalese customs and beliefs.

The blue border on Nepal's flag symbolizes peace and harmony. The two triangles symbolize the Himalaya Mountains and could also represent the two major religions, Hinduism and Buddhism. The red triangular flag has been a Hindu symbol of victory since the time of Ramayana and Mahabharata. The depiction of celestial bodies (sun and moon) represents permanence, the hope that Nepal will last as long as the sun and the moon. Another interpretation is that as long as the sun and moon are in the sky, Nepal will remain independent. The moon symbolizes that the Nepalese are soothing and calm, while the sun symbolizes fierce resolve. The moon also symbolizes the shades and the cool weather of the Himalayas, whereas the sun symbolizes the heat and the high temperature at the lower part (Terai) of Nepal. Another interpretation: The flag's shape could also symbolize a Nepalese pagoda as noted by local Nepalese, because placing a mirror at the side of the flag closest to the flagpole will generate an image of a pagoda. The flag of Nepal will always remind Olivia of the Nepal that she loves.

The men in Nepal whose occupation is to drive individuals, and often on treacherous roads, have countless hours of experience. They know the territory. Olivia told several of them that they really could be NASCAR drivers in the USA! The best driver she had ever hired and the most harrowing experience she had ever had was just months ago when her flight from the Gautam Buddha International Airport in Bhairahawa, 14 miles from Lumbini, Nepal (the birthplace of the Buddha

Shakyamuni) to Kathmandu was cancelled because of heavy smog. Olivia sat in the Lumbini airport for three hours before the call was made by airport officials: the smog was not going to lift. As a result, Olivia needed to take a cab back to the travel agent that had issued her plane ticket and then plan accordingly. She found that the hotel where she had been staying was now full, and the buses to Kathmandu, where she needed to be the next day, were also full. Thus, at 4:00pm in the afternoon a 19-year-old young man who drove for the travel agency offered to drive Olivia to Kathmandu in the smog on treacherous, narrow, winding roads, mostly in the dark with visibility that was nonexistent. Olivia was spellbound by the driving skills he demonstrated in the most precarious navigational situations. He could brake, swerve, and dodge like nothing she had ever seen, and it proved to be one of the most dangerous situations Olivia had ever been in. They arrived in Kathmandu nine hours later, stopping once in order to eat dinner. She believed that her driver was driving to a friend's house to spend the night but discovered the next day that after they parted he simply locked the doors to the car and slept for four hours, driving another eight hours back to Lumbini. His salary, per month, was approximately $60.00 (US).

En route to Pokhara, Deval and Olivia would change places in the front seat whenever a stop was made because sitting next to the rolled-down window provided some relief from the heat. They drove over the spectacular Seti River, its shallow water dotted with gray rocks and boulders, because the rainy monsoon season had not arrived. Pokhara was known to have the most rainfall in Nepal; thus, it was not surprising that upon approaching Pokhara, the landscape was speckled with haystacks elevated off of the ground by at least two feet, in order that the hay would not rot on rain-soaked ground. Not surprisingly, then, upon arrival in Pokhara, there was a downpour of rain with wind that made driving difficult for the driver. Olivia attempted to videotape banana trees dancing in the wind, ready to snap in half. Soon they arrived at another transportation hub and sought shelter while Deval quickly found a cab that took them to a hotel, located with a view of not only Fishtail Mountain (Machhapuchhre) and the Annapurna Himalayan Range, but a view of the famous Phewa Lake that holds 22 native species of fish.

The Cattle Egret bird. Olivia loved photographing this beautiful and unusual looking white, long-necked bird, approximately two feet in height, with tan feathers on its head, neck, and body during breeding season, and a long, narrow yellow beak. She and Deval were preparing to hike to the Pokhara Shanti (Peace) Stupa, a white Buddhist pagoda-style monument prominently displayed and surrounded by trees on a hilltop in the Ananda hill of Pumdi Bhumdi Village Development Committee, district of Kaski. They were told that there were three different routes to the stupa, but chose to take a cab part of the way and then climbed the many steps that led to the entrance of the stupa grounds. From there, the view of Phewa Lake was breathtaking, the lake appearing almost as a crater full of water surrounded by mountains, lush green foliage, and lavender flowers. There was repair work being done on the stupa, not because of the April 25 earthquake but, rather, a landslide in August 2014. Although there were large SILENCE signs stationed at the entrance, a woman was sitting on one of the steps of the stupa to inform visitors that they should not linger on the site because of its need of repair and instability; therefore, Olivia and Deval quickly climbed the stairs to the stupa, walked around it taking pictures of stunning gold Buddha statues placed in inlays, and made a quick exit.

On the way down to the parking lot, they stopped to take pictures with a holy man, a Sadhu, which means "good man." It is impossible to come to this part of the world and not occasionally see one of these unusual looking men; thus, it is prudent to know that a Sadhu is one who renounces all material attachments and chooses to live in caves, forests, or temples. They may also choose to live on the outskirts of society in order to focus on their spiritual practices and reach liberation, the final stage of life. This Sadhu, with a white beard and white hairline showing from an orange wrap around his head, also wore an orange cotton shirt, an orange wrapped skirt that fell past his knees, and sandals. A six-inch metal bucket full of donations was hanging below his waist by an orange scarf that was placed under the handle and wrapped around his neck. A black bag hung from his left shoulder, and a yoga mat was rolled and carried on his back. His hands were folded in gassho, holding a small bouquet of golden daisies and red flowers between his fingers. His front teeth were missing, as well as some other teeth.

A religious Hindu sign, a red mark (Tilak), was prominent at the Sadhu's Ajna Chakra between his eyebrows at the third eye (considered to be the spiritual eye). Worn by a priest, ascetic, or worshiper it shows which Hindu tradition one follows. The pastes are applied to the forehead and in some cases to the upper part of the head by hand or with a metal stamp, made with a variety of methods: using ash from a sacrificial fire (vibhuti), kumkum, sindhoor, sandalwood, paste, turmeric, cow dung, clay, charcoal, or red lead, and have not only spiritual but health benefits since it is located at the pineal gland; mystical traditions and esoteric schools have long known this area in the middle of the brain to be the connecting link between the physical and spiritual worlds. On a spiritual note, the color red is known to help retain the positive energy of the body and it is believed that it has the capability to keep you strong, healthy and positive throughout the day. A mark that is a decoration at the third eye, which could include jewelry, is called a bindi, whereas a red mark at the hairline of a woman is a tilak (a form of bindi) and indicates that she is married and not widowed.

Olivia and Deval saw a small restaurant where they ordered a soft drink and sat at a balcony area with a majestic, panoramic view of Phewa Lake. They browsed through a touristy shop where Olivia wanted to purchase a black, broken in half stone displaying a fossil—an ammonite, an extinct group of marine invertebrate animals that lived as long 175 millions of years ago. Deval didn't want her to purchase it, claiming that it was not a fossil, and he would find one for her that wasn't broken. She gave up on the "But, it's a fossil... I know a fossil when I see a fossil." "No, it's not" argument. However, she later did her research. A shaligram or saligram is a fossilized shell used in South Asia as an aniconic symbol and reminder of god Vishnu as the Universal Principle by some Hindus. The saligrams are collected only from the Gandak River in north Nepal, which Deval had mentioned. It is considered easy to carry and popular in certain traditions of Vaishnavism, as an aniconic representation of the divine, typically in the form of a spherical, usually black-colored ammonoid fossil; however, Hindus do not see them as "fossils" but as a representation of Vishnu; thus, the use of Saligrama in the worship of Vishnu has been a well-known Hindu practice; thus, they only want whole stones rather than ones that have been broken open. Simply put, Deval did not want Olivia to purchase the fossil because of her perception that it was a fossil. She later discovered that if she wanted a whole stone, short of going to the Gandak River, she could go to the Hindu Pashupatinath Temple.

Olivia also discovered that Shiva worshipers use nearly round or oval shaped saligrams to worship as Shiva Lingam. They are sometimes referred to as Shilas, with Shila being the shortened version. They are one of the most sacred stones of the ancient as well as the modern worlds, found only in the Narmada River in the Central Western part of India, a holy site for Hindus. In the movie *Indiana Jones and the Temple of Doom*, this is the sacred stone that the characters were desperately searching for! Accessible only during the dry season, these stones are collected from the riverbed by only a few families who have been trained to identify only the most special pieces. Once collected, these incredible artisans finally shape and polish the stones to bring out the natural markings which are inherent in their composition, much like a diamond cutter who cuts the rough material to bring out the best in the diamond; however, they are processed according to ancient Vedic tradition that has been passed down from one generation to another from Guru to disciple. The lingam is symbolic of the Divine Creative manifestation, and its shape is representative of the power of Shiva, the lord of creation, the masculine creative energy. The markings, known as the yoni, symbolize the feminine energy, the seed which is fertilized to manifest the creative power in the dance of the cosmos. Geologists theorize that the iron oxide of which the yoni is composed was impregnated in the riverbed millions of years ago by a meteorite. The quartz composition, along with basalt and agate, and the shape make them powerful energy generations appropriate for healing and unique tools for meditation and cleansing.

The nostalgic Devi's Falls was their next stop, a roaring waterfall that marks the point where the Pardi Khola stream vanishes underground. When the stream is at full bore after monsoon rains, the sound of the water plunging over the falls is deafening; however, because they were visiting prior to the monsoon season, the water was unusually low. The history of the falls includes the fact that a Swiss woman by the name of Mrs. Davis was with her husband at the falls, but fell and died on July 31, 1961. With great difficulty her body was recovered, and since then the falls have been called Davis Falls. Deval had seen the falls before and wasn't too interested in them, spending most of his time on his cell phone. He spent a lot of time on his cell phone, to the extent that his phone wasn't holding a charge for very long. Olivia believed in selective cell phone use and would avoid the use of them when she was with someone. If Earl Nightingale was correct in saying that the key to success was to make every person feel as though they are the most important person in the world, perhaps it was also true that the best way to make someone feel unimportant is to live on your cell phone in their presence.

After Olivia and Deval drank coffee and ate pastries at a German bakery, they enjoyed authentic Nepali food (dhindo instead of rice) at the Thakali Kitchen Restaurant. She kept her paper placemat that had a few Nepali conversational words written on it, which motivated Olivia to learn every single word before taking on the entire Nepali language. Perhaps she didn't need to be embarrassed for the rest of her life that she was like most Americans who only spoke one language; however, after mastering the greeting of Namaste and goodnight (shubha raatri), the Nepali language was put on her bucket list. Regardless, Deval ate at least two huge platefuls of white rice every day, a staple in the Nepalese diet; thus, Olivia was pleasantly surprised that he liked the pizza she ordered-in at the hotel. He also liked Mexican food and loved Caesar salad. Every morning they hiked up four flights of stairs to the roof of the hotel where breakfast was served—coffee, juice, toast with butter and jam, fresh fruit, and potatoes—as they looked straight ahead at Fishtail Mountain. Olivia had seen many pictures of this mountain over the years, nicknamed Fishtail because the two peaks at the top of the mountain did indeed appear to be a fishtail. For it to be in front of them, seemingly within their reach, felt like a dream-come-true moment. They also overlooked a spectacular view of Pokhara's colorful buildings dotting the mountainous landscape.

However, experiencing breathtakingly beautiful Phewa Lake, with those famous, colorfully painted row-boats parked near the banks, was a highlight of their stay in Pokhara. One of those boats can be rented for the entire day for 850 rupees (USD 8.50), and Deval wanted to do this. Olivia thought it would be a good idea to hire someone to row them on the lake but no, he wanted to do it all by himself. She warned him that she would be holding an umbrella, and wouldn't be able to row but he was determined. They buckled-up their lifejackets, stepped into the middle of the royal blue boat that was selected for them, and after Olivia sat down in the middle he sat down in the back and began to row. "Haven't you seen *The Notebook*?" he smiled. He first rowed them on a straight path to Baal Barahi Temple that is on a little island in the middle of Lake Phewa. Olivia couldn't resist buying birdseed to feed the birds while Deval entered the temple to complete some Hindu spiritual rituals. He acted annoyed and dismissive when she asked about what he was doing, and he never, ever discussed Hinduism with her.

Gingerly stepping into their boat again, Deval began paddling to Fishtail Lodge for lunch, a popular spot for the previous Royal Family. They passed fishermen standing along the banks with fishing poles. Olivia loved listening to the birds and crickets and recorded their sounds as Deval rowed in silence. He was beginning to get tired, and Olivia did try to help with the rowing but it was quite impossible while holding an umbrella, as she had predicted. Once they arrived at Fishtail Lodge, Deval had some difficulty parking the boat and needed assistance from a security guard; however, once out of the boat, they walked up a few steps, past stacks of kayaks, and entered a Shangri-La of a resort. The landscape was immaculately groomed with flowers and plants. After lunch, they toured the grounds, and Deval experienced his first hammock made with tan rope in a loose, open weave, tied to and hanging between two trees. He laid in it and laughed until his body shook, saying it was like a baby's cradle.

The journey paddling back to the boat dock where they needed to return the boat was magical. It felt as though they were lost on the lake all by themselves because there were few boats out and only one of them passed their way—a woman who was clearly skilled at paddling while a passenger sat, enjoying himself. Deval's shoulder and back muscles were getting sore. He would stop rowing, lay the paddle across his thighs, and ask, "What do you say?" Olivia would respond, "I love you, Deval." He would start rowing again, dipping the oar into the river outside the right side of the boat, pulling the oar backwards through the water, then lifting it out of the water and switching the same moment to the other side. After a couple of minutes he would stop rowing and ask, "What do you say?" She replied, "I love you, Deval." And thus it continued for about an hour, their words couched in the sound of Deval's oar being pulled through water, propelling them forward—until they reached the dock. Again, they snapped pictures, and started their 10-minute trek back to the hotel.

Their final morning in Pokhara was one last opportunity for Olivia to sit in stillness in a corner of the deck on the rooftop of the hotel, the warmth of the sun showering her face as she gazed straight ahead at the snow-covered Fishtail Mountain. At 22,943 feet it is considerably less tall than Mt. Everest, but definitely in illustrious company, stuck in the middle of the Annapurna Range of mountains. This morning there was moderate visibility—the best she had seen—since October, not May, is the optimal month for viewing mountains in clear skies. She sat there, one last time, in reverent awe of them, knowing she would soon depart. And then—astonishingly—Fishtail pierced through the smoggy haze, emerging as if painted on canvas. "Here I am," the mountain seemed to say. It reminded her of when she was in the freezing Mt. Everest region, believing she truly might not live until morning. In the middle of the night, she struggled out of two sleeping bags, unzipped the tent in order to find her way to the tent toilet, stepped out, and there in front of her, as though they were within her reach, were the Big and Little Dippers that she would search for when she was a child. The same surge of joy she felt then, which made her forget her discomfort, is the same surge of joy she felt now—as if the entire universe was with her—supporting her—understanding her. Not to her surprise, Olivia later learned that Fishtail Mountain is a sacred peak in the Hindu religion, associated with the god Lord Shiva, who is believed to live on the peak. As one of the last places on earth where human beings had never set foot, naturally Fishtail was a target for Western mountaineers, particularly the British, who had conquered Mt. Everest in 1953. In fact, it was a member of that expedition, Wilfrid Noyce, who came the closest to the summit on a 1957 expedition. The king of Nepal had asked Noyce to respect Hindu religious customs and not set foot on the summit; thus, he and his climbing companion, ADM Cox, turned back 150 feet short of the summit. This expedition produced the only climbing record of this mountain, a very rare book called *Climbing the Fish's Tail*.

Deval soon joined Olivia for breakfast but, understandably, wasn't nearly as captivated by the presence of Fishtail. After all, he was Nepalese and seeing Fishtail was an opportunity he had experienced many times over the years. She never heard him talk about the Himalayas or yearn to step foot on them, characteristic of Nepalis who do not trek or work in the tourism business. But Nepalis could not live without feeling the sacredness of these mountains, whether they realized it or not. They ate breakfast together in silence—she drank black coffee, and he, milk coffee. Then they posed for pictures and prepared to depart in a cab to the transportation hub for their minivan trip back to Kathmandu. Olivia wanted to visit the seven UNESCO World Heritage Sites that she had grown to love over the years, located in Kathmandu and the Kathmandu Valley: Irina Bokova, the Director-General of UNESCO had released a statement on April 27: "As we are receiving more information from the ground, I am deeply aggrieved by the magnitude of human loss caused by the earthquake in Nepal. I am also shocked by its devastating impact on the unique cultural heritage in the country, in particular extensive and irreversible damage at the World Heritage site of Kathmandu Valley." According to UNESCO's preliminary assessment on the ground, the monuments and sites within the Kathmandu Valley World Heritage property, as well as several other cultural and natural heritage sites located in the area, had been heavily affected. In particular, Durbar Squares of Patan, Hanuman Dhoka (Kathmandu) and Bhaktapur are almost fully destroyed. The seven UNESCO sites included the Durbar Squares of Kathmandu, Patan, and Bhaktapur, the Buddhist stupas of Swayambhunath and Boudhanath, and the Hindu temples of Pashupatinath and 3rd century Changu Narayan.

Part IV

Dark Clouds

Olivia visited what remained of the nine-story, 203-foot Dharahara or Bhimsen Tower in Kathmandu, a civic icon and lighthouse-like structure that collapsed during the Gorkha earthquake, killing at least 230 people. More people died at that site than at any other location in Nepal. It was convenient for Olivia to visit the Dharahara Tower because it was located next to the post office where she needed to pick up a box of flip-flop sandals that one of her donors from New Jersey had shipped for earthquake survivors. After a long, six-step process at the post office, which involved paying customs fees and the sandals being dumped onto a counter for inspection, Olivia walked across the street to what was once the historic Dharahara Tower. A tall red sign, depicting the white tower as it appeared before the earthquake, was framed in a black metal frame and stood near the entrance of the site that was now closed to the public. The tower was reduced to its base, a stump of tan-colored brick, approximately 33 feet in height. Tragically, at least 100 people were on the tower when it collapsed during the earthquake. Rescue workers were seen retrieving bodies from the debris as people on the spot desperately tried to dig through piles of bricks and dust with their bare hands.

The Dharahara or Bhimsen Tower was originally built in 1832 by Prime Minister of Nepal Bhimsen Thapa in a Mughal and European style, and then rebuilt following the 1934 earthquake. It was originally constructed for military use as a watchtower. When incidents of national importance occurred, bugles were blown from the top floor of the tower, a signal for soldiers to assemble. This tradition of bugle trumpeting continued until the first collapse of the tower in 1934. Olivia had never climbed the 200+ step spiral staircase of the white tower, topped with a bronze minaret and small statue of Lord Shiva, although it was a major tourist attraction. It had offered panoramic views of the Kathmandu Valley from the top of the minaret observation deck. Durbar Square, "place of palaces," refers to the places of Nepal's historical royal palaces, as Nepal was once a land that consisted of many small kingdoms; thus, Durbar Squares are exquisite examples of ancient kingdom lifestyle, and one is truly transported back in time while visiting them. Temples, idols, statues, open courts, and fountains along with other structures form part of Durbar Squares that have been witness to events of importance, including coronations of kings of the land. The three Durbar Squares in Nepal are Kathmandu (Basantapur) Durbar Square, Patan Durbar Square, and Bhaktapur Durbar Square, three of the seven landmarks in the area declared by UNESCO as World Heritage Sites. According to UNESCO, "the architecture which was developed over the past two millennia boasts of one of the most highly developed craftsmanship of brick, stone, timber and bronze in the world." They have also vividly showcased the skills of the Newar artists and craftsmen over several centuries. Thus, Nepal is truly a Land of Ancient Art and History, including Kathmandu being described in its traditional myths and legends. According to Swayambhu Purana, present-day Kathmandu was once a lake, drained by Manjushri, the Buddha of Wisdom, who established a city called Manjupattan and made Dharmakar the ruler of the land. Regardless, artifacts dating back 2,000 years have been unearthed by archaeologists and preserved.

This preserved history is one reason why it was so tragic to see massively damaged monuments and temples roped off and restricted to the public because of the danger that many of them could collapse at any moment. Wooden beams on the ground, propped against many of the structures at an angle, hoping to give them support, were now part of the landscape. An example of one of the saddest losses was at the Kathmandu Durbar Square, the home of Nepal's Royal Family until the 19th century, a complex of 50 temples, distributed in two quadrangles and representing the four kingdoms of Kantipur, Lalitpur, Bhaktapur, and Kirtipur. Several temples, including Kasthamandap, Panchtale temple, the nine-story Basantapur Durbar, the Dasa Avtar temple, Krishna Mandir and two dewals located behind the Shiva Parvati temple, were demolished by the earthquake. The city of Kathmandu was actually named after Kasthamandap temple, which stood in the Kathmandu Durbar Square before it collapsed in the earthquake. In Sanskrit, Kastha (काष्ठ) means "wood" and Mandap (मण्डप) means "covered shelter." This temple, also known as Maru Satal (in "Newar language"), was built in 1596 by King Laxmi Narsingh Malla. The two-story structure was made entirely of wood, and used no iron nails nor supports. According to legend, all the timber used to build the pagoda was obtained from a single tree.

Olivia snapped pictures of the temples and other structures at all of the Durbar Squares, suspecting that many of them wouldn't remain standing for much longer. She had a feeling of gratitude in her heart for these magnificent monuments, truly an enormous treasure house of art and sculptures, made of wood, stone, metal, and terra-cotta, replete with sacred history, while at the same time sadly saying goodbye. She stood in front of a stone structure in the Patan Durbar Square, believing it was the most breath-taking, exquisite piece of stone architecture in the entire world. She said goodbye—and in letting go, she felt the suffering of her attachment to it, realizing that it was more of the same. The Law of Impermanence does stare us in the face, and all extrinsic phenomena are temporary. Fortunately, the recently restored Sundari Chowk (courtyard), and the most important temple in the Durbar Square, the Krishna Mandir, survived. However, many smaller pagoda temples collapsed.

Walking through the narrow streets of Patan to see the Golden Temple (Hiranya Varna Mahavihar), a Newari Buddhist monastery, built in the 12th century by Vaskar Deva Varma, was not new to Olivia. She was relieved to see that it did not sustain damage in the earthquake; however, hidden away in the middle of the city, it was dangerous getting there, and Deval did not appreciate her dragging him there. He had actually never seen the Golden Temple. The very narrow streets were lined with beams supporting the walls of tall, thin buildings, standing cheek to jowl on the verge of collapse, which meant there was nowhere to run to safety. In attempting to find the Golden Temple (many come across it by accident) an identifying landmark is the two large lions in front of the ornately carved oval, wooden entrance gate. The nickname "Golden Temple" actually arose from tourism, more than the temple actually being made of pure gold. Instead, most of the temple and its doors are actually polished brass but a stunning sight to see, especially the two large brass guardian elephants and riders at the entrance. The main shrine (directly behind the smaller one) contains a statue of Buddha Shakyamuni. The prayer wheels and the detailed quality of bronze and silver work in and on the temple are amazing. Olivia was glad that they didn't forget to look up on their way out to see the Dharmadhatu Mandala, and Deval finally understood its significance, regretting that he had asked her, "Why are we here?"

A sprawling temple complex that was once home to royalty, Bhaktapur Durbar Square originally boasted 99 courtyards; however, it was severely damaged by the 8.0-magnitude earthquake that hit Nepal in 1934, leaving only six of the original courtyards, now damaged by yet another earthquake 81 years later. Bhaktapur, 12 miles east of Kathmandu, is the smallest of the three valley cities, but was the capital of the Malla Kingdom until the 15th century. The area actually consists of four squares: the durbar square; the Taumadi with its two main temples, the Nyatapola and the Kasi Biswanath; Dattatreya Square and Pottery Square. The Bhaktapur Durbar Square is where Olivia saw the strongest police and Nepalese Army presence, not only restricting areas to the public but protecting its treasures from possible theft. Eighty percent of the temples were destroyed in the earthquake, including the 18th century Vatsala Durga temple, a towering sandstone structure that evoked the peaks surrounding the city.

However, of all of the seven UNESCO Sites, Olivia also appreciated 5th century Boudhanath (Boudha) Stupa, six miles from Kathmandu, which sustained little damage during the earthquake. Olivia observed scaffolding around the spire to repair cracks, and the walkway around the stupa was being replaced. Because of its historical significance to Tibetan Buddhism, it is surrounded by more than 50 Tibetan monasteries and the home of thousands of Tibetan refugees in exile. Tibetans live a precarious existence in Nepal, particularly in Kathmandu and at Boudha, where the Nepalese authorities are under intense pressure from the Chinese government to curb Tibetan activities. In 2012 surveillance cameras were installed at Boudha after a monk attempted to self-immolate there the previous year. However, on August 6, 2013, a monk named Karma Ngedon Gyatso set himself on fire and died shortly thereafter. It was the second fatal self-immolation that year by a Tibetan monk. Drupchen Tsering set himself on fire on February 13, 2013, also at the Boudha. These events saddened Olivia for several reasons—the loss of life, the family and friends who grieved, and the people who were traumatized from witnessing such horror. It also meant increased security and surveillance at Boudha, which the Tibetans did not need.

Om Mani Peme Hung. Olivia had countless memories of Boudha: seeing innumerable Tibetan refugees, hearing the song *Om Mani Peme Hung* from the CD *Tibetan Incantations* constantly playing; lighting butter lamps at night; purchasing lotus seed, bodhi seed, rudraksha seed, bloodstone and other precious stone malas at the many mala shops; being fitted for Tibetan brocade dresses (chupas) by a Tibetan seamstress; meeting friends for coffee at the outdoor, ground level Flavors Cafe; sitting upstairs at Roadhouse Cafe, eating pizza for lunch while gazing directly across at the Buddha Eyes of the Stupa; circumambulating the stupa on the lower level, spinning many of the 500 prayer wheels with pilgrims from all over the world; circumambulating the stupa on the upper level and being told by a monk that she should not "cut corners," and purchasing her gold White Tara statue that was later filled at Swayambhu.

Olivia had a strong affinity for Swayambhunath Stupa, known as "Monkey Temple," which sits on a hill just west of Kathmandu. Swayambhu has rich historical ties to the Karma Kagyu Buddhist lineage. It is where her teachers Hannah and Ole Nydahl met His Holiness the 16th Gyalwa Karma in a Black Crown Ceremony. Swayambhunath had been so damaged in the earthquake that it was now a landslide risk, roped off, with access denied to tourists and the public; however, Deval spoke to a police officer (in Nepali) standing at the entrance, and the police officer granted them access. Olivia realized that when she was alone in Nepal, she understood about 50% of what was going on around her and saw about 50% of the picture. Yet, when she was with Deval, partially because he spoke Nepali, she got the full story, the full picture. The dichotomy left her perplexed, humbled, and eager to understand what was really transpiring among the Nepalese. Deval was expanding her worldview, and she appreciated him for that.

It was the first time Olivia had entered Swayambhu from a car road around the hill from the south leading to a southeast entrance. In the past, she had always walked to Swayambhu and climbed the long, steep stairway with 365 concrete steps, along with hundreds of other pilgrims in the morning before dawn. The first sight on reaching the top of the stairway is the largest Vajra (Tib: Dorje) one will ever see, with two large lions guarding the entrance before one begins a clockwise circumambulation of the stupa while spinning a row of metal prayer wheels on the right. From that vantage point, the view of the Himalayas and

Kathmandu Valley is breathtaking.

The first time Olivia had climbed the stairs to Swayambhunath was actually in the dark in order to attend a puja at the Kagyu monastery, and she was a little spooked by the barking dogs and lack of streetlights. By late morning, however, there were many vendors on either side of the steps selling mala beads and other artifacts. Olivia had once purchased a slate etching of a Tibetan couple riding a yak, marveling at how the artist could chisel away and produce such beautiful work. The 365 steps lead directly to the main platform of the temple, which is from the top of the hill to the east. It was on these stairs that a monkey had jumped on Olivia's back in 2011 and didn't want to let go! Yes, there are monkeys everywhere at Swayambhunath which, again, is why it is often called the Monkey Temple. Olivia had no food with her that would attract a monkey; thus, after she gave the incident some thought, she came to believe that the monkey really did recognize her from some other time and place.

Olivia could not believe the massive damage to Swayambhunath, the sight so evocative that it was the second time that Olivia had shed tears since the earthquake on April 25. The complex consisted of a majestic white stupa, which fortunately survived the earthquake, although the 17th century Pratapur Temple adjacent to the stupa, which was heavily damaged by lightning in 2011 and recently restored, appeared to be heavily damaged. A variety of shrines and temples, some dating back to the Licchavi period, the Kagyu Karma Raja Maha Vihar Monastery, the Drukpa Kagyu Monastery, museum, library, shops, restaurants, and hostels that were more recent additions, were mostly damaged beyond repair and in shambles.

Fortunately, there was not much damage to the stupa. The dome at the base of the white stupa represents the entire world. There is a large pair of eyes and eyebrows painted on each of its four sides, which represent Wisdom and Compassion. Above each pair of eyes is another eye, the third eye. Between them, the number one (in Devanagari script) is painted in the fashion of a nose. When a person awakes (represented by eyes of wisdom and compassion) from the bonds of the world, the person reaches the state of enlightenment. The thirteen pinnacles on the top symbolize that sentient beings have to go through the thirteen stages of spiritual realizations to reach enlightenment or Buddhahood. There are carvings of the Panch Buddhas (five Buddhas) on each of the four sides of the stupa. There are also statues of the Buddhas at the base of the stupas. Panch Buddhas are Buddha in metaphorical sense in Tantrayana. They are Vairochana (occupies the center and is the master of the temple); Akshobhya faces the east and represents the cosmic element of consciousness; Ratna Sambhava faces the south and represents the cosmic element of sensation; Amitabha faces west and represents the cosmic element of Sanjna (name); and Amoghsiddhi faces north and represents the cosmic element of conformation.

Olivia and Deval ate dinner together at a restaurant in Thamel. Olivia knew that he needed to visit his family in a faraway village and told him that he should go there without further delay. She told him that a cab would be waiting at the hotel to take her to the airport in two hours. Deval knew what this meant. It meant goodbye, and he hated goodbyes. He always told her to never say goodbye. But, how could it ever really be goodbye if their meeting was a play without an ending, another chapter in a never-ending book? Loving someone didn't have to "look" a certain way. Love didn't have to mean tying someone in chains with promises and programmed expectation that gives rise to disappointment. Loving someone meant freedom… freedom to grow… Love meant having the courage to embrace that freedom in order to give two people the wings they needed in order to soar above their circumstances. Love meant letting go of all of the glue, the attachment, the enmeshment, the craving—not detachment but non-attachment. She told him that this was the perfect moment—the perfect time—and it wasn't a goodbye but an invitation to move beyond the pain they had seen, and the pain they themselves felt because of their individual circumstances that held them in bondage. They had both seen so much suffering. Olivia didn't need to be convinced of the nature of suffering.

Olivia seemed to have gained clarity as to what had transpired between them, as if two specks in the universe had been brought together again when causes and conditions ripened—with a love that transcended lifetimes, and not accidentally, but because of their deep karmic connection. There were so many times over the past seven months that she almost said goodbye to Deval but past attachment kept her bound to him, her "I" attached to "him." She realized what a misconception it was for her to believe that this "I" existed because it was what kept her in samsara, an ocean of suffering. She looked closely at her thoughts that were feelings: "I need him… I want to be with him… I love him." Wasn't it those feelings that were causing her to suffer and not Deval? If feelings have no inherent existence, does this I self exist? According to Buddhist thought, things do exist, but only conventionally by designation, not powered from their own side. They exist only in dependence on causes and conditions. In other words, we do exist but in a relative way, but not in an absolute way. We exist interdependently. We are empty of inherent existence. The closer we look, the more we enlarge, blow up, the further away the object becomes, receding into the grain fragments into particles and then space. Selflessness of phenomenon is a natural consequence of the Four Noble truths because as Nagarjuna (Tsondru, 2011, p. XXIV 40) expressed:

The one who sees
Dependent origination
Sees suffering, its origin,
Cessation, and the path.

Deval and Olivia rode to the airport in silence as they held hands in the back seat of the cab. Once at the airport, Olivia could only manage to whisper, "Go to your village. Your family needs you." He knew he needed to go, as they clung to each other. Olivia opened the door of the cab with one hand and stepped out while he held her other hand in a grip. She turned and looked at him, as he slowly released her hand. She didn't want to leave him, and she didn't want to leave Nepal. This was her most difficult farewell, her most difficult exercise in letting go. She watched as her cab driver finished loading her luggage onto one of the metal carts that are abundantly available at the airport, and she pushed the cart to the airport entrance door. She didn't look back. She was near the very spot where she had stood when the April 25 earthquake hit Nepal. The impermanence of that experience, as well as her experience with Chris and Deval, seemed to echo the words of Shantideva:

> All that I possess and use
> Is like the fleeting vision of a dream.
> It fades into the realms of memory;
> And fading, will be seen no more.
> Nothing that has passed can be regained.
> Shantideva, *The Bodhicharyavatara* (2:36–39)

Olivia's trip back to the USA was necessary in order to process a long-term visa for India; however, it was an arduous trip over a period of two days because of the limited availability of flights departing from Kathmandu—an outcome of the earthquakes. She needed to spend the night not only in Guangzhou, China but in Los Angeles. Upon arriving in Utah, she quickly appeared in a Park City TV morning news show about Nepal, despite two weeks of serious East-West jet lag that she never experiences when traveling West-East, after arriving in Nepal.

Olivia began to heal through an acute case (less than a three-month duration) of PTSD (post-traumatic stress disorder) and learned that PTSD affects a part of the brain that we have absolutely no control over. Although some people were concerned that she would develop PTSD, she discounted those concerns until she experienced flashbacks while sitting on a plane that couldn't take off on a Baltimore Airport runway due to a lightning storm. Suddenly, she was back in the lightning storm in the village of Syaule in Nepal, and the anxiety she experienced was gripping. She also experienced flashbacks when seeing cracks on building walls, as witnessed throughout Nepal. While in New York to see the "Honoring Nepal" Exhibit at the Rubin Museum of Art, seeing the height of skyscrapers gave her anxiety, and she didn't believe she would be able to enter any of them. Clearly, she was experiencing anxiety that she didn't experience during the earthquakes. There were Vietnam veterans who reached out to her, believing that she would have to live with unpredictable flashbacks and traumatic memories, as they themselves had surrendered to; however, Olivia's meditation practice and her entourage of compassionate healers took it on, and after about a month, the flashbacks stopped; fortunately not an acute case.

At about that same time, Olivia passed out halfway through her first tattoo. While having dinner with her oldest daughter—who has a cute tattoo of a daisy on her ankle—they were discussing tattoos one minute, and 45 minutes later Olivia was dragged into a tattoo parlor up the street. A live band was playing deafening hard rock-metal music, and Olivia felt she was entering the Art Institute of Chicago. One of the tattoo artists was intrigued with her sign off, MUCH love. Olivia showed him the picture she took of the MUCH love she drew in the sand at Yamdrok Lake in Tibet. He reduced the image, and tattooed it on her upper back. She sat in a massage chair, hair pulled up on her head, feeling the sting as he stenciled away. He was zealous about capturing an unprecedented "sand" look with pebbles. However, as soon as the word love was complete, Olivia saw the wood floor beneath her rise, and she fainted. The artist believed they might have to quit halfway through without the MUCH but he wanted Olivia to try drinking water and eating sugar while her daughter laughed uncontrollably. Thirty minutes later Olivia visualized the chair as Mt. Everest Base Camp and she hung in there until the job was complete; thus her MUCH love sign off, exactly as she drew it in the sand at Yamdrok Lake, is now permanently on her back. Of course, Olivia didn't draw it meticulously at Yamdrok Lake so it doesn't look meticulous on her back; however, when her artist-younger-daughter sized it up as a "prison tattoo" all Olivia could say was that it was on her back, and she didn't have to look at it. The symbolism does mean a lot to her, and now she feels bonded with every person she sees who has a tattoo on their body—as if she joined a club.

Olivia returned again to Kathmandu on August 16, 2015, ignoring the fact that there was a cholera outbreak, which was not surprising given that most cholera cases occur during the monsoon season (June–October). The cases reported were mainly in the urban and slum areas due to contaminated water, inadequate supplies of safe drinking water, food sold in open spaces, and high rates of open defecation. She learned that Nepal had a history of cholera, the largest outbreak reported in 2009 in the midwest region of Jajarkot with more than 30,000 people affected. Tragically, more than 500 people lost their lives. More recently, during the 2014 monsoon, a cholera outbreak was reported in Rautahat in the Terai region adjoining northern states of India in which more than 600 people were affected. Olivia inquired as to where she could obtain a cholera vaccine but found that there wasn't one available in close proximity to her, and the CDC discouraged them because of their short-lasting effect that also wasn't guaranteed. Olivia resolved that she simply needed to be careful about water, which is how the disease is transmitted. Other than that, when was there ever a time that she had arrived in Kathmandu without "something" going on; thus, a cholera outbreak wasn't going to hold her back.

Upon arrival in Kathmandu, Olivia consciously retraced the steps she took at the airport on April 25 before and after the Gorkha earthquake hit, hoping that she could do it fearlessly and without flashbacks. Deval had left Nepal the previous month to further his education out of the country. That was the good news. The bad news was that Olivia had been contacted by an older, widowed European woman, and they subsequently engaged in hours of fact-finding communication. Deval had been "love bombing" foreign, older women for many years, hoping to marry one who would financially take care of him and serve as a "ticket" that he so desperately wanted out of third world Nepal. Via the Internet and social media he seemed to seek out spiritual but vulnerable, older women who were widowed, divorced, or separated. Although this woman's online relationship with Deval persisted for years and they Skyped frequently (he had two Skype accounts and one reported his age more than ten years older than he was), she never traveled to Nepal to meet him in person, and his attempts to obtain a visa in Nepal to see her in Europe were always denied. She experienced from Deval the same "love bombing"—undying professions of love—at the same time that Olivia had experienced them and yes, he wanted to marry her, also, which she refused to consider; however, unlike Olivia, she was out at least $5,000, most of it from her pension fund, and feeling duped. She wanted her money returned. "He never had any money," she said. She and Olivia learned about other women that Deval was maneuvering like an artist in an array of secretive worlds, and two of those worlds had just collided. Without expounding, Olivia wondered if she had been run over by a Mack truck but predicted that he would soon snare a financially-stable, older woman who would agree to marry him. A younger Nepali woman in poverty-stricken Nepal was never in the cards. She also wondered what her heroine Yeshe Tsogyal would do in such a situation. Would she open a Rehabilitation Center for Men or would she round them up in the O.K. Corral and tie them up in the noonday sun? Probably not.

Perhaps Olivia had made a lucky escape; her intuition once again proving to be accurate; however, continuing to work with her undeniable karma with Deval was an arduous challenge, particularly because she was genuinely concerned about his future, wishing that he would be a source of hope, strength, and inspiration to Nepal rather than a disappointment. After all, the Nepalese had experienced more than enough disappointment from their government; however, Olivia did give Deval an opportunity to explain. He was speechless, never understanding the meaning of the word forthright. He claimed that Olivia was his best friend, and he was fighting to salvage that friendship. She penned the words:

To Deval
Not that I do not understand poverty,
But fearful of your escape.
Not that I am not proud of your vision,
But wary of you actualizing it.
Not that I do not admire ambition,
But conflicted by your antics—

Wealth often wears a mask,
Camouflaging its callousness.
Immortal and growing, it digests
All that is intrinsic in its path.
Consumerism trumps love.
Cars replace walks on starlit nights.
Homes become mortgage-strapped houses.
Grasping defeats contentment.
Televisions muffle silence.
The voice of singing birds can no longer be heard—

Nor can mine.

Affluence can give rise to a lonely world.
Alas, you have taken leave—
An apprehensiveness stirs
That the village boy with only love in his heart
Will get trapped and lost in a maze
Of assiduous ambitious distraction
Before finding love that was lost.
Olivia

Fortunately, the sticky glue of retrospection and analysis was brief. Olivia reflected upon a teaching from one of her spiritual teachers that if we want to know a true Bodhisattva, injure or harm him/her, and we will benefit; however, being a Bodhisattva doesn't mean being a passive, enabling doormat. It takes discriminating wisdom to draw a line in the sand and demonstrate through skillful measures what it means to strive to live virtuously for the benefit of all beings. We must also be a little protective of our capacity to be of benefit to others, because if we are buried under with suffering, we can be of no benefit to anyone. More importantly, Olivia remembered the wise and comforting words of her greatest teacher, His Holiness the 17th Karmapa Trinley Thaye Dorje: "We can never know the causes and conditions for one's behavior so it is impossible to judge." Those words allowed Olivia to take the helium balloon full of hurtful, afflictive emotions and release it, letting it go, disappearing out of her heart and dissolving forever into space. She was able to check into the same hotel room in Kathmandu that had been designated as hers. There were no painful memories, but memories that made her feel that there was a period of time in her life—an upheaval—that was shared with someone. And somehow she was appreciative of that, regardless of its outcome.

And don't ever forget... Life is meant to be interesting.

Two days later, Olivia visited the new construction site of DRC and donated nearly $1,500 US dollars in Nepalese rupees to the Disabled Rehabilitation Center (DRC). She saw her children, including Tufan, in a green Adidas jersey with matching shorts. His hair was cut short almost to a buzz, and he wasn't feeling well because of a skin rash but he smiled when he saw Olivia, recognizing her with fondness. She met a new little boy, Harke, without arms, who had just arrived from the Mustang area near the border of Tibet. He had grabbed a live electrical wire and lost his arms. The government was working with the Rotary Club to get prosthetics for him from America, which should happen in about a year. Every child at DRC had a story. Every child at DRC had special needs.

Three and a half months later, on December 7, 2015, Olivia once again returned to Kathmandu. She wanted to observe firsthand the humanitarian crisis that was unfolding in Nepal because of its southern border dispute with India over Nepal's new constitution. This dispute had resulted in a border blockade nearly three months earlier in September. Driving from the airport to her hotel she saw vehicles that had been lined up in queues for miles outside petrol stations, sometimes for days. On the black market, petrol and diesel smuggled in jerry cans from India were selling for up to five times the normal price. Taxis were no longer an option for most because the price of hiring a taxi had increased six times. Thousands of people were lining up every day outside fuel depots with empty gas cylinders only to be told that tankers have not arrived. The rooftops of buses running on the streets were dangerously piled with people. Since there was no fuel for cooking, people were cooking with firewood, not only on the street for restaurants and cafes but in their homes, which posed health risks, including pneumonia, for babies and children because of the smoke it created. Young men were gathering boards to use as firewood from earthquake and garbage debris, loading them on carts or bicycles and transporting them through the streets. Women were seen carrying straw work baskets on their backs, loaded with firewood.

Because of this desperate need for firewood, rampant deforestation was underway, the land mafia grabbing forest land and felling trees for firewood. This would cause additional problems for Nepal, beyond the destruction of protected areas. Rural populations rely on rich forest biodiversity for subsistence and as a source of income, and forests are needed to reduce the threat for landslides. Nepal had already fallen victim to illegal timber processing; in many of Nepal's forests timber operations have illegally smuggled wood into India on both major roads and back roads. Nepal's forest administration had confiscated many trucks and tractors laden with timber from Nepal's forests. And now this.

UNICEF announced on November 30 that due to severe shortages of fuel, food, medicines and vaccines, more than three million children under the age of five were at risk of death or disease during the harsh winter months in Nepal. Hospitals were running out of medical supplies that simply were not arriving because of the blockade. The Government's regional medical stores had already run out of BCG vaccines against tuberculosis and stocks of other vaccines and antibiotics were critically low. And the situation was worsening by the day.

On December 11 the United Nations World Food Program (WFP), the world's largest humanitarian agency fighting hunger worldwide, issued a statement, calling upon all sides to ensure the free flow of food across all points of the India-Nepal border. Disruption of this flow from the blockade had caused the price of food to soar, and if continued, a serious humanitarian crisis would be nearly impossible to avoid. WFP also emphasized that Nepalis who are struggling on a day-to-day basis to feed their families should not be the ones who bear the burden of a protracted political standoff. The limited capacity of these families is glaringly apparent: 25% of Nepalis live on less than

$1.25 a day and spend about 60% of their income on food, which had increased more than 50% since last year. The price of food commodities in the remote areas of the country has increased even more. For example, in Gorkha, a sack of rice cost Rs. 5,000 ($48.60)—up from Rs. 2,500 ($23.40) before the blockade. Fuel prices skyrocketed across the country and a cooking gas cylinder had increased from Rs. 1,500 ($14) to Rs. 8,000–11,000 ($75 and $102), which is as much as a 630% increase. Olivia noticed the soaring prices of food, and most restaurants had restricted menus because of that fact.

Olivia wondered how much longer this situation could continue as winter approached and firewood became scarcer. The news media was doing a mediocre job of reporting the reality and seriousness of the situation. The resilient, non-complaining people of Nepal were on their knees, reeling from one more setback that was psychologically impacting them far worse than the Gorkha earthquake and its 421 aftershocks of magnitude 4.0 or greater, recorded in eastern and central Nepal, according to Nepal Seismological Center (NSC), as of December 18, 2015. The earthquake also triggered 4,312 landslides that were often death traps. The Nepalese simply had not been given time to recover. Schools and businesses were shut down, people didn't have fuel to cook food, and shortage of petroleum products was restricting the movement of people, goods, and earthquake relief aid. WFP was experiencing serious delays in getting food assistance to more than 240,000 people, and had only been able to deliver one-third of the supplies earmarked for distribution. As Olivia sat and talked with Nepalis, there was a sadness in the air that she had never before experienced in Nepal. They asked for her opinion as to what the future held for Nepal. Because their economy relies heavily on the tourism industry, which was already suffering, they feared it would plummet even more. Domestic airlines had reduced the number of flights, and hotels were not providing a full menu service. It appeased them when

Olivia assured them that adventurous people would never stay away from Nepal, even in the wake of calamity. The villages. Olivia knew she couldn't leave Nepal without making a run to some of the villages. She had made an assessment of what was transpiring in Kathmandu and Thamel but the people in those areas don't represent the majority of the Nepalese. Millions of Nepalis were in rural villages in remote areas. Fortunately, Olivia was invited to join a team of filmmakers who were producing documentaries. They loaded into a jeep at 6:00am one morning and headed for Sindhupalchowk District, one of the hardest-hit earthquake areas. They had to drive through at least ten landslide areas, four of which involved meandering through newly created rivers with large rocks and boulders. They were fortunate to successfully creep through one of those areas and not have to turn back, but even more fortunate that they could now make the attempt because the monsoon season was over. During the monsoon season it would have been risky at the least—and impossible at the most—to drive on muddy roads waiting for yet one more landslide. They drove through the villages of Mulpani, Thali, Indreni, Shakhu, Lapsephedi, Nanglevare, Fotaksila, Bansbari, Melamchi, Shikharpur and Jyamire, Lagarche, Bhotenamlang, and attended a program at a school where Team Nepal was donating ten computers with desks. In typical Nepali style they were received with khatas and garlands of marigold flowers that were placed around their necks. They also hiked up more than a dozen stone steps to a very earthquake damaged Shree Bhumeswory Higher Secondary School where tents provided temporary classrooms for students. They then delivered socks to another school and backtracked to Melamchi Village to spend the night at Little Angels Children's Home where 19 orphans live, 11 girls and 8 boys.

When they arrived at the Children's Home, the children were bundled up in their coats, scarves, and hats, sitting at three picnic type tables with a bench, diligently working on homework. All of the children throughout the day greeted them in gassho saying, "Namaste." Two Nepali women were squatting in front of a fire in the open kitchen area. Two large, silver metal teakettles were boiling water for tea. They were soon served a meal of the best vegetable soup Olivia had ever eaten, and rice and dahl. The cooks appeared a couple of times to serve more food. The children were polite, well mannered, and appreciative. She took pictures of their artwork that hung outside and in the building where they slept. She enjoyed them all but her favorite depicted the mountains with a bridge over a river, with houses, trees, and flowers.

Olivia shared her room with two other women, and yes, it was cold. She would sleep for a few minutes and then awaken from being so cold or perhaps the wooden platform she was sleeping on without a mattress was so hard that she needed to keep turning. She looked over at Jana and knew she was warm because she was sleeping with a flannel-covered hot water bottle, which would now be Olivia's next purchase item. After all, a hot water bottle was easy to pack; however, she appreciated the fact that a trip to the bathroom in the middle of the night meant simply walking down the hall to a bathroom with a sit-down Western toilet. So what if it required a bucket flush, filling one of two large buckets with water and pouring it in the toilet bowl. A pair of black rubber flip-flops were outside the bathroom door because the floor was wet due to an unenclosed shower with a dripping faucet. Regardless of slipping into the flip-flops that were provided, Olivia's merino wool socks got soaking wet while bucket flushing the toilet. She knew better than not to bring an extra pair of socks. But it was all okay—no problem—due to her sustained elation at having just used a Western toilet. Squat toilets were becoming increasingly difficult—almost tortuous—because of the previous knee injuries, the most serious one being a snow skiing fall that caused her to lose her right anterior cruciate ligament (ACL).

Groping the wall in the hallway, the top of the wall was lined with white, Scotch-taped sheets of paper displaying pictures that the children had drawn with crayons. Olivia would later take pictures of them. She walked past an open room where the men were sleeping, warm and zipped up in their mummy sleeping bags. Olivia hadn't broken down and purchased a sleeping bag yet because it was one more thing for her to pack; thus, back to blankets pulled up over her head. Breathing under blankets always seemed to help, and she did have her sage green satin-covered pillow under her head. It usually caused laughter or amusement when anyone became aware of the fact that since high school Olivia had traveled nowhere without her satin pillow.

Olivia didn't mind feeling that she was freezing to death because it was what the Nepalese people were now enduring. She had heard reports that although many people had received immediate assistance after the Gorkha earthquake, adequate clothes and shelter had not been provided to victims in Dhading. They were suffering, having tents without adequate bedding, and forced in live in the open, burning firewood throughout the night in the severe cold. Olivia remembered Dhading—where more than 1,300 households had been displaced. The government was making promises they were not keeping in regard to providing assistance. Of course, new mothers, the elderly, and children all over Nepal were being hit the hardest. From Lamjung, the District Disaster Rescue Committee had yet to distribute 700 blankets stored in the office of the District Development Committee. These kinds of reports were just beginning to surface, reinforcing the fact that people needed warm clothes and blankets, at the minimum.

A few days later it was reported that five elderly people had died in Dolakha due to the cold. After the May 12 Dolakha earthquake, many were forced to live in tents, susceptible to increasing cold and wind. As a result, many were ill.

There were complaints that although the government had announced it would provide Rs. 10,000 to those affected by the earthquake as immediate relief, many of them in the district were yet to get the government succor. According to the District Development Committee, it had asked Home Ministry to release Rs. 850 million for the earthquake victims in the district but only Rs. 500 million had been released. In Nepal, do as the Nepalis do—but when people are destitute, whenever Buddha time needs to be NOW. There was a desperate need for the government to work at an accelerated pace.

Knowing that a humanitarian crisis was unfolding in Nepal, Olivia found some solace the next morning in walking out on the second floor balcony to see the view of the river and breathtaking Himalayas. She gazed down at the wonderful, well-kept garden that included corn, radishes, carrots, and other greens. The black water buffalo onsite provided milk. The children were being taught to be self-sufficient, which the Nepalese people needed to do now in order to survive. She agreed that the children could use 10 beehives, 200 chickens, and a chicken coop. The fast approaching winter, in addition to the problems caused by the fuel blockade, had much to do with why the children so diligently executed their chore of stacking firewood each morning and night. Olivia enjoyed watching them, particularly Tisha, who was approximately six years old, reminding Olivia of her own six-year-old granddaughter. The cooks had carried up a large bucket of hot water for washing but Olivia had already used a makeup remover wipe. The cooks were also preparing omelets and noodle soup for breakfast and gave Olivia a hot cup of water for her Via Starbucks coffee that she drank black. Milk tea was the drink of choice, which Olivia avoided. Of course, milk meant water buffalo milk.

Late in the morning, as Olivia and her friends were departing, one of the cooks was suddenly next to Olivia with a Nepali smile and large metal plate with six white mum flowers surrounding a pile of red powdery substance in the center. She wore small earrings and was dressed warmly in a red shirt, topped with a gray velour zipped-up jacket, trimmed in lavender at the collar and wrists, and hair tucked up inside a beige, loosely-knitted cap that was pulled over her head. She smeared a red tilak on Olivia's forehead, wishing her a safe trip back to Kathmandu. No one had ever done this before for Olivia in Nepal, and she was touched by the gesture. They had burst out laughing together the previous night when she told Olivia that Olivia couldn't possibly be more than 32 years of age. The children were waving goodbye, and Olivia wished that she could have gotten to know them better. They quickly stopped by the hospital, a tent with two fold-up cots. Colm Harrington, MD, from Ireland was there, and Olivia spent some time talking with him. He had spent the past three months at the children's home, replacing Melanie Hennessee, another MD who helped earthquake victims until her visa expired, requiring that she return to Ireland. The two of them had cared for 8,000 sick and injured people since the Gorkha earthquake in April. In fact, Melanie hand carried medical supplies to the children's home during the monsoon season because no vehicle could drive on the treacherous roads. Immediately after the earthquake, she saw 100 patients a day. These kind of selfless volunteers are the true Bodhisattvas in action, and it warmed Olivia's heart.

As they drove back to Kathmandu, and as in the past, Olivia kept her eye out for an American Red Cross tent... not a single one but she did see a new tent—from Switzerland. Gassho to you, Switzerland. Scientific reports were being released that an even bigger earthquake might be coming to Nepal. The fault did not break all the way up to the Earth's surface; thus, the fault that ruptured still had energy equaling about 33 to 50 feet (10 to 15 meters) of motion that needed to be released, meaning that some strain that built up prior to the earthquake still needed to be unleashed, which could lead to even bigger earthquakes. The

April 25 earthquake caused the fault at the boundary of the Indian and Asian plates to shift about 10 feet (3 m), according to the US Geological Survey. The fault could release this energy with more earthquakes or by slowly shifting without triggering major temblors—a phenomenon called creep. Further studies will also help researchers understand how the earthquake stressed other faults on either side of the rupture.

The following morning at the hotel, Olivia was delighted at breakfast when she asked a European gentleman if he was in Nepal to trek. He replied, "Oh, no. I just came here because my friend said if I wanted to help Nepal, just go to support their economy." Yes, this is what will help Nepal. Visit Nepal, spend your vacation in cost-efficacious Nepal, experience its magical beauty, and feel the smiles of the Nepalese penetrate your heart. Olivia couldn't help but keep saying, "I love this place," although she realized the contextual parameters of her existence in Nepal. It will take generations before caste belief and behavior changes deep within the culture of Nepal, enabling a Western woman to thrive there. This is primarily due to the fact that there are far too many pre and post earthquake survival issues that must take precedence now. It reminded Olivia of when she was in Moscow in 1994 when the relevant, hot topic for Americans was Anita Hill and sexual harassment. When she mentioned it to Russian women they laughed at what they perceived to be insignificant in lieu of their dire circumstances and fear of starvation. Unfortunately, Olivia departed from Nepal without her broken ammonite fossil *and* a whole, unbroken saligram stone from the Narmada River in India. She would leave the Shivagram to Indiana Jones. She still paid attention to the all-so-intelligent, flighty squawking crows. And although she never figured out how to unlock her hotel room door—the struggle always made her laugh.

Letting Go

Olivia had remained close to Nepal, choosing to move to India in August to teach, write, and practice the Dharma. However, she first wanted to visit the UNESCO World Heritage Site Taj Mahal in Agra, which is a 2–3 hour drive from New Delhi. Years ago she had seen iconic photos of a melancholy Princess Diana sitting on a bench in front of the exquisite white marble mausoleum. Olivia wanted to sit on the very same bench, known as Princess Di's chair. She hired a private driver who was supposed to be English speaking but wasn't; thus, she had no choice but to enjoy sitting in the back seat of his car, gazing out at the scenery in silence—occasional monkeys and sheep by the side of the road, miles of stone-cutting businesses and brick factories with 20-foot tall brick kiln chimneys, dotting desolate land that wasn't suitable for agriculture. Olivia knew that over 850 brick kilns operate in Nepal, employing thousands of laborers from across the country as well as from neighboring India; however, the smoke-spewing towers were also an environmental concern, and New Delhi has been considered the second most polluted city in the world, next to Beijing.

Once in Agra, Olivia's driver pulled into a parking area at the Taj. Olivia proceeded to the entrance in a bicycle rickshaw peddled by a young man in a fairly straight path after stopping to allow Olivia time to purchase her admittance ticket. Once they arrived at the gate to the Taj, Olivia gasped in awe, thinking that pictures simply would never capture the magnitude of its beauty. Directly ahead of her, she saw Diana's bench, made a beeline for it, and sat down, touching the coolness of the white marble with her hands. She understood why those iconic photos depicted pain, loneliness, and isolation. Diana had gone to the Taj alone, without Charles, and they separated months later. Diana was already letting go, and Olivia seemed to know what she was thinking, beyond the fact that Diana took the courage to step out of the royalty box, express her opinions, and disclose her depression. Olivia remembered her words in a television interview with Martin Bashir in 1995, "There were three of us in this marriage, and it was a bit crowded."

What would it be like for a man to love a woman the way Mughal emperor Shah Jahan loved Mumtaz Mahal—to the extent that he would build the magnificent Taj Mahal monument in her memory? In that respect, it wasn't easy to be there, a reminder of love that could have been but wasn't—looking at the glass half empty instead of half full—feeling the double-edged sword—a knife being driven into the heart while at the same time marveling at the most stunning monument in the world with breathtaking inlay artwork of 4.3 million pieces, which took 20,000 artists 22 years to complete. Fortunately, in order to keep this artwork alive, UNESCO and the government decided to fund 460 artists. Olivia was actually able to watch some of these artists tediously working in order to create precious stone inlays in the white marble. It all represented the way things are: birth, sickness, old age, and death.

The cloud of foreboding sadness felt at the Taj Mahal was quickly replaced by the unforgettable experience of riding a white, male camel at the riverbank behind the Taj and later riding an elephant at the massive Amber Fort in Jaipur. Between riding a yak, camel, and elephant, the camel was by far the most difficult. Olivia had to delicately balance herself when sitting on the beige, burlap, makeshift saddle that sat on the camel's back, draped with an elaborate, red-trimmed silver cloth that was topped off by a smaller and simpler yellow, square piece of cotton fabric. The saddle was tied by ropes underneath him and around his neck, and a set of bamboo support posts were positioned at the front of the saddle for her to hold onto. In order for her to dismount, the camel descended to his knees, legs folded under him, which also meant that Olivia went flying forward while hanging onto the posts for dear life. She was even captured on film, nearly being thrown off, while the camel appeared to be laughing. How analogous to life: a balancing act that often requires clinging to a support in order to avoid a big, big fall.

There it was—where and when she would least expect it—waiting for her at the UNESCO World Heritage Site Red Fort in New Delhi—a perfect, black yang energy Shivagram, about five inches long, with a few faint striations of grayish color, the yin energy. Without hesitation, Olivia held it in her hand and then purchased it from a wonderful Hindu gentleman. He wrote a note: "The Cosmic Stones have been a fact of India tradition. They are from very deep banks in the riverbed. The river is Narmada. They heal, cure, and are positive, all at the same time. It is a symbol for the Lord Shiva." Legend says that the Narmada River is especially sacred for Lord Shiva, the Hindu God, because of its origin, and it is often called Shankari, i.e., daughter of Shankar (Lord Shiva). All the pebbles rolling on its bed are said to take the shape of his emblem with the saying, "Narmada Ke Kanker utte Sankar" (a popular saying in the Hindi belt of India), which means that "pebble stones of Narmada get a personified form of Shiva." These lingam shaped stones (cryptocrystalline quartz) called Banalinga also called (Banashivalingas) are much sought after for daily worship by the Hindus.

Yes, Motherland India was exotic and mystical. In the Vedic tradition thousands of years ago, the discoveries of sages were found in the Upanishads, documents that do not belong to a particular religion but to all mankind, and they are India's gift to humanity. They are not philosophical but, rather, the record of darshana: literally something seen, a view that is not of the world of everyday experience but of the deep, still realms beneath the sense-world, accessible in deep meditation. The Vedic sages preceded the Buddha's voice; India was the birthplace of that kind of spiritual treasure, and Olivia looked forward to reading and studying the Vedas and Bhagavad Gita. The longer Olivia was there, the more she delved into the heart of India's place in the world. It was the perfect milieu to learn about Hinduism, Islam, Sikhism, Bahaism and Jainism, where spirituality thrives among people who are living in spiritual harmony, appreciation, and tolerance. She came to terms with a lifetime of subliminal messages of stereotyping people, which included unfounded fears. One day when she was at a Muslim pilgrimage site, surrounded by buildings that had undergone artillery fire and left huge holes in the walls of buildings, Olivia couldn't quickly escape but was forced to observe hundreds of Muslims who were trying to be good people. She developed a deep respect for the personal discipline of the Jains and admired the human service of the Sikhs who feed thousands of people every day via volunteers working in their kitchens. And all of these people were so very kind to her. More than any other single event in her life, the people of India opened her heart to the people of the world.

Olivia especially noticed the words of American historian Will Durant at Swaminarayan Akshardham in New Delhi: "India was the motherland of our race, and Sanskrit the mother of Europe's languages: she was the mother of our philosophy; mother, through the Arabs, of much of our mathematics; mother, through the Buddha, of the ideals embodied in Christianity; mother, through the village community, of self-government and democracy. Mother India is in many ways the mother of us all. Nothing should more deeply shame the modern student than the recency and inadequacy of his acquaintance with India... This is the India that patient scholarship is now opening up like a new intellectual continent to that Western mind which only yesterday thought civilization an exclusive Western thing." Contrary to Western opinion, it wasn't just yoga that had its genesis in India but just about everything of significance, including the game of chess!

However, for Olivia, Nepal remained "home." She was once again in Kathmandu when the border blockade ended on

February 4, 2016, just after the 434th aftershock hit, a 5.5 magnitude that rocked her same hotel room as it had done so many times in the past. But now there was hope for recovery because the excruciatingly damaging and painful blockade was over.

This was an opportunity for Olivia to finally visit the authentic village of Changu Narayan, where people live their life as they have for generations. An elderly woman walked by, leading her three goats who were attempting to eat the greens she was carrying in her straw work basket. Another young woman was bent forward at the waist, washing her long, black hair at the public bath area and yet another woman, her red skirt matching the red tilak on her forehead, sat at her doorstep in pensive thought. The most important industry of the village is the several small workshops run by artisans; thus, the shops are full of colorful locally handmade products. At the mask shop a man was carving a food bowl with a hatchet. Several thangka painters, brush in hand, were diligently at work. While looking at the artwork Olivia learned about the Art of living in Changu Narayan, supported by Sunapati Thangka Painting School and the Historical Nepalese Masks Shop. Both offer free thangka painting and woodcarving classes and sponsor initiatives and projects. At least half a dozen silver metal containers and a plastic bucket were lined up underneath a pipe that was dripping a slow stream of water. Olivia knew that women would carry these containers on their backs, in their work baskets. Because she had seen women carry them for miles, she would never again waste water.

Most notably, the village is home to the oldest Hindu temple in Nepal (dating back to the 3rd century), Changu Narayan, a UNESCO World Heritage Site. Unfortunately, they didn't receive the attention that the other UNESCO World Heritage Sites did in and near Kathmandu. The smallest coin in the WORLD comes from this site (News, Guinness World Records). Upon entering the Changu Narayan complex, the damage from the earthquakes was glaringly apparent. There were enormous cracks in the entrance gate, and Olivia wondered if it would collapse on her as she scurried forward while holding her breath. There were areas stashed with exquisite artifacts, and displaced pieces lying throughout the compound, including a damaged, wooden chariot buried under a pile of rubble in an open, but roofed shed. The damage to all of the temple and structures was massive; some had collapsed completely, and the breathtaking Changu Narayan Temple was very close to collapse, needing much work to stabilize the structure that is now surrounded by propped beams and stilts giving it support. Built in the two-tiered pagoda style, the main shrine is guarded on all sides by pairs of mythical beasts—lions, elephants and ram-horned griffons—and its roof struts feature some amazingly intricate carvings of Tantric deities. Olivia liked the stone-carved elephants at one entrance, and as she sat on the steps in between them, she was transported back to ancient times. The locked, ornately decorated metal-plate doors are only opened for rituals that only Hindus may enter. Nearby, a team of four men were painstakingly working (one of them cleaning sacred pieces with a toothbrush) to reconstruct the collapsed Vishnu Temple. Olivia spent a great deal of time observing and talking to them about their project that would continue for the next six months.

Motherland India

Once again returning to India, Olivia had a dream shortly after she settled into her bed in India. She stood at the bank of a river on a sweltering hot day and felt enticed to remove her sandals, roll up her black, capri pants, and walk down into the refreshing water of the river; however, once standing in the water, the powerful force of the current grabbed her in a sweep and started to carry her downstream. She lost her footing, but with determination and perseverance, struggled out of the all-consuming current and crawled up the dirt bank on her hands and knees, creating a safe distance between her and the force of the river. The dream was a reminder of the nature, strength, and force of the Karma we create for ourselves, which can easily sweep us away if we are not mindful. Olivia had been oblivious to this reality, which was apparent when she expressed, "If Yeshe Sogyal could work for the benefit of others in charnel grounds, I can do this." However, a very wise, young woman heard Olivia, smiled at her and said, "But Yeshe Sogyal was an enlightened being." Yes, Yeshe Sogyal was an enlightened being, and until Olivia is an enlightened being, she needed to use great wisdom in skillfully recognizing and working with glue-like attachments and feelings—born from her mind—in order to uproot them. It was similar to walking away from a gripping reality show or the suspense-dripping *The Young and the Restless* soap opera that she watched with her maternal grandmother when she was a little girl.

With her nomadic spirit and sense of adventure, during times of love, loss, and letting go, Olivia now faces the greatest adventure of all—and perhaps the most challenging—knowing the knower rather than the unknown—exploring consciousness (mind) itself, empowered with methods, blessing, and protection. She has also discovered the freedom and spaciousness of another kind of love—not being in love with someone but rather, being love—a love that begins with self, extending to loved ones, friends, teachers, strangers, enemies, and finally, towards all sentient beings. That kind of love is metta—love without the suffering that arises from attachment. With discipline and perseverance, she sits in stillness; however, she believes that there is always something waiting for us—just around the next corner—if we remember to remove the frame around our existence and open our most magnificent door to the world. Olivia seems to have accomplished opening this door in India because months later, when she departed, she wrote these words:

"I am leaving Motherland India today for America, and what an unforgettable, transformative eight months it has been. I have awakened every morning to the sound of birds singing. That is probably what I will miss the most, next to being a hop, skip, and a jump away from my Nepal.

When people say that India brings you to your knees, no one really knows what that means because it is such a uniquely different experience for everyone. Yes, it brings you to your knees adjusting to a world that functions so differently than the West; however, for me, I was brought to my knees whenever I realized that I thought I knew something about people, only to discover that I knew so very little. I believed that I had always opened my door to the world until I lived in India and saw that I was in a box, replete with unconscious fears and stereotypical beliefs. Perhaps I had received too many messages from the US State Department warning Americans not to travel abroad or perhaps subliminal messages from biased media reporting had influenced me.

The elaborate, henna-painted hands of women are not a disease but an auspicious sign that brings good luck. I didn't know what Jainism, Sikhism, Islamism, or Bahaism meant, really, and I understood little about Hinduism; however, I was soon touched by how these different religions truly live in harmony with each other. And, when I was forced to look closely enough, I discovered their commonality: they were comprised of good people trying to be good people. I couldn't come up with a negative impression. The Sikhs serve food to 100,000 people a day in New Delhi… they are kind, selfless humanitarians. Their head turbans and unkempt beards didn't make me feel uncomfortable anymore. I learned so much about head coverings! The Jains have a bird hospital that admits at least 60 patients a day. I cannot count how many strings Hindu priests tied around my wrist as they said prayers and mantras for me or how many temple bells I rung. I gently touched the preserved foot imprint of Mohammed and saw pages from the original Quran, and although I was among thousands of Muslims, none of them were radical. I grew to love people more, not less. As I observed and experienced the spiritual people of India, I came to understand that being different and diverse are not just okay but magical. I was elevated to a different place in this marvelous web of humanity. This is India's most indelible gift to me, and I shall never forget her kindnesses."

Beyond her meditation practice, Olivia begins each day by making strong wishes for the benefit of others. She believes that this practice is not only self-empowering but a positive action that is life-changing. The focus on "me" shifts to "others" and the distance created away from self becomes a buffer, providing space that allows one to take the ups and downs of life not so personally. In wishing for the indestructible happiness of others, a broadened perspective develops, steeped in a wisdom that fuels a greater capacity to forgive, love, let go, and move on—but always moving on with the karma we have created for ourselves—karma that often needs to be purified. We discover that pain lessens to a sting, and it becomes more fleeting. We roll better, crash less often, and with each relapse we come one step closer to never relapsing again. As life continues to unfold in such an interesting and joyous way, we hope for opportunities to accumulate as much positive merit as possible. We talk less or not at all... we simply go—and with diligence, do what needs to be done.

In the meantime———— Olivia's most fervent wish remains forever embedded in the deepest chambers of her heart:

May all sentient beings possess happiness and the causes of happiness.

May they be free from suffering and the causes of suffering.

May they never be separate from the superior joy that is beyond suffering.

May they remain in great equanimity beyond attachment or aversion for anything.

The Four Immeasurable Thoughts (Buddha, 2013, p. 34)

References

Atisha (2015) "Aspiration prayer for lamp offering." New Delhi: Karmapa International Buddhist Institute

Buddha (1985) *The Dhammapada*. (Dharma publishing staff, Trans.) Berkeley: Dharma Publishing

Buddha (2002) "Dhammapada: Path of Truth" in *Wisdom Bible*. (S. Beck, Trans.) Santa Barbara: World Peace Communications

Buddha (2013) *In four foundation sadhana: Preliminary practice of Mahamudra*. New Delhi: Karmapa International Buddhist Institute

Buddha. *Majjhima Nikaya Sutta* No. 63

Buddha, G. (2009) Samantabhadra's aspiration prayer found in *The King of Prayers: A Commentary on The Noble King of Prayers of Excellent Conduct*. (Shamar Rinpoche, Trans.) USA: Bird of Paradise Press

Diagnostic and statistical manual of mental disorders (DSM-IV) (1994). Arlington, VA: American Psychiatric Association

Dorje, TT (June 5 & 6, 2009) Teaching on Shantideva. Karma Guen, Spain

Dorje, TT (2007, August 29) Personal communication. Kalimpong, India

Dowman, K. (1988) *The Power-Places of Central Tibet: The Pilgrim's Guide*. London, New York: Routledge & Kegan Paul

Dowman, K. (1994) *Sky Dancer: The Secret Life and Songs of the Lady Yeshe Tsogyel*. Ithaca: Snow Lion

Dreyfus, G. (2001) "Procedure and Rules of debate." Tibet: Tibetan Monastic Education. Retrieved on November 2, 2015 at: http://www.thlib.org/places/monasteries/sera/essays/#!essay=/dreyfus/drepung/monasticed/s/b41

Dyer, W. (2005) *The Power of Intention*. Carlsbad: Hay House

Gampopa (1998) *The Jewel Ornament of Liberation*. (Khenpo Konchog Gyaltsen Rinpoche, Trans.) Ithaca: Snow Lion

Publications

Goldman, J. (2002) *Healing Sounds*. Rochester: Healing Arts Press

Gyaltsen, S. (2007) "Meditation practice." *Buddhism Today*, 20, 38–41

Hicks, E. and J. (2006) *The Law of Attraction: The Basics of the Teachings of Abraham*. Carlsbad: Hay House

Hoffman, A.; David, M.; Livingston, J. (1949) *A Dream Is a Wish Your Heart Makes*. (From the film score for *Cinderella*.) Hollywood: Walt Disney Productions

Kalu, R. (1986) *The Dharma*. Albany: State University of New York Press

Kalu, R. (1994) *Gently Whispered*. Barrytown, NY: Station Hill Press

Lawrence, D.; Perri, C.; Yeretsian, B. (2010) *Jar of Hearts*. Lyrics © Warner/Chappell Music, Inc., BMG RIGHTS MANAGEMENT US, LLC

LEL, Lindsey Erin (2014) Lyrics and song, *Om to Nepal*. Brunswick: MN

Milarepa (1962) *The Hundred Thousand Songs of Milarepa*. (Garma CC Chang, Trans.) Secaucus, NJ: Carol Publishing Group, Inc.

Newland, G. (2008) *Introduction to Emptiness: As Taught in Tsong-kha-pa's Great Treatise on the Stages of the Path*. Ithaca: Snow Lion

Nydahl, H. (2008) Hannah Nydahl on the 16th Karmapa, "His Way of Teaching Was Very Skillful, Part II." *Buddhism Today*, 21, 16–25

Nydahl, O. (1999) *Entering the Diamond Way*. Grass Valley, CA: Blue Dolphin

Patrul, R. (2010) *The Words of My Perfect Teacher*. New Haven: Yale University Press

Plamintr, S. (1995) *Getting to Know Buddhism*. Boynton Beach: Dummy Book Co.

Rinchen, GS (2015) *How Karma Works: The Twelve Links of Dependent Arising*. (R. Sonam, Trans., Ed.) Boston: Shambhala

Rinpoche, S. (1994) *The Tibetan Book of Living and Dying*. San Francisco: HarperCollins

Seifert, K. (2007) "The Power of Wishes." *Buddhism Today*, 20, 32–37

Shantideva (1979) *A Guide to the Bodhisattva's Way of Life*. (Stephen Batchelor, Trans.) Dharamsala: Library of Tibetan Works and Archives

Shantideva (2012) *The Way of the Bodhisattva*. (Padmakara Translation Group, Trans.) Boston: Shambhala

Shields, C. (Ed.) (1951) *Plato's The Apology*. New York: Penguin

Stewart, JM (1994) *The Life of Gampopa*. Ithaca: Snow Lion

symbolsdiction.net. retrieved at http://symboldictionary.net/?p=1706 October 31, 2015

Thoreau, HD (2004) *Walden*. New Haven: Yale University Press

Tsondru, MJ (2011) *Ornament of Reason: The Great Commentary to Nagarjuna's Root of the Middle Way (Mulaamadhyamakakarika)*. Ithaca: Snow Lion

Warren, C. (2014) "The Chronicles of Chogyam Trungpa Rinpoche." Retrieved on October 31, 2015 at: http://www.chronicleproject.com/stories_460.html

Washington, N. and Harline, L. (1940) *When You Wish upon a Star*. (From the film score for *Pinocchio*.) Hollywood: Walt Disney Productions

White, PG (2005) "East is West." *Tricycle: The Buddhist Review*. NY: The Tricycle Foundation

Wilson, CA (2011) *Healing Power Beyond Medicine*. UK: O-Books

About the Author

Carol A. Wilson taught English after a brief career in journalism. She received a PhD in Health Education from the University of Utah and completed a Postdoctoral Fellowship in Clinical Psychology, awarded to her by National Institute on Drug Abuse (NIDA). She taught more than 30 different health and psychology classes at the University of Utah, University of Virginia, University of Nevada, Las Vegas (UNLV), and Utah State University, and was nationally and internationally recognized for her published medical research on premenstrual syndrome (PMS) in mothers and their first-born adolescent daughters. She published her first book *Healing Power Beyond Medicine* (O-Books) in 2011. Dr. Wilson bridged Eastern and Western approaches to healing as Founder of Carol Wilson Organization where she facilitated workshops and taught hundreds of students in complementary and alternative approaches to medicine. She is a Vajrayana practitioner in the Karma Kagyu Buddhist tradition and has traveled extensively to Bhutan, Thailand, Nepal, Tibet, and India. When she is not in the USA visiting her parents, Peggy and Carl Wilson and enjoying her children and grandchildren, Chelsey (husband, Brian), Braxton, Nyah, Taytum and Grayson; Lindsey (husband, Peter), twins Autumn and Emmett; and Colby (wife, Sarah), Cicily, and twins Agnes and Oliver; she is in Nepal or teaching Academic English Writing at the Karmapa International Buddhist Institute (KIBI) in New Delhi, India.

BOOKS

O-BOOKS

SPIRITUALITY

O is a symbol of the world, of oneness and unity; this eye represents knowledge and insight. We publish titles on general spirituality and living a spiritual life. We aim to inform and help you on your own journey in this life.

If you have enjoyed this book, why not tell other readers by posting a review on your preferred book site?

Recent bestsellers from O-Books are:

Heart of Tantric Sex

Diana Richardson

Revealing Eastern secrets of deep love and intimacy to Western couples.

Paperback: 978-1-90381-637-0 ebook: 978-1-84694-637-0

Crystal Prescriptions

The A-Z guide to over 1,200 symptoms and their healing crystals

Judy Hall

The first in the popular series of four books, this handy little guide is packed as tight as a pill-bottle with crystal remedies for ailments.

Paperback: 978-1-90504-740-6 ebook: 978-1-84694-629-5

Take Me To Truth
Undoing the Ego
Nouk Sanchez, Tomas Vieira
The best-selling step-by-step book on shedding the Ego, using the teachings of *A Course In Miracles*.
Paperback: 978-1-84694-050-7 ebook: 978-1-84694-654-7

The 7 Myths about Love...Actually!
The journey from your HEAD to the HEART of your SOUL
Mike George
Smashes all the myths about LOVE.
Paperback: 978-1-84694-288-4 ebook: 978-1-84694-682-0

The Holy Spirit's Interpretation of the New Testament
A course in Understanding and Acceptance
Regina Dawn Akers
Following on from the strength of *A Course in Miracles*, NTI teaches us how to experience the love and oneness of God.
Paperback: 978-1-84694-085-9 ebook: 978-1-78099-083-5

The Message of A Course In Miracles
A translation of the text in plain language
Elizabeth A. Cronkhite
A translation of *A Course in Miracles* into plain, everyday language for anyone seeking inner peace. The companion volume, *Practicing A Course In Miracles*, offers practical lessons and mentoring.
Paperback: 978-1-84694-319-5 ebook: 978-1-84694-642-4

Rising in Love
My Wild and Crazy Ride to Here and Now, with Amma, the Hugging Saint
Ram Das Batchelder
Rising in Love conveys an author's extraordinary journey of

spiritual awakening with the Guru, Amma.
Paperback: 978-1-78279-687-9 ebook: 978-1-78279-686-2

Thinker's Guide to God
Peter Vardy
An introduction to key issues in the philosophy of religion.
Paperback: 978-1-90381-622-6

Your Simple Path
Find happiness in every step
Ian Tucker
A guide to helping us reconnect with what is really important in our lives.
Paperback: 978-1-78279-349-6 ebook: 978-1-78279-348-9

365 Days of Wisdom
Daily Messages To Inspire You Through The Year
Dadi Janki
Daily messages which cool the mind, warm the heart and guide you along your journey.
Paperback: 978-1-84694-863-3 ebook: 978-1-84694-864-0

Body of Wisdom
Women's Spiritual Power and How it Serves
Hilary Hart
Bringing together the dreams and experiences of women across the world with today's most visionary spiritual teachers.
Paperback: 978-1-78099-696-7 ebook: 978-1-78099-695-0

Dying to Be Free
From Enforced Secrecy to Near Death to True Transformation
Hannah Robinson
After an unexpected accident and near-death experience, Hannah Robinson found herself radically transforming her life,

while a remarkable new insight altered her relationship with her father; a practising Catholic priest.
Paperback: 978-1-78535-254-6 ebook: 978-1-78535-255-3

The Ecology of the Soul
A Manual of Peace, Power and Personal Growth for Real People in the Real World
Aidan Walker
Balance your own inner Ecology of the Soul to regain your natural state of peace, power and wellbeing.
Paperback: 978-1-78279-850-7 ebook: 978-1-78279-849-1

Not I, Not other than I
The Life and Teachings of Russel Williams
Steve Taylor, Russel Williams
The miraculous life and inspiring teachings of one of the World's greatest living Sages.
Paperback: 978-1-78279-729-6 ebook: 978-1-78279-728-9

On the Other Side of Love
A woman's Unconventional Journey Towards Wisdom
Muriel Maufroy
When life has lost all meaning, what do you do?
Paperback: 978-1-78535-281-2 ebook: 978-1-78535-282-9

Practicing A Course In Miracles
A Translation of the Workbook in Plain Language and With Mentoring Notes
Elizabeth A. Cronkhite
The practical second and third volumes of *The Plain-Language A Course in Miracles*.
Paperback: 978-1-84694-403-1 ebook: 978-1-78099-072-9